HISTORY

Curriculum Bank

KEY STAGE TWO
SCOTTISH LEVELS C–E

HISTORY: I

ROMANS, ANGLO-SAXONS AND VIKINGS IN BRITAIN

ANCIENT GREECE A PAST NON-EUROPEAN SOCIETY

MARTIN FORREST WITH PENELOPE HARNETT

Published by Scholastic Ltd,
Villiers House,
Clarendon Avenue,
Leamington Spa,
Warwickshire CV32 5PR

7890 12345

AUTHOR
MARTIN FORREST WITH PENELOPE HARNETT

EDITOR
JANE BISHOP

ASSISTANT EDITOR
SALLY GRAY

SERIES DESIGNER
LYNNE JOESBURY

DESIGNER
CLARE BREWER

ILLUSTRATIONS
DAI OWEN AND ANNABEL SPENCELEY

COVER ILLUSTRATION
JONATHON BENTLEY

INFORMATION TECHNOLOGY CONSULTANT
MARTIN BLOWS

SCOTTISH 5–14 LINKS
MARGARET SCOTT

Designed using Aldus Pagemaker

British Library Cataloguing-in-Publication Data
A catalogue record for this book is available from the British Library.

ISBN 0-590-53397-5

Contents

Introduction

Scholastic Curriculum Bank is a series for all primary teachers, providing both an essential planning tool for devising comprehensive schemes of work as well as an easily accessible and varied bank of practical, classroom-tested activities with photocopiable resources.

Designed to help planning for and implementation of progression, differentiation and assessment, *Scholastic Curriculum Bank* offers a structured range of stimulating activities with clearly-stated learning objectives that reflect the programmes of study, and detailed lesson plans that allow busy teachers to put the ideas into practice with the minimum amount of preparation time. The photocopiable sheets that accompany many of the activities provide ways of integrating purposeful application of knowledge and skills with differentiation, assessment and record-keeping.

Opportunities for formative assessment are highlighted where appropriate within the activities, while separate summative assessment activities give guidelines for analysis and subsequent action. Ways of using information technology for different purposes and within different contexts, as a tool for communicating and handling information and as a method for investigating, are integrated into the activities where appropriate and more explicit guidance is provided at the end of the book.

The series covers all the primary curriculum subjects with separate books for Key Stages 1 and 2/Scottish Levels A–B and C–E. It can be used as a flexible resource with any scheme to fulfil National Curriculum and Scottish 5–14 requirements and to provide children with a variety of different learning experiences that will lead to effective acquisition of skills and knowledge.

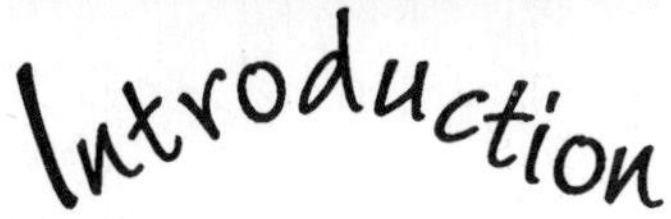

SCHOLASTIC CURRICULUM BANK HISTORY

This *Scholastic Curriculum Bank History* is designed for teachers of Key Stage 2 History. It provides a range of activities which are closely linked to the requirements of the Programme of Study of the History National Curriculum. Scholastic's *Curriculum Bank History* Key Stage 2 is divided into two volumes; this book covers Study Units 1, 4 and 6; Study Units 2, 3 and 5 are covered in *Curriculum Bank History: II.*

Aims of this book

Curriculum Bank History has been designed to help teachers plan, teach and assess history activities in the classroom. The lesson plans include background information and suggestions for developing children's historical skills and understandings. The lesson plans identify the Study Units and the Key Elements of the History Key Stage 2 Programme of Study. There are suggestions to help assess children's learning in relation to the History Attainment Target. Advice is provided on differentiation to take into account the children's abilities and stages of maturity at Key Stage 2.

The activities take into account the cross curricular nature of the primary school curriculum and links with other subject areas are identified on page 160.

Curriculum Bank History also provides guidance for planning a scheme of work at Key Stage 2. Criteria are suggested for the selection of historical content. Planning for progression is also addressed and advice is given on record-keeping and monitoring National Curriculum History.

Using this book

The book can be used in a variety of ways. The overview grids on pages 24–28 provide a summary of the activities. They can be used to select activities most suitable for the particular historical focus being developed in the classroom. The main chapter headings are linked to the Study Units in the Key Stage 2 Programme of Study. In this book, *Curriculum Bank History: I*, these are Study Unit 1. **Romans, Anglo-Saxons and Vikings in Britain**, Study Unit 4. **Ancient Greece**, and Study Unit 6. **A past non-European society**. The activities suggested for Study Unit 6 can be adapted to cover the different historical periods and societies mentioned within the unit. Make a sample recording sheet such as the one below to keep a record of the activities completed.

DIAGRAM 1

Name of child	Study Unit 4 Ancient Greeks			Activities			
	1	2	3	4	5	6	etc

Lesson plans

Detailed lesson plans are included for historical activities. They are designed to provide appropriate material for immediate implementation in the classroom. Some lesson plans are quite short, whereas others provide a basis for a sequence of learning activities. The structure for each lesson plan is as follows:

Activity title box

The information contained in the box at the beginning of each activity outlines the following key aspects:

▲ Activity title and children's learning objective – Each activity identifies learning intentions for the children. Reference is made to the Study Unit and particular Key Elements in the Programme of Study for history.

▲ Class organisation/Likely duration – Icons and indicate the number of children involved in the activity and the approximate duration. The book contains activities suitable for individual, paired, group and whole class work. Many activities involve whole class introductions prior to individual or group work. Some activities will continue and be extended over more than one lesson.

Previous skills/knowledge needed

Information is given here when it is necessary for the children to have experienced particular skills or acquired knowledge before undertaking the activity.

Key background information

This section provides information to extend teachers' historical knowledge and awareness about the activity. It is designed to set the activity within a broader historical framework and to elaborate on the context and skills addressed by the activity.

Preparation
Advice on preparation needed prior to the lesson is provided. Preparation of particular materials and photocopiable sheets is included as well as the organisation of a display or similar stimulus.

Resources needed
All of the materials needed to carry out the activity are listed so that the pupils or the teacher can gather them together easily before the beginning of the teaching session.

What to do
Clear instructions are provided for carrying out the tasks. Specific questions to ask children are included and points to develop through discussion are identified.

Suggestion(s) for support/extension
Advice on how the activities might be adapted to meet children's different learning needs is included. Modifications for both the less and the more able are included. Sometimes suggestions for extension describe further aspects of the same topic.

Assessment opportunities
Key questions are provided which can be used to help assess children's learning in history.

Opportunities for IT
The icon 💻 indicates where the activity might be extended to include opportunities for children to include information technology in their work.

Display ideas
Diagrams and notes for display ideas are incorporated within the activity plans as appropriate.

Reference to photocopiable sheets
Where photocopiable sheets accompany an activity a small reproduction is included in the lesson plan. Guidance notes for the use of the sheet are included if appropriate.

Cross curricular links
The History National Curriculum is closely linked with the English National Curriculum and provides many opportunities for developing children's speaking and listening, reading and writing abilities. Links with other curriculum areas are identified in the grid on page 160.

Photocopiable worksheets
Many of the activities are accompanied by photocopiable worksheets. These can be used to develop historical skills and concepts and to provide opportunities for children to record and communicate their historical knowledge and understanding. Some worksheets can also be used as historical sources to provide the children with historical information. Others provide material for craft/colouring/ painting or modelling activities designed to stimulate children's interest in the past. Certain worksheets have been identified as appropriate for assessment purposes and would be useful as records to include in portfolios of children's work to monitor their progression in historical understanding.

NATIONAL CURRICULUM HISTORY KEY STAGE 2

Programme of study
The focus statement which is set out at the beginning of the programme of study, underpins all the teaching at Key Stage 2 and should be used as the guide for planning and teaching. The historical content to be taught is outlined in the Study Units. The Key Elements describe ways of developing children's historical understanding.

History Study Units
Curriculum Bank History covers all the Key Stage 2 Study Units.

This book *Curriculum Bank History: I* provides activities linked with:
- ▲ Study Unit 1 Romans, Anglo-Saxons and Vikings in Britain;
- ▲ Study Unit 4 Ancient Greece;
- ▲ Study Unit 6 A past non-European society.

Curriculum Bank History: II covers:
- ▲ Study Unit 2 Life in Tudor times;
- ▲ Study Unit 3a Victorian Britain;
- ▲ Study Unit 3b Britain since 1930;
- ▲ Study Unit 5 Local History.

Key Elements
The Key Elements act as a guide for planning work within the Study Units. The Key Elements may not be developed in all the Study Units, but should be covered by the end of Key Stage 2, consequently schools will need to consider where particular elements are going to be addressed in their

curriculum plans and history schemes of work. For advice and points to consider in developing whole school plans see page 12.

Key Elements have been identified within all the Curriculum Bank activities and can be developed in the different lesson plans in *Curriculum Bank History.*

There are five Key Elements:

1. Chronology
2. Range and depth of historical understanding
3. Interpretation of history
4. Historical enquiry
5. Organisation and communication

Chronology

The ability to sequence events and place objects in order is important in the study of history. Across Key Stage 2 children need to develop a chronological framework so that they can place events and different periods within time, and also recognise the relationship of different events and periods with each other. Language is central for children to communicate their understanding and to describe the passage of time. Particular vocabulary and terms for Key Stage 2 children to become familiar with would include: ancient; modern; AD; BC; the Vikings; and the Romans. Numerical skills are also important for more precise recording of time, including BC time. Children need a variety of experiences to help them develop a vocabulary of time and to become familiar with using numerical skills to locate events in time past. Such experiences could include:

▲ providing opportunities for children to place objects or pictures in historical order. Beginning with the oldest and finishing with the most recent.

▲ creating personal timelines for children to sequence their own experiences and changes which have occurred in their lifetimes.

▲ creating class timelines to show features of the different Study Units covered.

▲ maintaining a class timeline which the class starts in Year 3 and which they complete as they progress through years 4, 5 and 6, so that children can relate new historical experiences to more familiar ones.

As the children progress in Key Element 1 you will notice that they are increasingly able to sequence events and objects in the correct order. Children will progress from simple sequences employing terms such as yesterday/today, now/then, past/present, long ago, to using more complex vocabulary linked with the passage of time, including reference to particular dates, terms and periods of history.

Range and depth of historical knowledge and understanding

A broad range of historical knowledge and understanding is included within this Key Element. Such a range takes into account the beliefs, attitudes and ideas held in the past, and the experiences of different sections of society. Children will learn about different aspects of past societies, such as their cultural, social, religious and ethnic diversity. Key historical ideas such as identifying reasons behind events and explaining their effects, and recognising changes and similarities are incorporated within this Key Element. As children begin to acquire knowledge of different periods of history they will be able to recognise some of the characteristic features of particular periods of time. For example they may start to recognise various features of Roman architecture, styles of costume worn by the Romans, or intricate Anglo-Saxon patterns found on a range of different artefacts.

Classroom experiences to develop the range and depth of children's historical knowledge and understanding would include:

▲ learning about different aspects of society and researching particular areas.

▲ discussing why things happened and why particular events occurred.

▲ comparing and contrasting different events and features of periods across time.

▲ providing opportunities to recognise similarities and differences between present and past ways of life. Why have some of the changes in our ways of life taken place?

As the children progress in Key Element 2 you will notice that they become increasingly able to recount details and information about episodes and ways of life in the past. They will learn to recognise some characteristics of different periods and will be able to relate this understanding to knowledge which they have of other periods in time. Children will begin to recognise reasons for events in the past and to identify the results of main events and changes.

Interpretations of history

Children can learn about the past from many different sources. Essentially this Key Element emphasises the importance of secondary sources of information. These sources are dependent to some degree on interpretation: how the past has been perceived by people living at a later date. Artists' drawings and illustrations in history books provide examples of particular interpretations of history: how do artists know what to draw? Some parts may be based on historical evidence but some will be dependent on the artists' imagination.

Children viewing films or TV programmes are looking at the producers' versions of the past. Are these accurate interpretations of events? The contents of museum displays are influenced by the available artefacts and also by the views of the museum curators who arrange the display.

This Key Element provides opportunities for children to question how historical knowledge and information about the past is handed down. In the classroom this Key Element can be developed through:

▲ encouraging children to question how we know about the past. Discussing the different sources of information available and encouraging children to begin to identify whether the source is primary (drawn from a particular period of time) or secondary (that is an interpretation of an event/way of life which was created at a later date).

▲ discussing the sort of information which can be learned from different sources of information. Draw attention to the fact that some sources might be more reliable than others.

Progression in Key Element 3 will involve children recognising the different ways in which they can gain information about the past. They will begin to recognise that the past can be interpreted in different ways.

Historical enquiry

This Key Element emphasises the importance of primary source material as evidence for ways of life in the past. At Key Stage 2 such sources include documents and printed sources, artefacts, pictures and photographs, music, buildings and sites. Different Study Units will provide opportunities for children to encounter varied source material – for example the Study Units in this book provide many opportunities to work with archaeological sources. In the classroom this Key Element can be developed through:

▲ encouraging children to raise questions and look for answers from a range of source material.

▲ organising collections of different objects for children to investigate and to handle. Such collections can include both original items and replicas of objects. Organising visits to local museums to view their collections; see if they operate a loan service. Pictures of objects from books and posters are also useful. Collections of old postcards and photographs can provide information about a locality.

▲ organising visits to different buildings and sites. Looking for clues about past ways of life on short walks in the locality.

▲ providing examples of written sources of information; for example old maps of the locality, copies of the school log book. Older children enjoy trying to decipher old writing. Transcripts of some of the writing might also be helpful.

As the children progress in Key Element 4 you will notice that they are able to identify the different sources they have used to find out about the past. Children progress from simple to more detailed observations of particular sources and develop skills to make generalisations and to draw conclusions about life in the past from different sources.

Organisation and communication

This Key Element emphasises the importance of providing different opportunities for children to communicate their understanding. It also suggests ways for children to organise their understanding and includes particular terms for children to become familiar with. In the classroom you can develop understanding in this Key Element through:

▲ providing opportunities for children to talk and to share their historical understanding in class, group and paired discussions. Listen to their comments and ideas to develop your own awareness of their understanding.
▲ providing children with opportunities to record their understanding in a variety of ways: for example painting, drawing, modelling, collage, photography, using audio or video tape recorders.
▲ organising resources in the classroom to encourage role-play activities to develop children's historical imagination.
▲ helping children plan structured accounts and narratives of the history which they have studied.
▲ providing opportunities to develop children's understanding of historical terms and to use them in appropriate contexts.

As the children progress in Key Element 5 you will notice that they begin to make some decisions on the best way of presenting the historical information which they have learned. They will begin to structure their work and use dates and terms appropriately.

The History Attainment Target

The History National Curriculum has one Attainment Target to assess children's progress in historical knowledge and understanding. The level descriptions provide a means of recording children's progress in history throughout Key Stage 2 and are linked closely with the requirements for teaching history listed in the Key Elements. Children's progress is recorded by the level which provides the best description of their attainment at the end of Key Stage 2.

Curriculum Bank History has identified clear learning objectives within the classroom activities and assessment opportunities which relate closely to these learning objectives. The suggested questions in the activities can be used for both formative and summative assessment purposes.

Use the suggested assessment opportunities to acquire information about children's current skills, knowledge and understandings. The information gained from such assessments can help inform the planning of further learning activities designed to ensure children's progress in history.

At the end of the Key Stage it will be necessary to ensure that enough information has been gathered concerning children's progress to make a summative assessment of their attainment. Make a grid such as the one in Diagram 2 (below) to provide a record of children's progress and different historical experiences.

Curriculum Bank activities suggest a range of learning objectives and you can select those which you wish to use for assessment purposes. Provide space on the grid for you to write down the learning objective together with the names of the children in your class. You may like to devise your own coding system which relates to children's learning. For example a scale ranging from A to E, describing children's understanding from excellent, to satisfactory, or even none. Leave some space on the grid for any other comments you wish to include.

You will not want to use all activities for summative assessment purposes. However, a grid like this provides opportunities to keep an ongoing record of selected activities which will provide a useful source of information for determining the level which provides the best description of children's attainment across Key Stage 2. Children will need to have acquired a range of historical knowledge for their attainment to be recorded on the higher level descriptions.

Ways of assessing history at Key Stage 2

Children's progress in history can be assessed in many ways. Listening to children talking about the past and expressing their own points of view is important. *Curriculum Bank History* provides several activities where children are able to talk and express their opinions about what they have found out.

DIAGRAM 2

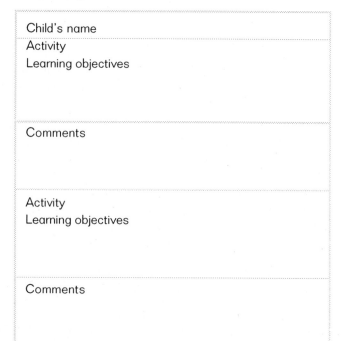

Child's name
Activity Learning objectives
Comments
Activity Learning objectives
Comments

DIAGRAM 3

QUESTIONS TO CONSIDER WHEN USING ARTEFACTS OR PICTURES

Describe

- ▲ What can you see?
- ▲ What is happening in the picture?
- ▲ What is it made of ?
- ▲ What does it feel/smell like?
- ▲ How big is it?

Purpose and function

- ▲ Why was it made?
- ▲ What was it used for?

Evidence

- ▲ What does it tell us about life in the past?
- ▲ Similarities between then and now; then and other historical periods?
- ▲ Why has it survived?
- ▲ Is it unique?
- ▲ Is it complete?
- ▲ Why was it made?
- ▲ Is it authentic/or is it a replica?
- ▲ Is it a reliable source of information?
- ▲ Were there many of them?
- ▲ What else would you like to know about it? (Relate to other sources of information, for example, oral testimony, documents, buildings etc.)

Time

- ▲ How old is the picture/object?
- ▲ How does it relate to other sources of information

Working with timelines provides opportunities to assess children's understanding of the passage of time and their ability to describe it with particular words and phrases. Modelling and painting activities can be helpful for assessing children's observational skills and to see what they consider are important features in the source materials from which they are working. Structured narratives and written accounts can enable assessments to be made on children's abilities to organise and communicate historical information.

Developing historical activities

The suggestions included here provide further guidance and ideas for extending children's historical experiences in the classroom.

Timelines

The concept of time is a very abstract one and timelines can provide opportunities for children to visualise the passage of time in less abstract ways. Organise timelines to include different sources of information; for example pictures, artefacts, children's own comments and research. In-depth timelines can illustrate the chief events and features of a particular period (for example the 'Persian War' sequencing activity, page 78). More extensive timelines covering a long period of time enable children to develop a broader chronological framework and help them to appreciate the relationship of different events with each other (for example 'Invasions' on page 32). Timelines can provide a useful device for describing how different features have changed, for example transport. Children will also need to consider how to depict continuity. For example people have walked on foot and ridden horses from earliest times until the present. Comparison charts provide other means of comparing different periods of time. The coming of the railway in the 1840s marks a major change in the way people have travelled by land through the centuries. The invention of travel through the air marks a similarly dramatic watershed. Involve children in discussion on the scale of the timeline and what items they think they should include.

Artefacts and pictures

Encourage children to look closely at different artefacts and pictures. Magnifying glasses are helpful. Placing an acetate sheet, divided into sections, over detailed pictures can be helpful to concentrate children's observations on particular areas. Children can be encouraged to make detailed drawings involving careful observation of different source material. Sometimes providing an outline for children to complete may help children record greater detail. Encourage children to recognise the significance of particular artefacts or pictures by relating them to other sources of information available during the same period as well as at other times. Begin by asking the children to explore the artefact/picture on their own. What questions do they raise? Diagram 3 (left) suggests ways to develop children's questioning skills. Children can be encouraged to review their current knowledge and to decide on what else they would like to know (see Diagram 4 below).

DIAGRAM 4

LOOKING AT A GREEK POT
I have found out There were pictures on Greek pots. Some of the pots have patterns. The pots are black and orange.
I want to know Who made the pots? Did everybody have pots like this?

Using books in the classroom

Many fictional stories are set in the past and provide opportunities for children to learn about different ways of life and different values. Illustrations in picture books can also provide useful historical information for children. Myths and legends can support teaching and learning in the Study Units in this book. An example of an activity which includes myths and legends is 'Gods and Goddesses' on page 66.

There are many excellent historical reference books and children can be encouraged to examine the pictures for detail as well as the written text. Children can also extend their information-retrieval skills, by using content pages and indices to find answers to their particular historical enquiries.

Role-play in history

Role-play can provide opportunities for children to imagine and to experience more fully what life might have been like in the past. Conflict resolution activities (for example building the Roman road, page 35) enable children to explore different viewpoints and to use information to develop particular lines of argument. All children can participate in such activities. Children can work in pairs and then join with another pair of children to share their points of view. Work can be extended from the two pairs of children working together to larger group work and finally whole class discussion. Historical re-enactments provide further opportunities to develop children's historical understanding, (for example 'The end of Roman Britain', page 44). Encourage children to consider what props they would need to re-enact such scenes and to research information from different sources.

Ranking activities

Ranking activities help children to appreciate the importance of particular events and changes. Reasons and effects can be recorded on to separate pieces of card. The children can then rank them in a variety of ways, such as order of importance; long and short term effects; most important *now* contrasted with most important *at the time.* Other ways of ranking ideas include using a triangular shape with the most important point at the top, or causation circles with a central main point and ripples representing less important features radiating out.

Planning the history curriculum at Key Stage 2

'The most effective teaching at Key Stage 2 was characterised by careful planning and clearly defined learning objectives related to the Attainment Targets'. (Report from the Office of Her Majesty's Chief Inspector of Schools. *History Key Stages 1, 2 and 3,* Second Year, 1992–1993, page 7).

Curriculum Bank History aims to aid planning and the identification of clear learning objectives. In planning National Curriculum History, decisions will need to be made both at whole school and classroom levels.

At school level consideration will need to be given to:

Whole school curriculum

▲ the allocation of time to cover the different Study Units.

▲ the links with other subject areas and themes being developed in the school.

▲ the records of children's historical experiences across Key Stage 2

Historical content

▲ the selection of Study Units to be made, for example Victorian Britain or Britain since 1930.

▲ the choice of a past non-European society to be studied in Study Unit 6.

▲ the relationship of the Local History Study Unit 5 with content of other Study Units.

▲ the sequence in which the Study Units are to be taught across Key Stage 2.

▲ the historical perspectives which can be developed through different Study Units; for example, political, economic, technological and scientific, social, religious, cultural and aesthetic.

▲ the coverage of the different Key Elements within the Study Units at Key Stage 2.

Children's learning

▲ the assessment and recording of children's progress in history.

▲ the progression of children's historical understanding from Key Stage 1 and into Key Stage 3.

▲ differentiation to meet children's different needs and abilities.

Resources

▲ the resources available within the school and the community.

In the classroom

Teachers will need to consider:

▲ the selection of activities which cover the content of the Study Units and provide opportunities for children to experience the Key Elements.

▲ the ways in which children's historical language and vocabulary can be extended.

▲ the differentiation of activities to meet individual/group needs and abilities.

▲ the selection of appropriate historical source materials.

▲ the ways in which children's work can be assessed and used for planning future historical activities.

▲ the records of children's progress and attainment in history.

Historical approaches

This chapter explains the basis on which *Curriculum Bank History* has been grouped into two separate books and how the study units have been split between the books. It also analyses the common features which make it appropriate to consider Units 1,4 and 6 together. The range of activities which might be particularly (though not exclusively) relevant within the context of these three Study Units is then explored. Consideration will therefore be given to specific ways in which these three Study Units in particular can contribute to the delivery of the Key Elements identified in the National Curriculum documentation for Key Stage 2.

In developing the Key Elements through Units 1, 4 and 6, it is inevitable that greater emphasis will be given to some Key Elements rather than others. Taken together the Key Stage 2 *Curriculum Bank History* books (*I* and *II*) should enable primary school teachers to pay attention to all the Key Elements, in an equal and balanced manner, as set out in the Statutory Orders for History at Key Stage 2.

RATIONALE FOR STUDY UNITS 1, 4 AND 6

The arrangement of the Study Units into two separate books has not always resulted in a 'neat and tidy' packaging of the two groupings. For example the importance given in this book to archaeological techniques could readily be applied to the Tudor or Victorian periods, for example, the under-water excavation and retrieval of *The Mary Rose*, is a topic which many schools might wish to consider within Study Unit 2. Having said that, the following principles have been used in identifying the group of Study Units to be included in the two books.

Chronological division

There is not a strictly chronological division between books I and II. The Benin civilisation of West Africa and the Aztec civilisation of central America are, after all both roughly contemporary with Tudor England. Where appropriate, links have been made between the non-European societies and their British (and European) contemporaries.

Myths and legends/archaeology

There are two major features which are given emphasis in the lesson plans and supporting rationale for the Study Units dealt with in this book. These are firstly, myths and legends which are in most societies, the precursors of historical writing, and secondly, archaeology, including some contexts where written evidence is thin or even non-existent.

Extended time scale

The Study Units in this book, offer many opportunities for thinking about chronology on an extended time scale and an opportunity to work with human history which is located in time long before the Christian Era as well as that which occurred after Christ's birth. Opportunities will therefore arise which are particularly useful for giving an emphasis to ideas of chronology as referred to in Key Element 1. Units 1 and 5 and five of the possible topics included in Study Unit 6 all include, to a greater or lesser degree, subject matter which is located before the Christian Era and some of the non-European civilisations take us into the realms of several millennia BC.

TIMELINE

Unit 1	Unit 4	Unit 6
BC		
		Egypt/Indus Valley/Sumer
	Greece	
		Assyria
		Maya
Prehistoric Britain		
AD		
Roman Britain		
Anglo-Saxons		
Vikings		
		Aztecs
		Benin

Topic selection

The rationale which underpins Book I and the particular emphases given in this book are explained here. This discussion may help teachers to decide which of the three elective topics they choose to tackle in greater depth in Unit 1 and which of the seven possible non-European societies they choose to tackle in Study Unit 6.

Common strands

There are a number of links between the three Study Units covered in this book.

Location in time

In studying these three units there is ample opportunity for children to operate with dates which are BC as well as AD and to use the term *millennium* as well as *century* in reverse order from the norm. Thus in learning about the ancient Athenians at their heyday in the fifth century BC they will be moving through the years from 499 to 400 BC (similarly the 3rd millennium BC embraces the centuries from 2,999 to 2000 BC). There will also be opportunities for considering the different ways people through the ages have identified the years. The ancient Greeks dated their years by reference

to the first recorded Olympic Games in 776 BC. The Romans dated their years from the founding of Rome in 753 BC.

When the first Europeans came into contact with the indigenous peoples of the Americas, they found very different forms of calendar (see Maya, page 108). Note that the term BCE (Before the Christian Era) is now widely used to indicate that Christianity is only one of the great world religions and that other societies used alternative dating systems.

Early exploration and investigation

In these units there will be many opportunities for children to see how archaeology has developed over time. The beginnings of archaeology in the eighteenth and nineteenth centuries AD, often represented little more than plundering by wealthy European explorers. Examples of Europeans bringing back sometimes spectacular finds from Greece and the near East have been included in lesson plans for Unit 4 (Ancient Greece) and Unit 6 (past non-European societies). In Britain, 'Barrow openers' and treasure hunters were the predecessors of serious scientific archaeology, which only began to develop towards the end of the nineteenth century, but which has been transformed beyond all recognition during the twentieth century. Our museums today are full of the results of these early ventures, for example the British Museum and many provincial museums have Egyptian mummies and some museums also have objects from nineteenth-century barrow openings and from the plundering of Roman villas.

There were, however, a few early pioneers who attempted to study field antiquities using more systematic methods such as Stukeley (eighteenth century) who was interested in prehistoric sites such as barrows and stone circles and Atkyns (nineteenth century) who uncovered and recorded Roman mosaic floors. Stories of early exploration and discovery often provide interesting historical narrative in their own right (for example the excavations of Heinrich Schliemann at Troy and Mycenae in the 1870s and Howard Carter and his financial sponsor Lord Carnarvon rediscovering Tutankhamun's tomb in the 1920s).

Early attempts at interpretation and reconstruction of buildings, are today often open to challenge and to alternative interpretation following either further systematic work or a more scientific reinterpretation of the evidence. Some opportunity will be given for children to see some of this process for themselves. Excavation during the twentieth century provides copious illustration of the evolution of scientific archaeology and for contrasting today's systematic and meticulous methods of investigation (which now draw upon many branches of science) with the crude looting and destruction of sites in earlier times.

Where does prehistory end and history begin?

This is a difficult area for children to appreciate at this stage of their development; it can be complicated for adults to understand. A conventional definition of **prehistory** is 'the account of events or conditions prior to written or recorded history' (*Oxford English Dictionary*). **History** must therefore be particularly concerned with periods of time which have been documented using written evidence. However, it is not always as simple as this and there is often no clear-cut boundary between prehistory and historical time. Traditionally we have depended on literate societies to tell us about their non-literate neighbours or those societies with which they first came into contact, for example the earliest written records pertaining to Prehistoric Britain are from Greek and Roman writers. A similar situation arises with the Spanish conquest and obliteration of Aztec culture in Mexico, where we are heavily dependent upon early post-conquest Spanish sources for our information about Aztec society as it had previously existed.

Myths and Legends are a crucial source of early history in many societies. Where precise attempts to catalogue events are lacking, myth and legend can often supply rich sources of information, which may combine a genuine reflection of past events with a degree of creativity. For example two of the earliest pieces of Greek literature to be set down in writing after the invention of a Greek alphabet were the Homeric poems, *The Iliad* and *The Odyssey*. When it comes to written records for the Benin society, we depend entirely upon European sources and oral traditions of the Beni themselves.

Information sources

Our word 'history' is a Greek word, first used by the historian Herodotus and it means enquiry and investigation. This is precisely what the subject should be about and the principles of investigation based on evidence are now firmly enshrined within the Key Elements for History as a National Curriculum subject. Any historical investigation will depend upon a wide range of information sources, not simply written records (see Key Element 4a). During study at Key Stage 2, children will be helped to appreciate the weakness of relying solely on documentary sources. Many children will also be able to appreciate that the written sources which do survive are often a haphazard selection of what was written and that they are solely the product of those who had the necessary skills to record events at the time.

Even with early societies which are better documented there are problems which arise partly from the long periods of time which have elapsed and partly from the limited access to writing skills at the time. For example: for Anglo-Saxon England the major sources for Alfred the Great are from people who were very close to the man himself. Egyptian records were set down solely by the class of scribes who were trained to write. As the historian E. H. Carr reminds us, a study of the ancient Greeks is dependent upon the chance selection of documentary evidence that survives; the bulk of our written sources were in fact written by upper class Athenian men! Reliance on written records alone therefore is bound to paint an unbalanced picture of the ancient Greeks. This illustrates the value of archaeology as a counterbalance to written records alone and how study of it can reduce the degree of distortion in information.

Importance of archaeology

Introduce children to techniques of surveillance (including aerial photography and field walking) and help them to appreciate that excavation now plays a major role in historical study, even more so in studying earlier societies. Through various activities children can explore the concept of stratification and the detailed techniques now developed for studying archaeological evidence. These skills have been acquired through excavation or by chance discovery using a range of scientific techniques – the study and conservation of artefacts (including *objets d'art*) and of animal and plant remains. The use of reconstruction techniques provides a fuller picture and attempts at reconstruction itself alter with time as new evidence is acquired and as techniques are continually improved.

Written records

Almost all the societies dealt with in this book used written records in one form or another. There will be plenty of opportunities for considering how these came to survive (for example copies of manuscripts made by medieval monks or clay tablets which were accidentally baked in fire), the process of their decipherment (in most cases) and the translated messages that they reveal.

APPROACHES TO WRITTEN EVIDENCE

Two main categories of written evidence will feature in the lesson plans.

Manuscripts

Particularly relevant to Study Units 1 and 4 are the huge quantity of documents which survive through the tradition of copying manuscripts. These form the major source of our written information about the ancient Greeks and the Romans and about the early English and Viking periods in Britain. They are written either on papyrus or on animal skins (vellum or parchment) in the case of the former and on animal skins in the case of the latter. The surviving texts are frequently copies of earlier copies, which in turn were copied from earlier versions. Many of these manuscripts have survived in monasteries where they were preserved by monks and nuns during the Middle Ages. Some manuscripts will have been copied several times over many hundreds of years and will have suffered to a greater or lesser extent in the hands of careless copyists. It should be noted that the copyist may not always have understood what he/she was copying, thus increasing the risk of inaccuracy. In some cases the text might be smudged or damaged, sometimes making the process of accurate copying very difficult.

In school explain to the children that the only way to make copies of written records in the days before printing was to copy by hand, normally using a quill pen and ink. Invite the children to imagine a time when there were no photocopiers, computers or even printing presses. Demonstrate the problems by choosing a number of children to represent copyists from different periods of time. One child can act as an original Roman writer. The second child could act as a copyist from the fourth century AD whose task it is to try to write out the text. This copy can then be copied in turn by another child (tenth century) and so on up to, say, the sixteenth century. Finally compare the resulting copy with the first version. Explain to the children that the original might no longer be available and they will be able to see how we depend on much later copies of manuscripts for our information about early periods of history.

Most of us today will get our information from translations of Greek, Latin or Anglo-Saxon texts. Some children in the future may have the opportunity for studying these languages and for translating these texts themselves. The activities on pages 42 and 85 provide opportunities for developing language awareness in relation to the ancient languages of Latin and Greek which form the basis of the majority of the documents referred to in these lesson plans.

Archaeological finds

Relevant to almost all the societies studied in these three Study Units will be documents which have been dug up as the result of archaeological activity: inscriptions on clay tablets, stone, metal and occasionally (if the circumstances have been right) organic materials such as papyrus or wood.

The range of inscribed or epigraphic evidence, as it is often termed, is considerable and a number of activities have been suggested relating to this category of evidence (for example, 'Anglo–Saxon writing' on page 50). Children of this age are particularly fascinated by codes, and so the hieroglyphs of ancient Egypt, the alphabet of the ancient Greeks (first letters alpha and beta!), the cuneiform script used in Assyria, or perhaps even, the glyphs of the Maya will provide an absorbing subject for translation (in both directions). Children can attempt to translate simple messages from the original scripts. At the same time they can also use these scripts to write out their own names and other simple messages.

APPROACHES TO ARCHAEOLOGY

It is a requirement of Study Unit 6 that children should be made aware of the 'use of archaeology in finding out about the people and society' which they are studying. However, the use of archaeology is also very central to the societies to be studied in Units 1 and 4 and will feature strongly in activities proposed for these two study units. The crucial importance of archaeological evidence can be seen from some of the lesson plans for Units 1 and 4 which are included in this book.

The excavations at the Roman Vindolanda, a fort on the Northern frontier system which predates Hadrian's Wall, have in recent years resulted in a whole new batch of written evidence. Similarly, work by the Egypt Exploration Society earlier this century resulted in the recovery from the sand of vast numbers of ancient papyri stored in baskets at the Greek town of Oxyrhynchus. These papyri have been translated over the years and they are able to tell us in detail of the life of a community which spanned a number of centuries both before and after the Christian Era.

The archaeologist's spade has sometimes provided a rich collection of evidence to set alongside the written record. Anglo-Saxon burial cemeteries of the fifth and sixth centuries AD, in the eastern half of England, have yielded pottery which can be closely compared with pottery styles in the Germanic homelands from which the early Angles, Saxons and other settlers came. This evidence can be used to assess statements made about the English settlers in the writings of the eighth century Venerable Bede.

Ship burials including the Anglo-Saxon burial at Sutton Hoo and a number of examples from Scandinavia have enabled us to learn not only about burial customs, but to piece together aspects of everyday life including the construction of ships. Such evidence can be linked with written evidence about ship burials, notably the early English poem *Beowulf* and other literary sources which provide glimpses of life in the Anglo-Saxon and Viking periods.

Excavations on the Athenian Acropolis have provided stratified pottery evidence of its destruction by the Persians just before the Battle of Salamis in 480 BC. Pottery of this type which is so closely dateable becomes an invaluable source for dating other archaeological deposits which include similar material.

In Study Unit 6, there will be many examples of cases where archaeological evidence has to stand on its own, particularly in contexts where no written records exist (for example the early periods of most of these civilisations), or where written records have not yet been deciphered (for example the Indus Valley or early Sumer).

Introducing archaeological investigation

Here are some evidence games based on activities that have been carried out in primary classrooms. This type of activity is a good way of introducing the idea of archaeological investigation in class.

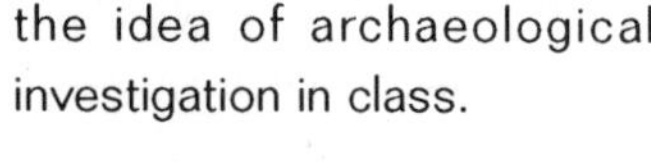

The dustbin

Present the children with a few selected items which could come from a present-day dustbin. Invite them to dip into a suitable container and to take out one item. Working in pairs, ask the children to consider what they think their item tells them about the person who threw it away. Articles can then be passed around the class so that each pair has a chance to handle and think about a number of items of evidence. There are two key questions to be considered as a whole class:

▲ What do these objects tell us about the people who threw them away?

▲ If a visitor were to arrive from outer space, what would this evidence tell them about the people of Britain today?

The ancient burial

Chose a number of items such as an old coin, some pottery, and several other artefacts which are more difficult to identify and place them in a large cardboard box in a corner of the classroom. Tell the class that they are going to investigate an ancient burial.

Build up the idea of undertaking an excavation. Invite individual children to extract the finds and ask them to interpret what they have found. The items can then be tabulated on the board or on sugar paper and notes can be made about each item. Next ask the children to draw conclusions from the finds contained in this burial. Discuss together what kinds of materials survive in the ground and which generally do not. What do the children think has happened to the body which would have accompanied the goods in the burial?

This activity could subsequently be linked with real examples (for example the Tolund Man buried in a Danish peat bog 2,000 years ago whose body, quite extraordinarily, was found intact). Alternatively the activity might be used to introduce one of the relevant activities included in this book (for example Tutankhamun's tomb page 97 or the Sutton Hoo burial page 51).

The time capsule

Invite the children to choose a selection of objects which could be buried in the ground, to represent our way of life today. Imagine what people in 1,000 years time would learn about our life-style? What items would the children choose for the time capsule and why?

Buried artefacts

This activity could link with science work. Choose a number of items made of different materials; items of food, paper, wood, bone, pottery and metal. Bury them all in a piece of ground at school, near to the classroom. Leave the items for a month or two before digging them up. Examine together the effect of the burial on the different materials.

Archaeological field work

Work with maps

Study a local Ordnance Survey map (as large a scale as possible) showing the school's locality. Can you identify any items of archaeological interest: prehistoric barrows, Roman sites, moated farms (medieval) etc? Use this information to make a wall map on which sites of archaeological interest are recorded using a key. Are there any local place names which are of historic interest? (see Early Angle and Saxon settlers, page 46). If so list these place names and add them to the identified sites on your wall map. Are there any aerial photographs available for the area around school? Do they provide any extra information which could be added?

Field work

If there are known field antiquities in the locality, you could photograph them or possibly make drawings using simple surveying equipment. In rural areas, there may be ploughed fields which you could take the children to during the winter months, (with permission from the land owner or tenant farmer). This could provide an opportunity for studying miscellaneous objects (old pottery, horseshoes etc.) if found during the visit. Back in school these can then be cleaned, drawn, photographed and identified as in a real excavation. Any finds which appear to be important should be reported to the local museum for checking.

Work on aerial photographs

If possible collect aerial photographs from published books, from periodicals or from newspapers which show evidence of earlier settlements. Ever since the invention of the aeroplane, there have been attempts at studying archaeology from the air. Every year, more and more new sites are discovered in this way. During the hot dry summer of 1995, more than 2,000 new sites were discovered in Britain as the result of aerial reconnaissance.

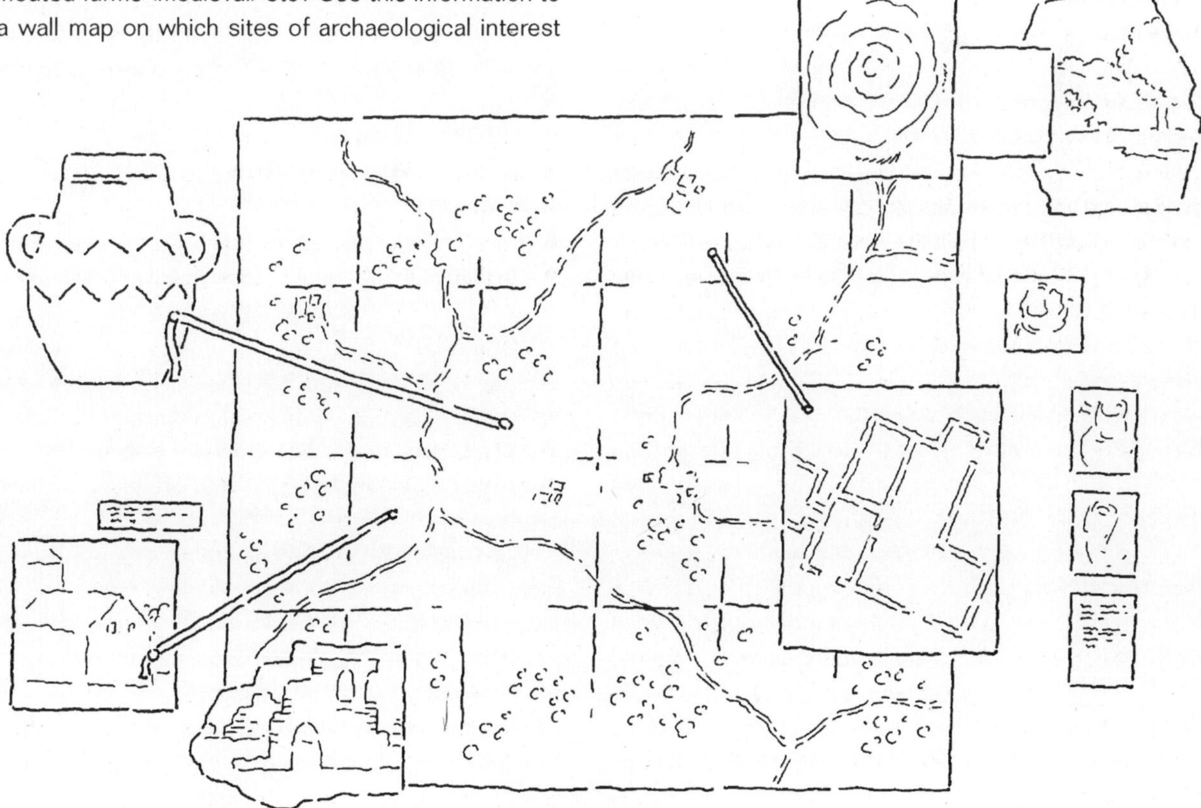

There are several ways in which ancient sites show up when seen from the air, for example, crop marks, soil marks and shadow sites.

Use whatever photographs are to hand to talk about these different phenomena and the value of being able to identify sites from the air. What sorts of buildings or other features such as ditches or pits may be identifiable in the photographs you have?

Simulating excavations

A simulated archaeological site

Use a square or rectangular container (one with transparent sides such as an unused aquarium tank would be ideal) and build up layers of different 'soils' in it, using peat (or peat substitute), soil, sand, etc. Place objects such as pieces of a broken pot, coins and other objects at different levels within the container as the soil level is built up. Once the container has been filled to the top, children can take it in turns to excavate, removing each layer at a time and recording the coordinates of objects they find. Have tape measures handy for the children to use to identify the levels. This simulated excavation will provide children with practical experience of stratification. The real thing – excavating in the ground – can lead to disappointment.

A small piece of ground

If a small piece of land is available in the school grounds or, for example on a nearby piece of waste ground, a small-scale excavation can be carried out similar to that undertaken by archaeologists. Any piece of land will be suitable except that this activity should **not** be undertaken on a known archaeological site.

Mark out a small area in the shape of a square using string and set squares to make sure that the corners are right angles! If the site is covered with turf, this should first be carefully removed. Children can then proceed to excavate in a similar manner to the activity undertaken in school with the filled tank.

Further work on interpreting artefacts

Imaginary civilisations

Split the children into two groups and ask each group to collaborate to make up an imaginary society and then create a selection of artefacts for the other group to interpret. The ensuing exercise in interpreting the evidence will provide an excellent substitute for the real thing.

Archaeological artefacts

Many museums have small collections of 'hands on' material which are available for schools to borrow. These can include items that relate to one period or which span a long period of time and these can be used for work on chronology, building of timelines (from flint implements to Victorian flat irons.)

Work on artefacts might include:

▲ accurate observation, drawing and written descriptions;

▲ developing an enquiry methodology for 'interrogating' artefacts, to ask key questions:

▲ what is it made of?

▲ is something missing?

▲ is it really old or an imitation?

▲ what kind of person might have used it?

▲ what might it be?

▲ how old is it?

▲ using artefacts as a starting point for historical investigations;

▲ developing stories from artefacts (autobiography of a pot for example);

▲ making replica artefacts in the classroom – for example, mosaics, pots and coins.

Interpretation of larger artefacts items – sites and buildings

The approaches used for reconstructing archaeological sites have changed over time. In studying particular sites (for example Roman St Albans), opportunities may arise for considering the differences between an artist's reconstruction made between the world wars and a modern day example. Investigate how interpretations have changed and why this should be so.

SOME EMPATHETIC APPROACHES

There are a range of practical approaches to the teaching and learning of history which may be adopted occasionally by the Key Stage 2 teacher and which are broadly associated with the word 'empathy'.

Recently this term has come under fire mainly from non-teachers, who are still committed to the view that history should be concerned with the presentation of predigested 'facts' to be learned, rather than with the process of actually 'doing history' and engaging in the process of investigation. The term 'empathy' although it does not currently appear in official documentation, is concerned with encouraging children to 'step into the shoes' of people living in the past, often through role play. This approach must continue to have a significant part to play in the process of teaching history at any level.

A wide variety of approaches are possible from which the teacher can select, according to the Study Unit undertaken. These might range from a fully developed dramatic representation or role play (for example, 'Roman Roads' on page 35); on the children's own interpretation of historical material; engaging in a series of 'hands on' activities such as the spinning, dyeing and weaving of wool; an interactive approach to museums or archaeological sites in which children become involved with the archaeological evidence in practical ways or the use of modern materials to make a model of an archaeological feature such as the Athenian Acropolis (see page 84). A further approach might be made using computers, for example using software programs such as 'Extra'.

One simple and fun way of introducing the idea to children of learning to empathise with people from another time in history is to assign them or ask them to choose a name appropriate to the topic being studied. For example if you are working on a Study Unit about Roman Britain you could give a child the name Portia, for work on Anglo-Saxons – Cuthbert; Vikings – Thorsten; Ancient Greece – Chloe.

Textiles

Work with the processes of textile manufacture could grow naturally from many of the Study Units that are included in this book. For today's children knowledge of textiles will be largely confined to their appreciation of the finished article as bought 'off the peg' from a high street store. Learning at first hand about some of the processes of making thread and then turning it into cloth can make a deep impression on children. If this work is undertaken in the context of studying history, the experience can be doubly satisfying. Archaeological finds frequently include items concerned with textiles such as spindle whorls, loom weights and, occasionally other items such as weaving combs or weaving tablets. Spindle whorls made of pottery, shell or faience with rounded tops and flat or slightly concave bases have been found at Mohenjo Daro in the Indus Valley. These are too light to have been used for the spinning of a springy substance such as wool and would almost certainly have been used for the spinning of cotton thread. Cotton material has in fact been found in Britain in archaeological deposits. Cotton was also used by the Assyrians from around 700 BC and flax was also spun into linen thread in Egypt.

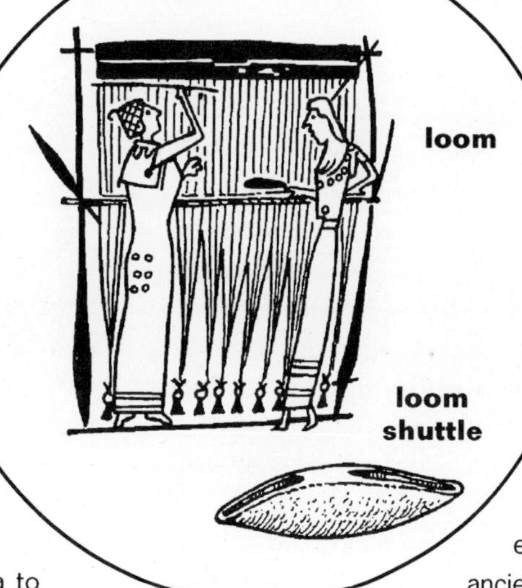

Work on Ancient Greece provides a rich context in which to integrate the making of thread and cloth with historical sources. There is much evidence of cloth making in ancient Greece.

artefacts. The children can then classify the instruments according to how the sound was created: percussion, strings, wind etc. Modern instruments which correspond to these early predecessors can then be used by the children to produce the range of sounds that would have been familiar in those early times. To reconstruct the actual tunes played we would need the equivalent to our sheet music, nevertheless the importance of music in other societies can still be appreciated through this work. An attempt to reproduce musical accompaniment for a Greek theatrical performance or for the burial of an Egyptian Pharaoh (see page 97) would be well worth exploring.

The preparation of food

We are fortunate in that a Roman recipe book written by the first century AD Apicius survives and a few items could be singled out for the children to cook in order to create a modern day Roman dinner party. However, some work has been undertaken on food preparation in other early societies such as during the time of the Aztecs (maize, porridge and guacamole) and this could form the basis of practical activity.

Pottery and jewellery making

Children should have opportunities to copy some of the shapes, textures and patterns that occur on artefacts from periods looked at in the relevant Study Units.

There are some important Graeco-Roman documentary sources for the manufacturing processes, including the elder Pliny's account of how to extract the purple dye from shellfish, that was highly prized in the ancient world.

The story of Athene and Arachne (as told by Ovid in his *Metamorphoses*) can also provide a dramatic accompaniment to a practical lesson based on spinning wool and preparing it for use.

Music

At first sight 'music' may be one of the less obvious sources of information from which to find out about early civilisations. However, some study of music has been undertaken by archaeologists and by musicologists. Archaeologia Musica have published audio-tapes of conjectural music based upon actual instruments that have survived from early times. Tapes have been produced of Roman and Viking music which can be used for the children to consider as sources. We know that instruments and replicas of their instruments can be used to reproduce the sounds that would have been heard in those early times: more difficult is the matter of how these sounds were then used to make music.

Some reconstruction work could be usefully undertaken by asking the children to identify visually different kinds of instrument, for example from Egyptian tombs and in fresco paintings or from Mexican excavations of Aztec and Mayan

Interactive work – sites and museums

At its simplest this approach involves a child holding a piece of a Roman mosaic or a Roman lamp and imagining that someone many hundreds of years ago made this artefact. The notion of hundreds of years is difficult to grasp, even for adults, but children can be encouraged to think about the processes involved in making the item and in the use of the artefact all those centuries ago. An extension of this can be to ask the children to write a biographical story supposedly written by the artefact itself (I am a Roman pot and I was born on a potter's wheel etc.) in which its life long ago is described in detail: what the item experienced was used for, what kind of people owned it and so on.

Children can also be involved in practical activities at archaeological sites in Britain if it is possible to arrange a visit. For example, measuring the dimensions of the Roman barrack blocks or the amphitheatre at Caerleon or other sites. Back in school the children can reconstruct their own version of archaeological sites such as the Roman Baths and Sacred Spring at Roman Bath.

Other 'hands on' activities

These might include writing using a variety of techniques from clay tablets to experimenting with inks of various kinds on different kinds of writing surface. Finding out what makes the best writing surface and what makes the best ink might be appropriate questions for fair testing in science. Teachers often look for a good opportunity to link history topics with science (for example a study of the seafaring Greeks could provide an opportunity for studying forces and for investigating floating and sinking).

Staged events

The staging of Roman days or re-enacting the awesome conditions of a Victorian classroom have become widely popular in schools in recent years. A staged event linked to a particular history topic can provide an invaluable way of pulling together all that the children have learned at the end of a Study Unit. Here is one example of a Year 5 class rounding off their study of ancient Greece:

'The whole class first of all took part as citizen members of a democratic assembly at Athens, where they undertook the task of electing a general. They then participated in a series of activities related to ancient Greek life including an Athenian schoolroom, where they learned the Greek alphabet and used it themselves and also used an abacus, a *palaestra* (exercise yard) where they were put through their paces under the fierce eye of a *paidotribes* (trainer). They rowed on an imaginary *trireme* (ancient Greek warship), visited the Delphic Oracle seeking advice about the future and paid a visit to the underworld.'

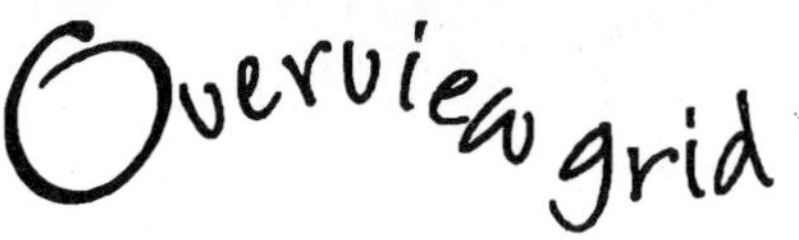

Learning objective	PoS/AO	Content	Type of activity	Page
Romans, Anglo-Saxons and Vikings in Britain				
To place the changing nature of British society from late prehistoric times to the Norman invasion in a chronological framework. To use dates and terms relating to the passing of time.	1a/1b ***People in the past:*** *Time and historical sequence (D)*	Sequencing events in chronological order. Looking at invasions and settlements.	Pairs or small groups, making timelines.	32
To understand and use the term invasion appropriately.	5b ***People and place:*** *Making & using maps...* (D)	The story of Claudius' invasion from different accounts.	Whole class activity involving discussion and mapwork.	34
To reinforce the concept of invasion and to explore the idea of conquest and what it might mean.	5b *As above (D)*	Exploring a conflict between Britons and Romans with regards to building a Roman road.	Whole class role-play activity. Studying and using Ordnance Survey maps.	35
To learn about the causes and consequences of an historical event. To learn about bias in how events have been recorded.	2b ***People in the past:*** *Change, continuity...* (D)	Learning about Boudicca's revolt through story and different accounts. Examining bias in written sources.	Whole class followed by group and individual activities. Considering different viewpoints.	37
To introduce the characteristic features of Roman towns (in Britain) and the experiences of men and women living in these towns.	2a ***People and place:*** *Locations, linkages...* (D)	Examining life in Roman-British towns.	Whole class activity followed by individual or paired work. Making a town plan.	39
To find out about Roman mosaics and how they were made and to communicate this knowledge.	2a/5c ***People in the past:*** *Historical evidence* (D)	Studying, designing and making 3D mosaics.	Art–based project extending over a few sessions.	41
To find out about the language the Romans used and to notice some differences and similarities between their language and modern English.	2a/2b ***People in the past:*** *Change, continuity...* (D)	Comparing Latin words and their modern English equivalents.	Individual or paired activity. Using referencing and investigation skills.	42
To use the term invasion and to compare it with the earlier examples of the Roman invasion of Britain.	5b ***People in the past:*** *Historical evidence* (D)	Considering the end of Roman Britain by listening to accounts and reflecting on archaeological evidence.	Whole class followed by individual and group activity. Making a personal response to the concept of invasion.	44
To find out about the early Anglo–Saxon settlers using documents and artefacts.	4a *As above (D)*	Comparing archaeological and place-name evidence with documentary sources.	Whole class followed by group and individual activities. Using mapwork, referencing and investigation skills.	46
To learn about and use the term conversion.	5b/5c ***People in the past:*** *Change, continuity...* (D)	Learning about and discussing the conversion of the Angles and Saxons to Christianity.	Whole class activity. Retelling and interpreting a story.	48

Learning objective	PoS/AO	Content	Type of activity	Page
To find out about the Anglo–Saxons using original documents.	4a **People in the past:** *Historical evidence* (D)	Comparing modern English with the Anglo–Saxon alphabet. Looking at examples of decorative and illuminated manuscripts.	Group and individual activities. Experimenting with writing materials and scripts.	50
To find out about the Anglo–Saxons using sites, artefacts and documents. To consider the beliefs and attitudes of the Anglo–Saxons towards burial and religion.	2a/4a *As above (D)*	Learning about the Sutton Hoo burial ship. Using archaeological evidence to make conclusions.	Whole class paired and individual activities. Handling archaeological evidence.	51
To find out historical facts from documents. To consider the different ways in which the past is represented.	3a/4a *As above (D)*	Learning about the life of Alfred the Great from accounts such as the Anglo–Saxon Chronicles.	Whole class activity. Using documentary sources critically.	54
To find out about Viking raids using documents and artefacts. To study ways in which the Vikings have been represented.	3a/4a *As above (D)*	Learning about Viking raids on the English coast. Looking at representations of the Vikings.	Whole class followed by individual and group work. Handling documents and archaeological evidence.	56
To find out about some of the characteristic features of Viking times.	2a *As above* **People and place:** *Effects of places on people (D)*	Investigating different aspects of Viking life.	Group work. Investigation using primary and secondary sources.	58
To research the extent of the Danish settlement in England. To select and record relevant information.	4a/4b/5b **People and place:** *Making and using maps (D)*	Finding and recording place names on a map: comparing this with Danelaw.	Working in pairs. Mapwork.	59
To find out about cultural and religious diversity in Viking times.	2a/4a **People and place:** *Effects of places on people (D)*	Retelling the story of Authen and the Polar Bear.	Whole class followed by individual and group activities. Using saga and archaeological evidence.	61
Ancient Greece				
To place events and people in a chronological framework and to use dates which are BC. To understand and use the terms decade, century, settlement, and conquest.	1a/1b/5b **People in the past:** *Historical sequence, people, events and societies (D)*	Making a timeline of events in ancient Greece.	Pairs or small groups with whole class feedback. Sequencing events chronologically.	65
To find out about some of the characteristic features of Greek religious beliefs and attitudes.	2a **People in the past:** *Historical evidence (D)*	Learning about the myths and legends of Greek gods and goddesses.	Whole class activity followed by individual and group work. Using research and reference skills.	66
To communicate knowledge and understanding using narrative and description. To examine interpretations of the past.	5c/3a *As above (D)*	Learning about the myths and legends of Greek heroes and heroines.	Whole class followed by group and individual activity. Interpreting stories.	69

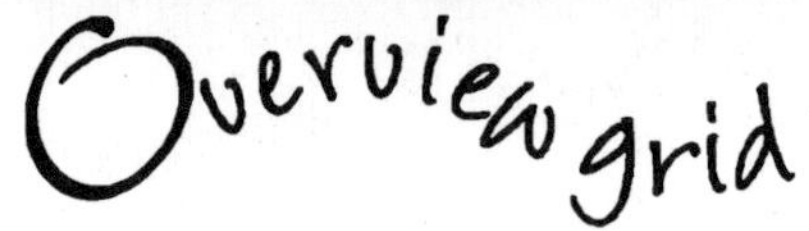

Learning objective	PoS/AO	Content	Type of activity	Page
To learn about everyday life in Attica and about Athenian society.	2a/5b **People and place:** *Effects of place on people (D)*	Considering the occupations of people in Attica and their locations geographically.	Whole class followed by individual and paired activity. Mapwork and data handling.	71
To learn about Athenian Government and understand the terms democracy and parliament.	2a/5b **People in the past:** *Societies of significance (D)*	Learning about Athenian government through role-play, debate and speech writing.	One session with the whole class and individual work. Whole class debate, role-playing.	73
To learn about some of the characteristic features of ancient Sparta and to consider the reliability of written sources.	2a *As above (D)*	Learning about life in Sparta for girls and boys. Examining life in a military unit.	Whole class followed by individuals. Studying and interpreting literary sources.	75
To find out about Greek traders using documents and artefacts and to use the terms 'settlement' and 'trade'.	4a/5b **People and place:** *Making and using maps (D)*	Learning about Greek traders. Examining settlement patterns and trade routes.	Whole class introduction and individual activities. Mapwork and role-play.	76
To learn about the reasons for the wars between the Greeks and the Persians and to place events into a relative chronological framework.	1a/2b/5b **People in the past:** *Time and historical sequence (D)*	Learning about the Persian invasions. Sequencing a chain of events to link the issues of cause and effect.	Whole class followed by a paired activity. Sequencing events and examining maps.	78
To find out about and investigate ancient Greek painted pottery as a source.	4a/4b **People in the past:** *Historical evidence (D)*	Looking at themes represented in vase paintings. Making own vase paintings.	Whole class and individual activity. Evaluating artwork as a source.	82
To find out about the ancient Greeks and their beliefs from surviving temple buildings.	2a/4a **People in the past:** *People, events and societies (D)*	Examining different aspects of religion: gods and goddesses, statues and temples. Looking at the development of temples over time.	Whole class, group and individual activities. Writing accounts and model making.	84
To learn about the language used by the ancient Greeks by studying their alphabet and documents.	2a/4a **People in the past:** *Historical evidence (D)*	Examining the Greek alphabet, deciphering names and words.	Paired and individual activities. Comparing languages.	85
To describe the ancient Olympics and to make links between the ancient Olympics and their modern day equivalent.	2a/2c **People in the past:** *Change, continuity... (D)*	Comparing the ancient Olympics with the modern day version.	Whole class and individual or group activity. Using reference skills and making comparisons.	87
A past non-European society				
To place the major events, people and changes in that society within a chronological framework. To use the terms relating to the passing of time appropriately.	1a/1b/2a **People in the past:** *Historical sequence (D)*	Investigating a non–European society in the past. Considering time and place.	Individual followed by whole class activity. Using timelines, raising initial questions.	90

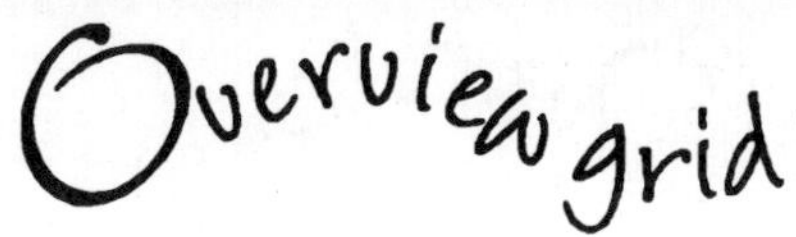

Learning objective	PoS/AO	Content	Type of activity	Page
To consider how past civilisations and their artefacts are represented and interpreted.	3a ***People in the past:*** *Historical evidence (D)*	Learning about a society and its buildings and artefacts.	Whole class activity. Studying some artists' reconstructions.	92
To find out about aspects of the society using a range of sources; documents, artefacts, buildings and sites.	4a/4b *As above (D)*	Investigating primary sources. Looking at evidence from aerial photographs/excavations.	Pairs, followed by whole class feedback/ discussion. Investigation work.	94
To communicate knowledge and understanding: by planning and presenting structured narratives, descriptions and displays.	5c *As above (D)*	Learning about the early European excavators.	Individual followed by whole class activity.	96
To find out about the ancient Egyptians including their beliefs, using artefacts.	2a/4a *As above (D)*	Finding out about Howard Carter's exploration and rediscovery of the tomb of Tutankhamen.	Whole class followed by individual activity. Studying artefacts.	97
To find out about the characteristic features of people in the past and the experiences of men and women using documents and artefacts.	2a/4a *As above (D)*	Considering the burial of a poor man from ancient Egypt. Making a replica of a mummified Egyptian.	Whole class followed by individual work. Study of artefacts, accounts and documentary evidence.	99
To find out about the characteristic features of the Sumerians and about the everyday lives of men and women.	2a *As above (D)*	Finding out about the ancient Sumerians.	Work in small groups of three to four children. Investigation and research.	100
To find out about Sumerian society using artefacts.	4a *As above (D)*	Examining the 'Royal Standard of Ur'. Studying artwork as a source.	Whole class followed by individual activity. Interpreting visual images.	102
To study the ways in which the Assyrians have been represented in different sources.	3a *As above (D)*	Comparing interpretations of the Assyrians.	Working in pairs. Raising questions.	104
To find out about the characteristic features of the Indus Valley society and their achievements.	2a/4a *As above (D)*	Investigating aspects of Indus Valley civilisation, paying particular attention to their technology, including the water supply and sanitation.	Investigation work in small groups.	105
To find out about the Indus Valley people using artefacts.	2a/4a *As above (D)*	Learning about the Indus Valley people from excavated artefacts.	Individual work. Model making.	107
To find out about some of the characteristic features of the ancient Maya, including the Mayan ball game.	2a/4a *As above (D)*	Learning about the Maya from documentary and archaeological evidence.	Working in pairs. Investigating different sources of evidence.	108

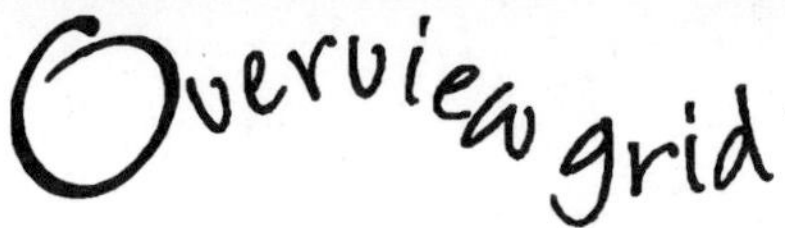

Learning objective	PoS/AO	Content	Type of activity	Page
To identify and give reasons for the different ways in which the Aztecs are represented and interpreted.	3a ***People in the past:*** *Change, continuity... (D)*	Finding out about the market at Tenochtitlan from different sources. Making drawings of the market place.	Whole class and individual work. Evaluating different types of evidence. Writing lists.	109
To investigate some of the characteristics of Benin society using a variety of sources.	2a/4a ***People and place:*** *Making and using maps (D)*	Investigation of Benin society. Map making.	Whole class and group work activities. Using reference and investigation skills.	112
To learn about Benin art and technology by studying their artefacts.	2a/4a ***People in the past:*** *Historical evidence (D)*	Finding out about Benin art and technology and contemplating the achievements of the Benin society.	Individual work. Close observation and drawing of artefacts.	115

Entries given in italics relate to the Scottish Environmental Studies 5–14 (Social Subjects: Understanding people in the past) National guidelines.

Romans, Anglo-Saxons & Vikings in Britain

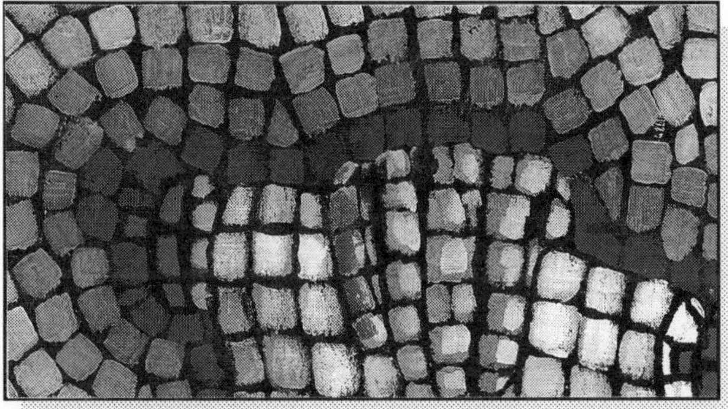

This Study Unit is crucial to an understanding of the history of Britain for today's children for many reasons.

Firstly, it covers a lengthy time span; from prehistoric times to the Norman Conquest. You may either begin with a brief introduction to prehistoric times or with the arrival of Julius Caesar at the shores of southern Britain in 55BC. Due to the length of the time span covered there is much scope for tackling Key Element 1 in the Key Stage 2 programme of study.

Secondly, the cultural changes are important to an understanding of present-day Britain. Children will see that at no point in recorded history has Britain been populated by a single cultural or ethnic group. Instead, the people of Britain and their culture has been created from a series of traditions. The 'inheritance' aspect is emphasised in the history programme of study.

Thirdly, there are opportunities for considering reasons for cultural change: invasion, conquest and settlement. The emphasis may be placed on any of the three cultural changes: the prehistoric Celtic Iron Age/Romanisation; Romanised Britain/Anglo-Saxon settlement or Anglo-Saxon/Viking settlement. The longer study over time will provide examples of the influences that played their part during the first thousand years of the Christian era.

Fourthly, documentary evidence for this Study Unit, in contrast to some others, is comparatively thin and surviving sources depend on many chance factors and often contain bias. Archaeological evidence has an important part to play throughout this Study Unit. There are several specifically archaeological activities suggested in Chapter 2.

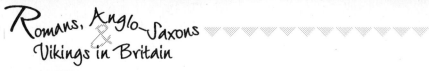

KEY FACTS

Time line distinguishing the different periods in this Study Unit.

Prehistoric Britain	Roman Britain	Anglo-Saxon England	Viking Britain	Norman Conquest
To AD 43	AD 43 to 410	AD 410 to 1066	(during the Anglo-Saxon period)	AD 1066

Prehistoric Britain

The first Roman invasion took place late on in the Prehistoric period. Julius Caesar was the first Roman soldier to lead an invasion of Britain (in 55 BC). Whilst campaigning in Gaul (now roughly modern France) he brought a second expedition to Britain the following year in 54 BC. Caesar's invasions did not lead to a permanent settlement of Britain.

The English Channel was known as the stream of Ocean and was considered to be the boundary of the civilised world! Caesar wrote an account of his campaigns in Gaul and Britain including a description of what he had learned about the Britons. A very large number of sites have been excavated which show that the people of late prehistoric Britain were skilled metal smiths who worked with bronze, iron, silver and gold. In many parts of Britain large-scale agriculture was practised, although in many parts of Britain, the chief source of food and wealth was pastoral farming. The Britons, in common with most other parts of pre-Roman western Europe were Celts.

Roman Britain

The first permanent Roman settlement in Britain came in AD 43 with the arrival of an expedition sent by the Roman Emperor Claudius. Gradually military occupation was extended to the far south west, to Wales and to the north, and the exploitation of Britain's mineral resources began. Lowland Britain began to be 'Romanised': the familiar network of roads and trading links with the continent was established and towns were built in the traditional Roman style. The Romans applied to Britain a number of well-established techniques for consolidating their hold on Britain. The highland areas of Wales and Scotland were never fully subdued, but in the lowland parts of Britain, they established a number of *coloniae* (singular: *colonia*) or settlements of retired soldiers and their families.

The Roman authorities also ensured that the leaders of each tribal community maintained their status at least to begin with and received some of the benefits of Roman rule. We are told that their sons began to learn the language of the Romans (Latin) and that they came to enjoy the more luxurious aspects of Roman society.

The garrison of Roman legions and auxiliary troops which came to Britain at this time was to remain in Britain until towards the end of the fourth century AD. By this time however, many of the soldiers were recruited locally and many changes had taken place, including the building (in the second century AD) of a frontier in Northern Britain (Hadrian's Wall). During the fourth century, the earliest raids were made on the shores of Britain by groups of people that were regarded by the Romans as 'barbarians'. There were many communities which lived beyond the Northern frontiers of the Roman Empire and who were regarded by the Romans as a serious threat. In the second century AD, the Emperor Marcus Aurelius campaigned against the tribes who occupied territory beyond the Rhine and Danube frontiers. In the end, as the power of the Romans weakened, these barbarian peoples were to break through the frontiers of Rome on the continent of Europe and to sack the city of Rome itself in AD 410, thus bringing to an end the power of Rome in the West.

In AD 367 Britain was threatened by groups of people from overseas and later in the century, the garrisons were withdrawn from Britain because they were urgently needed elsewhere. Before the end of the century groups of Germanic people had been recruited to fight as mercenaries in Britain in order to defend the island against attack from overseas.

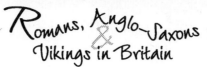

Anglo-Saxon England

Some evidence for early settlement in Britain by Germanic peoples has been based by archaeologists from artefacts that have been found in the military sites which were built to defend Britain from attack. The traditional date for the end of Roman Britain is AD 410. At this date, we are told that the Emperor Honorius told the communities of Britain that they must from now on be responsible for their own security and could no longer depend upon Rome. The earliest Germanic settlements in the fifth and sixth centuries have been identified in very large numbers from the evidence of pottery and other distinctive grave goods.

Written sources for the early settlement are with one exception much later in date than the period of settlement, but are likely to have been based upon local traditions. Place name evidence is complex, but it provides important confirmation of the earliest areas to be settled by Saxons (from Saxony in Germany), Angles (from Angeln in Schleswig Holstein, North Germany) and other Germanic peoples. It is impossible to speak of an 'invasion' in the same way as the Roman invasions of Julius Caesar and Claudius. By the early fifth century, centralised control had almost vanished, though some communities including some towns were able to keep going. All the evidence points to small groups of invaders, each under its own leader travelling to the shores of Britain by sea and settling along part of the coast or in some inland place accessible by river. It is possible to identify some settlements as distinctively Angle in origin and others as distinctively Saxon. Archaeologists have demonstrated that other cultural groups such as the Jutes (from Jutland in Northern Denmark) are also represented, as suggested by the Venerable Bede in the eighth century.

By the end of the fifth century our written sources and some archaeological evidence suggests that the new settlers were by now meeting some resistance from the Britons (the remnants of Romano-British society) who were making their stand against the new settlers. According to the Anglo-Saxon Chronicle, the Battle of Deorham in 577 was decisive and led to the loss of Cirencester (once the second largest town in Roman Britain), Bath and Gloucester. By the seventh century, much of England as we now know it (deriving its name from the Angles) was divided up into a number of kingdoms each with its own ruler. Up to the Danish invasion of 865 to 878, those kingdoms south of the River Humber were united under an overlord known as *Bretwalda* or ruler of the Britons. Rulers in different parts of England took it in turns to be overlord but by the eighth century, the country was dominated by the powerful rulers of Mercia, Ethelbald and Offa. Between the ninth and tenth centuries the Danish settlers were to dominate much of the Midlands and northern England, although Wessex under King Alfred had succeeded in resisting the Danes. In the tenth century the Kings of Wessex re-conquered the areas ruled over by the Danes, known as *Danelaw*, and thenceforth ruled over a united England.

The Anglo-Saxon period continued until the Norman invasion under William the Conqueror in 1066.

The Vikings

Our major source for the Viking invasions and settlement of Britain is the Anglo-Saxon Chronicle. There are also letters written by church leaders during this period. The people of the north who attacked and then settled in Britain from the mid-ninth century came to dominate the later history of Anglo-Saxon England. Viking raids began towards the end of the eighth century. We are told that the 'Heathenmen' attacked the Isle of Sheppey in Kent in 835. From this time on, there were invasions by increasingly large groups of seaborne invaders along the shores of Britain and between 855 and 858 the Vikings stayed in England over the winter for the first time. In 878, Alfred, King of Wessex, was victorious in south western Britain, but by this time Danish people in large numbers had begun to establish settlements in East Anglia, the north east Midlands and Northumbria. A large part of England in the Midlands and the north was ruled by the Kings of Denmark as Danelaw until the middle of the tenth century.

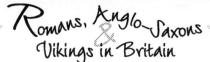

The traditional portrayal of the Vikings as violent marauders needs to be set alongside evidence of life and society during the Viking period. Archaeologists have shown evidence for a settled way of life in Greenland, Iceland, Scandinavia and most recently York which became the Danish capital of Danelaw. We also have vivid accounts of Viking life in the surviving sagas of Icelandic and Scandinavian origin.

CHANGE OVER TIME: INVADERS AND SETTLERS

To place the changing nature of British society from late prehistoric times to the Norman Invasion in a chronological framework. To distinguish between the terms BC and AD and to use the terms: Prehistoric, Roman, Anglo-Saxon, Viking and Norman to define particular periods of early British history.

Pairs or small groups.

45 minutes.

Previous skills/knowledge needed

If this activity is undertaken near to the beginning of the Study Unit, you will have to depend upon the children's general knowledge. If on the other hand this activity is undertaken as an introduction to the unit the children will need to be able to identify the items shown on the photocopiable sheet on page 118.

Key background information

This activity can be undertaken as an introductory activity, but is probably more effective if used as a summing-up lesson at the end of Study Unit 1 or as a continuing activity throughout the time that Study Unit 1 is being undertaken.

Preparation

The nature of preparation for this activity will vary: if the class has already been working on the content of this Study Unit for some time, there will already be material to hand for use in this exercise. If on the other hand this activity is undertaken as an introduction to the Unit use photocopiable sheet 118 to make up sets of cards which can be mounted on card, cut out and coloured, for the children to work on in pairs or small groups. Make a timeline from a strip of sugar paper at least 500cm long. Mark off the centuries on the timeline from 600 BC to 1000 AD.

Resources needed

Photocopiable page 118 and timeline strips, one per child.

What to do

Approach 1 – introduction to the Study Unit

First explain to the children the nature of the topic that they are about to begin. It is likely some children will have heard of 'the Romans' and some will know of the other terms to be used. Explain that the period they are going to study covers more than 1,000 years. It will be worth at this point making sure that they realise that 1,000 years is made up of ten centuries. The children can work in pairs or in small groups of three/four children. Give each group a set of the nine picture cards. Ask them to try to identify each picture: tell them there are two Iron Age/two Roman/two Anglo-Saxon/ two Viking and one Norman. Now ask them to place the items in chronological order. Finally, they should be asked to consider which events happened BC and which AD. You will need to explain the significance of these abbreviations and the associations with the coming of Christianity. Consolidate the children's efforts by putting together one set of pictures on the large timeline. The timeline could be divided into phases, each given a different colour and it could also be extended to show how the period relates to the late twentieth century AD.

Approach 2 – to be included in the middle of the Study Unit

Make a form of chronological framework either by using sheets of sugar paper as described above or by creating a 'washing line' stretched diagonally across the classroom onto which may be 'pegged' pictures of personalities and events contributed by members of the class at the appropriate intervals. To do this, stretch a piece of string across the

classroom and attach labels for example – Romans, Anglo-Saxons and so on, onto the string with pegs. Children can cut pictures from the photocopiable sheet and add them to the timeline. As the children acquire knowledge about the different periods they can draw pictures on card, or write other labels and attach them to the 'washing line'. Consequently, the use of a line permits children to add fresh events, personalities and other information as their study develops, to a chronological framework.

Suggestion(s) for extension

Ask the children to look for gaps in the timeline as it is being developed and find examples of events, personalities or buildings which could be incorporated. Discuss why there might be gaps (for example, during the earliest period). Ask the children: Might this be due to lack of written records in prehistoric times?

Suggestion(s) for support

The number of time phases could be limited to two or three at a time. Children needing support could be grouped with more able members of the class.

Assessment opportunities

Listen to what the children say as they arrange the cards. Do they refer to historical periods and dates using the correct terms for periods of time, for example Romans, Anglo-Saxons? Do they also use the terms BC and AD correctly? Create a larger selection of events and personalities for children to arrange in order as a summative assessment.

Opportunities for IT

Use a commercial Timeline package or a word processor to make a vertical timeline of the period, or a drawing package to create a diagrammatic timeline. If children use a word processor introduce them to the idea of 'tabs' to separate the dates from the text.

Alternatively a desk-top publishing package could be used with two vertical frames set up, one for the dates and the other for the information. For both approaches children can easily include their own pictures either scanned in or created using an art or drawing package.

Children could also create a computer database of all of the events of the period using a simple set of fieldnames such as year, AD/BC/King/Ruler, Event. Children could use a range of other resources including CD-ROM encyclopaedias to find as many events as possible to include.

Display ideas

Alternative ways of displaying representations of change over time might include the construction of a pictorial frieze to show the main events, personalities and aspects of ways of life around the classroom wall.

Reference to photocopiable sheet

The photocopiable sheet on page 118 shows nine illustrations from different periods for the children to order correctly. The pictures can be mounted on card and then cut up, or cut up as they are. The correct order is Prehistoric Britain before the conquest; Roman Britain; Anglo-Saxon England; Viking Britain and Norman Conquest.

Changes in Britain

▲ Cut out the pictures and arrange them in order. Start with the oldest.

Roman legionary

Viking ship

Norman castle-keep

Iron-age shield

Roman mosaic

Viking saga

Anglo-Saxon ruler

Iron-age hillfort

Anglo-Saxon helmet

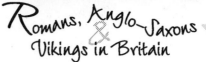

CLAUDIUS' INVASION

To introduce the term invasion.

Whole class followed by individual activity.

A 30 minute session followed by open-ended individual tasks.

Previous skills/knowledge needed

It would be helpful if children were already aware that the Romans invaded Britain.

Key background information

To the Romans, Britain was very remote indeed. In Rome many rumours circulated about what the Britons might be like! Julius Caesar's expeditions to Britain in 55 and 54 BC were almost equivalent to the first men on the moon and were a great propaganda coup!

The Roman historian Dio Cassius is a major source for the Claudian invasion. The invasion took place in AD 43, a long time after Julius had first come to Britain. The immediate excuse was that a Briton called Bericus had been driven out of the island and he had appealed to Claudius for help. This was how the invasion began.

At first Claudius had great difficulty in getting his soldiers to cross the Ocean and beyond the limits of the known world. The general in charge, Aulus Plautius, sent the army across in three groups. During the voyage the ships were blown off course. When they got to the coast, the Britons had been given the wrong information and were not expecting them.

The army landed and after some difficulty the Romans caught up with two of the British leaders, Caractacus and Togodumnus. They were rulers of a tribe called the Catuvellauni. The Romans defeated them in battle and forced them to flee. Plautius left some of his army in their lands and marched on towards a river.

When the Romans were in sight of victory, Plautius sent for the Emperor himself. Claudius travelled river, sea and land via Massilia (Marseilles) from Rome and reached Britain with a large army. He was well-equipped with four legions and auxiliary troops and even had elephants with him. Claudius took charge and attacked the Britons in a final battle. He captured their capital Camulodunum (Colchester).

Preparation

Read the background information to Claudius' invasion which is supplied above, together with any other available sources.

Resources needed

A map of Europe showing Italy, France and Britain including the location of Marseilles.

What to do

Tell the children the story of Claudius' invasion using the background information and including reference to the route taken by the Emperor himself.

Ask the children to each make a map of Britain showing Roman ships carrying food back to Rome. You may wish to distribute an outline map of Britain to help them.

Now read the following accounts out loud to the children to tell them what the Romans already know about Britain:

▲ Julius Caesar, a Roman general wrote these words: 'The shape of the island is a triangle and one of its sides faces Gaul. One corner of this side is Cantium, where almost all the ships from Gaul come in to land. Cantium faces east and the other corner that is lower down points south. This side is about 500 miles long.

The second side runs in the direction of Spain and the West where Hibernia lies. This is an island which people think is about half the size of Britain. About mid-way between is an island called Mona...The length of this side is about 700 miles long, so local people say. The third side points northwards...it is supposed to be 800 miles long...Most of the Britons who live inland do not sow grain but live on milk and meat and dress in animal skins. All the Britons, certainly, dye themselves with woad which makes a blue dye and makes them look wild in battle.'

▲ A Greek geographer called Strabo wrote: 'Most of the island is flat and is covered with forests, although there are

many hilly areas. Grain, cattle, gold, silver and iron are found on the island. The Britons export them as well as hides, slaves and fine hunting dogs .'

Suggestion(s) for extension

Children can consider the quotations above from Julius Caesar and Strabo and try to draw a map of Britain using just this information. This represents the kind of information that the Roman army in Claudius' day would have had. How useful would it have been to an invading army? What other information about Britain would have been useful to an invading army?

Suggestion(s) for support

Some children may need help in tracing Claudius' route from Rome to Britain.

Assessment opportunities

Children should have an opportunity to explain what they understand by invasion. The role-play suggested in 'Roman Roads', (next activity), could be used to reinforce this.

Display ideas

Pin up a large map of Britain comparing the actual shape of the British Isles with Caesar's description. Then add the written information given by Caesar and Strabo to the map. Make a class frieze showing Roman ships crossing the channel with a sponge-painted sea in the background.

ROMAN ROADS

To reinforce the concept of invasion and to explore the idea of conquest and what it might mean.

Whole class (divided in two).

60 minutes.

Previous skills/knowledge needed

Experience of role-play would be useful, although not essential.

Key background information

For evidence of where the Romans actually built roads, refer to the Ordnance Survey Map of Roman Britain. The Romans built roads, generally in straight lines between their settlements. The alignments of these roads have often left an indelible mark on the landscape and some stretches of Roman roads are still used today for example the Fosse Way.

The building of roads would have been among the earliest tasks facing the victorious Roman army. Movement of troops as quickly as possible would have been a key to the conquest. The activity involving the building of a Roman road will serve to explore what it was like for the Britons to be conquered by an invading force.

The illustration shows Roman soldiers using a surveying instrument called a *groma* to help them build their roads in straight lines.

Preparation

Identify one group of children in your class to represent Roman invaders. (This could be as many as half the class.) This should be done, without reference to the rest of the class (arrange it during play time). You will need to have some means of identifying them as Romans; this could be as elaborate as you wish or at its simplest, coloured badges will be sufficient. Roman names could also be given (such as Tiberius, Claudius, etc.). Identify the other half of the class as Britons and provide a similar set of badges together with Celtic names (for some examples see the *Asterix* series of cartoons). Prepare photocopiable page 119 for each child.

Resources needed

Badges and/or other items of clothing to distinguish half of the class as Roman invaders and the other half as Britons. Photocopiable page 119.

What to do

Introduction

As class teacher you have the option of playing the role of the Roman general (Claudius) or of briefing the 'Roman' members of the class before the lesson. During play time label the classroom door 'Britannia' and brief the Roman half of the class that they are to play the role of Roman invaders. When the rest of the class returns the 'Romans' must announce that they have invaded and that they have taken over control of the classroom (Britain).

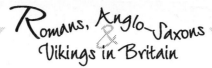

Tell the rest of the class that they are to pretend to be British farmers living in the countryside and that they will now have to obey orders from the Roman Emperor. At this point badges could be distributed to the Britons.

Development

Distribute the photocopiable sheet to all the children . Tell the class that as part of their plan to conquer Britain, the Romans intend to build roads (see illustration) which will make transportation much easier. They intend to build a road right through the area where the Britons live. Ask each child to look at the statements on the photocopiable sheet and, as a Roman or a Briton, to decide which views they agree with. Tell them to write agree or disagree next to each statement as they decide. Once the children have done this, ask them to group together as Romans and Britons and discuss their conclusions. Within the British camp there is likely to be a division of opinion, but they will need in the end to argue out their differences. Hopefully, there will be considerable opposition to the Roman plans. Although there may be some sympathy for the Britons in the Roman 'camp', army discipline and the power of the Emperor will determine one course of action, namely that the road must go ahead for strategic reasons (in order to move troops as quickly as possible from one place to another).

Now introduce a whole-class discussion of the pros and cons of building the road. This can be done in the form of a debate with the two sides ranged against one another.

Finally, the class can be invited, assuming that there is a serious disagreement over whether the road should be built or not, to suggest ways in which the conflict between the Britons and Romans might be resolved. Each member of the class could be asked to write his/her proposed solution on the reverse of the photocopiable sheet and the list of suggestions can be collated and presented to the class.

In reality, it was the power of the conquering Romans which would have ruled the day, although some British tribes were more friendly to the invading Romans than others. The Romans were able to divide and rule.

Suggestion(s) for extension

Study a map to see the limits of the Roman Empire. What modern countries were part of the Empire? Make a list of them. Try to identify any examples of Roman roads near to the school, using the local Ordnance Survey sheet.

Suggestion(s) for support

Some children can work in pairs with more able readers, when working on the photocopiable sheet.

Assessment opportunities

Assuming the activity 'Claudius's invasion' has been followed previously can the children explain how the Romans invaded Britain? What would the Britons have felt like? Ask the children to write out or record on audio tape, an argument between a Briton and a Roman about whether a road should be built.

Opportunities for IT

Children could use an art or drawing package to draw and label a typical cross-section of a Roman road, which could be included in a word-processor account.

A word-processor can be used to draft out their arguments about the pros and cons of building the Roman road. They could use the 'cut and paste' or 'drag and drop' commands

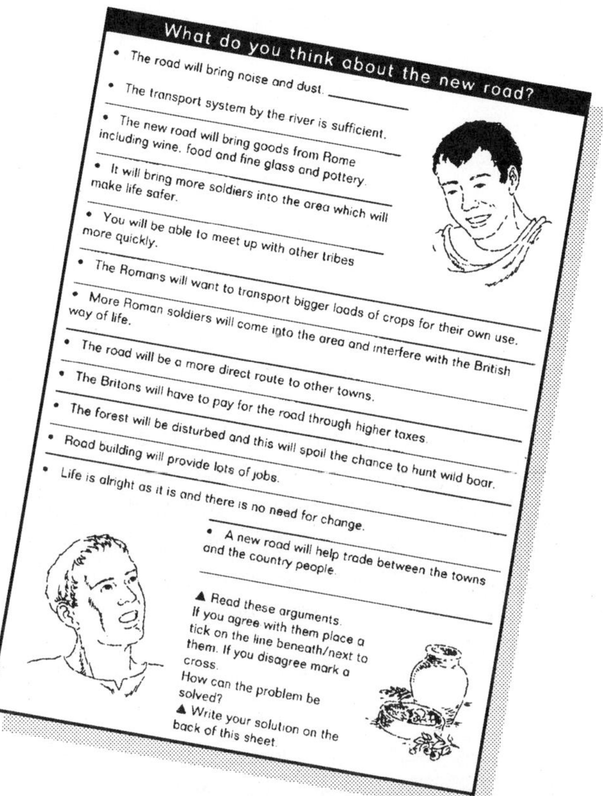

What do you think about the new road?

- The road will bring noise and dust.
- The transport system by the river is sufficient.
- The new road will bring goods from Rome including wine, food and fine glass and pottery.
- It will bring more soldiers into the area which will make life safer.
- You will be able to meet up with other tribes more quickly.
- The Romans will want to transport bigger loads of crops for their own use.
- More Roman soldiers will come into the area and interfere with the British way of life.
- The road will be a more direct route to other towns.
- The Britons will have to pay for the road through higher taxes.
- The forest will be disturbed and this will spoil the chance to hunt wild boar.
- Road building will provide lots of jobs.
- Life is alright as it is and there is no need for change.
- A new road will help trade between the towns and the country people.

▲ Read these arguments. If you agree with them place a tick on the line beneath/next to them. If you disagree mark a cross. How can the problem be solved?

▲ Write your solution on the back of this sheet.

to help them structure and organise their arguments into a logical order.

Use a CD-ROM encyclopaedia to search for information about Roman roads in England.

Display ideas

Combine a Roman road build-up scene, with a map showing Roman roads in Britain. Arguments could be tabulated for and against the building of a Roman road through British territory and displayed alongside the map.

Reference to photocopiable sheet

The photocopiable sheet on page 119 provides arguments for and against road building. Children can record their attempts to resolve the conflict on the reverse of the sheet.

THE REVOLT OF BOUDICCA

To learn about the reasons for and the results of an historical event. To learn about bias in how events have been recorded.

Whole class followed by group and individual activities.

Introduction 15 minutes; main activity 45 minutes.

Previous skills/knowledge needed

Children should be familiar with some of the advantages and disadvantages derived from Roman rule – see previous activity.

Key background information

The revolt of Boudicca in AD 61 is told by Tacitus who was a Roman historian. Boudicca's husband had been king of the Iceni. When he died, his wife Boudicca was flogged by the Romans and her two daughters were attacked. The chief men of the Iceni had their farms taken away from them. The king's own family were treated like slaves. Angry at what had happened and afraid of worse things to come, the Iceni called on their neighbours the Trinobantes to join their rebellion against the Romans. In particular they hated the retired Roman soldiers because they had driven out the Britons from their land calling them slaves and they had also taken their homes from them.

The rebellion alarmed the Romans. The rebels set light to and destroyed the towns of Londinium, Verulamium (St Albans) and Camulodunum (Colchester). Tacitus, a Roman historian, says that the Britons were hell-bent on bloodshed, and hangings and on burning and crucifying. Following the revolt, the Emperor Nero was said to have seriously considered withdrawing his army of occupation from Britain.

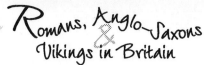

Preparation

Prepare a version of Boudicca's story to tell the children. (A more detailed account can be found in Tacitus *Annals* XIV 31-7, Penguin Classics.) Prepare enough of the photocopiable sheet on page 120 for one per child.

Resources needed

Black sugar paper, scissors, adhesive and red, yellow and orange tissue paper, photocopiable page 120.

What to do

Tell the whole class the story of Boudicca's revolt against the Romans. Consider the arguments given by Tacitus for the revolt. How might the list of British grievances be extended? Ask the children to work in groups to make a frieze showing Roman buildings silhouetted against the sky, being licked by brightly coloured flames.

Distribute the photocopiable sheet and ask the children to read the description of Boudicca carefully and then complete the statement made by Britorix. Explain that people in the Roman Empire were not used to being ruled by women. Tell them that Dio Cassius was a historian and was himself a member of the Roman senate long after Boudicca's time. Discuss the issue of bias in written sources and consider the different viewpoint that a Briton would have had from that of Roman writers. Let the children continue at their own pace to design a recruitment poster based on the verbal description of Boudicca.

Suggestion(s) for extension

Consider the statement that the Emperor Nero seriously considered withdrawing from Britain as a consequence of Boudicca's revolt. Invite the children to discuss and make a list of all the reasons why Nero might have considered withdrawing. They may think of:

▲ The initial threat to security (dissident Gauls fleeing to Britain) has vanished;
▲ The Britons are uncontrollable without extra forces;
▲ The amount of gold and silver does not appear to be as much as previously thought;
▲ Corn needed by the army is only available in the lowland areas;
▲ The costs do not outweigh the benefits;
▲ Britain is a very long way from Rome and the troops are unhappy.

Working in groups of four or five, each group can then write out each argument on a separate piece of blank card. Having done this ask each group to produce a 'Causation circle'. They should draw a series of concentric circles and decide which is the most important argument for withdrawal and place it in the centre. The lesser reasons should then be placed further from the centre according to their importance.

Finally, ask the children to consider the counter arguments which helped to persuade the emperor not to withdraw.

They may come up with:
▲ The emperor would lose face and seem weak;
▲ Rome would lose British supplies of slaves, and precious metals;
▲ There would be a renewed risk of insecurity from across the channel;
▲ The army needs to be kept occupied.

Suggestion(s) for support

Look at examples of historic war posters, for example, from the First World War Kitchener: 'What did you do in the war, daddy?'. Read through Dio's description of Boudicca very carefully. Encourage the children to underline words which describe Boudicca's appearance. Discuss what she might have looked like before asking the children to make a drawing of Boudicca.

Assessment opportunities

Ask the children to draw their own pictures of Boudicca and say why it is different from Dio's account. Which parts of the description would be more/less reliable? Can the children explain the reason for and the result of Boudicca's revolt? For those doing the extension work, can they suggest historical reasons why Nero might have withdrawn? Do they recognise that some reasons might have been more important than others?

Opportunities for IT

Some groups or individuals might use a word processor to draft and write arguments about whether the Romans should stay or leave, and these can then be developed into a structured piece of writing. You may like to create a writing frame, giving the children a series of prompts for their writing. This could be set up in advance and saved so that children could be shown how to load it into the word processor.

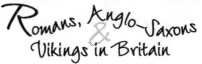

Display ideas

Display the silhouette frieze of burning buildings.

Reference to photocopiable sheet

The photocopiable sheet on page 120 gives Dio's account of Boudicca and shows a statement made by a British warrior for the children to complete.

Supporting Boudicca

▲ Dio wrote a history of the Romans. This is what he said about Boudicca:

"Boudicca was a Briton of royal descent. The rebels thought her their best leader. She was much more intelligent than women usually are. She was tall, and she was terrifying to look at. She had a fierce look in her eyes and a raucous voice. A huge mass of yellow hair hung down to her hips. Around her neck she had a huge torque of gold and she wore a dress of many colours, pinned together with a brooch. This was how she normally dressed."

My name is Britorix. I am a soldier in Boudicca's army. We are fighting the Romans because.....

▲ Draw your own picture of Boudicca. How far will it be different from what Dio tells us?

LIFE IN TOWNS

To introduce the characteristic features of Roman towns (in Britain) and the experiences of men and women living in these towns.

Whole class followed by paired activity.

Introductory session 30 minutes; 30 minutes for the activity on photocopiable worksheet page 121.

Previous skills/knowledge needed

Knowledge about the invasion and conquest of Britain by the Romans would be necessary.

Key background information

As the Roman army moved through lowland Britain into Wales and towards the Pennines, the process of building towns began. Some of these towns included large numbers of retired legionary soldiers who were given land and encouraged to settle within its boundaries. Examples of these *coloniae* (singular *colonia*) are: Camulodunum (Colchester), Glevum (Gloucester), Lindum (Lincoln) and York (Eboracum). Londinium (London) developed on the River Tamesis (Thames) as a major port but most other towns were built as capitals of the British tribes.

Towns varied tremendously in size but most of the larger towns would have had many features in common. A glance at the Ordnance Survey map of Roman Britain will show that the towns of Roman Britain were closely situated to villas. This suggests that the town and the country dwellers closely depended on each other. Towns were connected together by the network of roads built by the Romans. At a later date, walls and gateways were added to the many towns.

There are a number of things that you would expect to find as part of most Roman towns: roads laid out as a grid pattern, houses, shops and workshops, a *forum* (market place), a cemetery, boundary walls and ditches, gateways, religious buildings, roads leading to and from the town. Also sometimes you would find a theatre, an amphitheatre, baths and an aqueduct.

Preparation

Collect together information about the different parts of a Roman town. It will be particularly helpful if use can be made of guidebooks, postcards or information from museums and Romano-British town sites. Create an outline plan of a Roman town, using the photocopiable page 121 as a guide and enlarge it onto a sheet of white paper, or prepare a version of the plan for an overhead projector or board. Include the street grid but not other features. Write out a card for each of the features you might find in a town (identified above). Photocopy the sheet on page 121 sufficient for one per child.

Resources needed

A large outline plan of a Roman town (use page 121 as a guide), guidebooks, postcards or information from museums and Romano-British town sites, photocopiable page 121. General reference books.

What to do

Use the enlarged Roman town plan with the outline and street network only to introduce the layout of a Roman town and to identify some of the features that you might have expected to see in one. Distribute the cards bearing the different features of a Roman town to pairs of children and ask each pair to place their particular feature on to the plan. Some key questions to ask are: Which do you think were the most important places in a Roman town? Would some things go together? If the children already know something about Roman towns, for example, as the result of a trip, then try to use this additional knowledge too. The guidebooks available and other reference materials could also be considered for ideas.

Distribute the photocopiable sheet and ask the children to follow up the general discussion by making their own town plan inserting the appropriate buildings, using the sheet as an example.

Suggestion(s) for extension

Some children could go on to use reference books to find out about other elements of a Roman town such as shops and commercial outlets or the town water system.

Suggestion(s) for support

Limit the number of items you would find in a Roman town but include the forum, temple, baths and houses. Let the children talk into a tape recorder about each feature of the town in turn or alternatively make a pictorial guide to the different parts of the town.

Assessment opportunities

Children will discuss in their pairs the arguments for excavating urban amenities in particular situations. They can be asked to give reasons for their choice. Summative assessment: how many things can you remember that you would expect to find in a Roman town?

Opportunities for IT

Children could use a drawing package to design the layout for their own Roman town. They could add different buildings using pictures taken from clip art collections, scanned from their own line drawings or photographs or created using an art package.

Alternatively children could use a floor robot like 'Roamer' or 'Pipp' and instruct it to move around a floor-sized map of a Roman town; issuing the commands to move from one named building to another.

Display ideas

Make a large-scale table top model or wall display. Children can contribute models of different parts of the town.

Reference to photocopiable sheet

Photocopiable page 121 shows a Roman town plan.

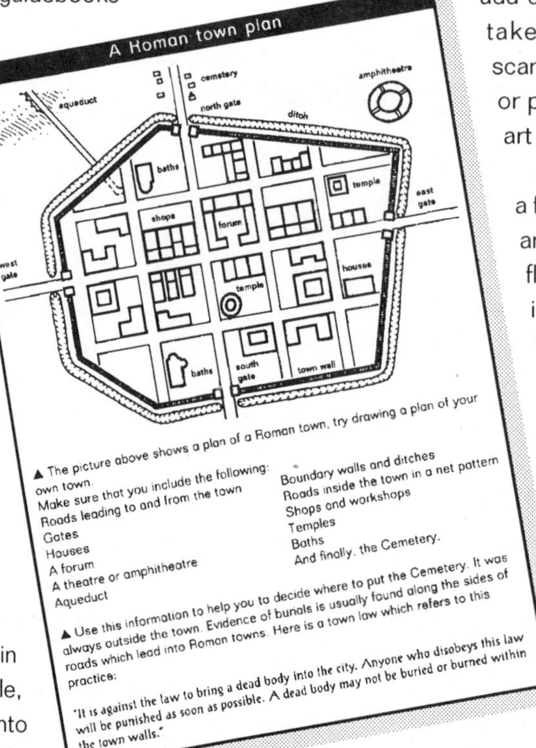

A Roman town plan

▲ The picture above shows a plan of a Roman town, try drawing a plan of your own town.

Make sure that you include the following:

Roads leading to and from the town
Gates
Houses
A forum
A theatre or amphitheatre
Aqueduct
Boundary walls and ditches
Roads inside the town in a net pattern
Shops and workshops
Temples
Baths
And finally, the Cemetery.

▲ Use this information to help you to decide where to put the Cemetery. It was always outside the town. Evidence of burials is usually found along the sides of roads which lead into Roman towns. Here is a town law which refers to this practice:

"It is against the law to bring a dead body into the city. Anyone who disobeys this law will be punished as soon as possible. A dead body may not be buried or burned within the town walls."

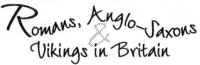

MAKING ROMAN MOSAICS

To find out about Roman mosaics and how they were made and to communicate this knowledge.

Whole class followed by collaborative and individual activity.

Four sessions spread out over a week or more. Session one (introduction) – 60 minutes. Sessions two and three will vary in length and will depend on the quantity of tesserae made and the number of colours used etc. Session four – 45 minutes.

Previous skills and knowledge needed

Children will need to be familiar with using self-hardening clay and poster paints. They will also need to have an awareness of mosaics and what they were used for.

Key background information

The art of making mosaics was not unique to the Roman World. For example, the Aztecs used small pieces of turquoise to make a form of mosaic and the people of ancient Sumer decorated their temples in a form of mosaic decoration (see pages 109 and 101). Some of the best examples are those which survive from the Byzantine empire. In Britain, as elsewhere, the floors of houses of the wealthy in town and country alike were decorated with mosaics. These took the form of pictures compiled from a very large number of small squarish stones of contrasting colours. The Romans learned the art of mosaic making from the Greeks who began by using coloured pebbles. In Britain the range of colours used for mosaics was limited to the available stones, though they frequently used baked clay for red. The small stone pieces called tesserae were arranged to form abstract patterns or representations of animal and plant forms including scenes from stories.

Preparation

Obtain some examples of good quality photographs of Roman mosaic which are detailed enough to show the individual tesserae. Transparencies are ideal for this purpose, although some examples of postcards which can be used as reference material will also be very helpful. Try to get examples of abstract designs as well as those depicting human, animal and plant forms.

Resources needed

Squared paper (graph paper), coloured crayons or pencils, pictures of mosaics, shallow polystyrene trays (the type that you get from a supermarket), self-hardening clay, poster paints, adhesive and glazing medium.

What to do

Session 1

Show the class some good photographs of Roman mosaics from Britain and elsewhere. Choose examples which show clearly the separate tesserae and which indicate how the picture has been constructed from many small stones. Discuss with the children how this could be done in the classroom and then invite them to use a sheet of squared paper to design their own pictures, using the small squares for different coloured stones. Stress that the British mosaic makers were often restricted to a limited range of colours, perhaps: black/blue stone, white stone, yellow stone and red (baked clay).

Session 2

Roll out pieces of self-hardening clay to a thickness of about half a centimetre and then score it deeply into squares. Leave each piece of scored clay to dry out.

Session 3

Next apply one colour to each scored piece of hardened clay.

Session 4

Once the paint has dried, each scored piece of clay can be carefully broken up into cubes to represent tesserae. The class will have a large selection of different coloured tessarae from which to compose their mosaic pictures.

Tell the children to draw an outline of their designs on the base of a polystyrene tray or card base. They can then stick the tesserae to the base. Once this has dried, the completed mosaic can be coated with a glaze to finish it.

Suggestion(s) for extension

Investigate the stories portrayed in some of the large mosaic pictures from Roman times, for example 'Orpheus and the animals' was popular in Roman Britain.

Suggestion(s) for support

If children are having trouble designing their own mosaics then suggest that they try very simple geometric shapes.

Assessment opportunities

Can the children explain the process of making mosaics step by step? Let them make a set of instructions to show the processes they used.

Opportunities for IT

Children could use an art or drawing package to create their own Roman mosaics, using the copy or duplicate functions to reproduce one section and rotate it to create a symmetrical pattern. If children use an art package they can 'zoom' into the pattern so that they can identify each pixel in its own grid of squares and edit or alter their pattern in great detail. Alternatively *My World 2* software can be used to create mosaic patterns.

More dedicated software such as the *Art Machine* or *Tiler* which automatically creates symmetrical patterns on screen is also available.

Display ideas

Completed mosaics can be used to form an impressive display beside photographs of real Roman mosaics for comparison. Alternative methods to those suggested above might substitute coloured sticky paper or egg shells. However, the simulated tesserae provide a much more authentic experience of the mosaic makers task.

THE LATIN LANGUAGE

To find out about the language the Romans used and to notice some differences and similarities between their language and modern English.

Pairs and individuals.

Several sessions of 30–40 minutes each.

Previous skills/knowledge needed

Ability to use a dictionary.

Key background information

The English language owes an enormous debt to Latin. The incoming Angles and Saxons spoke an early Germanic language which is distinctively different from Latin. However, the Normans brought large numbers of words of Latin origin into Britain at the time of the Conquest, because they spoke an early form of French which was derived from Latin. Many of the words came into use during the Renaissance. Some whole Latin words remain in modern English (terror, animal, arena, via, item, maximum/minimum), as well as many terms which are now abbreviated n.b., i.e., e.g., etc.; mottos; words on coins; medical terminology; legal terminology. Whole categories of words such as those ending in -ation and -ion also come from Latin roots.

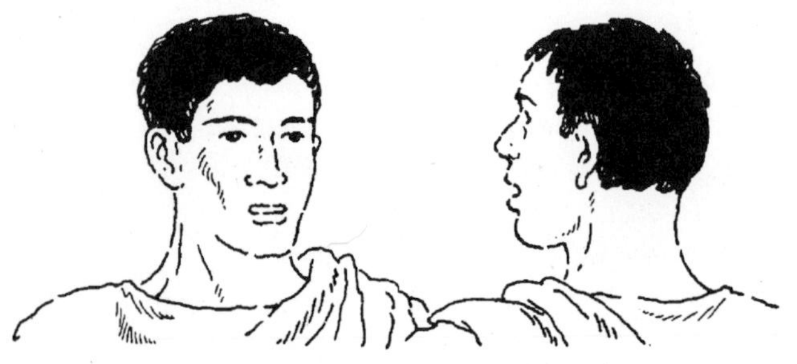

Preparation

Copy sufficient numbers of the photocopiable sheet on page 122 for each child to work individually.

Resources needed

Photocopiable sheet on page 122.

What to do

Begin by explaining to the whole class that the Romans spoke a different language from English, some children will have heard of 'Latin'. The Latins originally occupied an area around Rome (Latium = today Lazio). There is a well known modern day Italian football team - Lazio! The Romans left behind their language in Europe because Latin was the official language in the western part of the Roman Empire, even though the lower classes would have continued to use their traditional Celtic language. Large numbers of words in English come indirectly from Latin, for example: Roman numbers. Use these to illustrate how words with Roman origin are still used today in English.

Roman numbers

I *unus* – unicorn; united.
II *duo* – dual; duet.
III *tres/tria* – triangle; trident.
IV *quattuor* – quarters.
V *quinque* – quins; quincentenary.
VI *sex* – sextuplets; sextet.

VII *septem*
VIII *octo*
IX *novem*
X *decem*

The months September – December were originally the 7th, 8th, 9th and 10th in the calendar before the Romans added July (Julius Caesar) and August (Augustus Caesar).

IC *centum* – century; centipede.
M *mille* – millenium.

Encourage the children to use dictionaries to look up further examples. How many English words can they find which are connected with Roman numbers?

Hand out the photocopiable sheet and ask the children to match the Latin words with the correct English translations as a matching exercise.

Flash cards could also be made with the Latin words written on, and used by the whole class.

Suggestion(s) for extension

Use published Latin courses such as Unit 1, Stage 1 (set in a Roman house in Pompeii) of the Cambridge Latin Course and let children work through some of the early sections. More able pupils even in Year 3 should be able to cope with these early stages.

Suggestion(s) for support

Choose a few English words which derive from Roman numbers and let the children match up the two lists:

quinque – quins
duo – duet
decem – decimals
centum – century

Assessment opportunities

Provide a list of Latin words; can the children recognise English words within the list?

Opportunities for IT

Children could use a hand-held electronic dictionary or the spell checker dictionary on their word processor to search for other words with a Latin derivation. They may need to be shown how to include an unknown 'wildcard' in their search, or to set up a search on the dictionary which includes words of a particular kind or with a particular start. They could create and print out a list, with the Latin stem as the title and then a list of other related words and their meanings. These could be used in a classroom display.

Display ideas

Make a chart to show Latin words which are derived from English. Create a diagram like a family tree to show how Latin is related to other languages.

Reference to photocopiable sheet

The photocopiable sheet on page 122 requires the children to match up the Latin and English word strips by joining them with arrows. Correct translations are: Villa=house; Magister=Teacher; Servus=Slave; Milites=Soldiers; Flores=Flowers; Herba=Grass; Agricola=Farmer; Navis=Ship; Libri=Books; Mus=Mouse; Femina=woman.

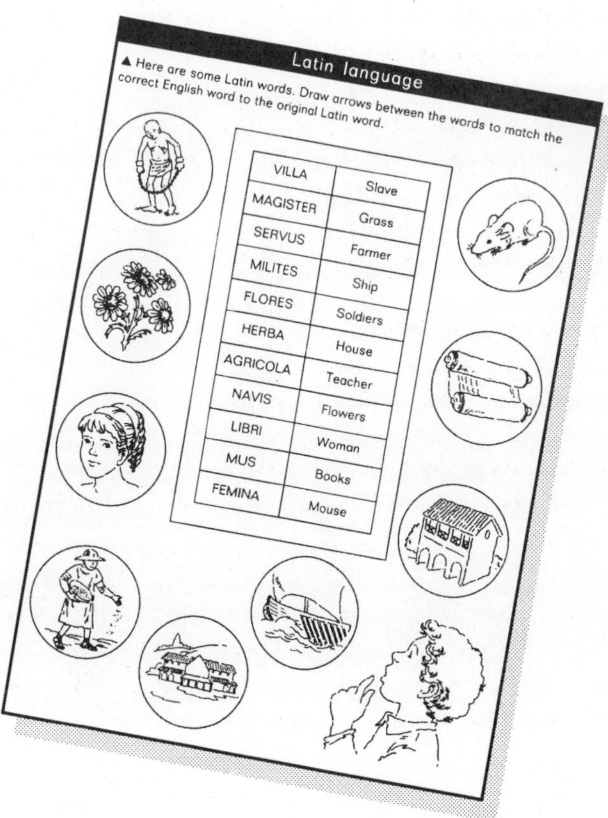

Latin language

▲ Here are some Latin words. Draw arrows between the words to match the correct English word to the original Latin word.

VILLA	Slave
MAGISTER	Grass
SERVUS	Farmer
MILITES	Ship
FLORES	Soldiers
HERBA	House
AGRICOLA	Teacher
NAVIS	Flowers
LIBRI	Woman
MUS	Books
FEMINA	Mouse

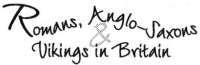

THE END OF ROMAN BRITAIN

To use the term: invasion and to compare it with the earlier examples of the Roman invasion of Britain.

Whole class followed by individual and group activity.

60 minutes and follow-up work.

Previous skills/knowledge needed

It will be helpful if the children have studied interior pictures of a reconstructed Roman villa in colour (for example the rooms of a villa on display in the Corinium Museum, Cirencester). It will also be useful if they have looked at other examples of invasion such as the Roman invasions of Julius Caesar (55 and 54 BC) and Claudius (AD 43).

Key background information

This activity provides a specific context in which the children can recognise the idea of an invasion of a hitherto peaceful settlement by an alien group of people.

By the middle of the fourth century AD, the relative peace of the northern Roman empire was shattered by increasing activity of many peoples who sought to invade and to establish settlements. By land, the main northern frontier of the empire along the Rhine and Danube rivers had long been under pressure but now there was a serious threat by sea also. It would not be long before the Roman authorities would be forced to withdraw their troops from Britain in order to defend other parts of the Empire where help was urgently needed. They would thus leave the people of Britain to defend themselves as best they could against all comers. These early invasions by groups of Saxons and other 'barbarian' peoples were to pave the way for future settlements in Northern Europe for example Saxons in southern Britain, Scots (from Ireland) in Scotland, and Franks in France. Also other groups not referred to here, principally the Angles in East Anglia and the Midlands (Mercia).

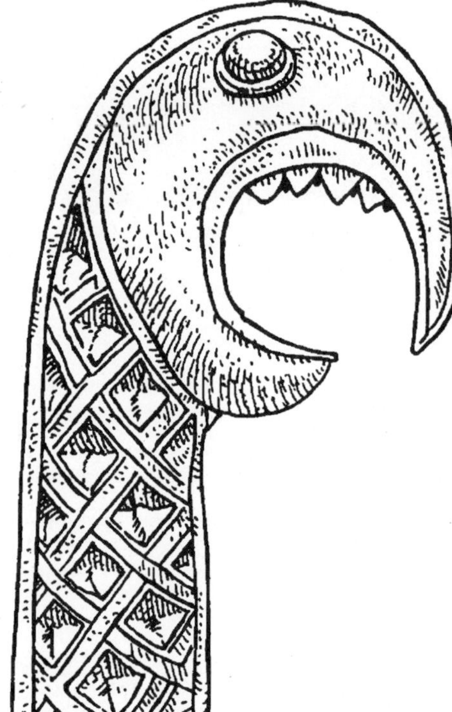

Preparation

If practicable, involve the children in decorating one wall of the classroom in the Roman style, with blank spaces left for windows. If this is undertaken, offcuts of surplus wall paper (reverse side) or lining paper can be used to cover the wall chosen and attempts could be made to use marbling inks and different combinations of colour to represent the Roman style of wall painting. Sponge printing might also be used. Photocopy sufficient numbers of the photocopiable sheet on page 123, one per child.

Resources needed

Pictures of Roman wall paintings for reference. Photocopiable page 123.

What to do

Invite the whole class to imagine that they live in a Roman villa in Britain in AD 367, at a time when the country is being invaded by bands of sea raiders. Use the information supplied on the photocopiable sheet either to tell a short story about invaders being sighted from one of the windows of the villa or present them with the actual words of the Roman historian. The strangers are seen rowing their long boats up the river, coming closer and closer all the time. Discuss with the class their feelings as these raiders approach their house. Invite the children to write down their first reactions. Their responses could be used to make a choral poem.

Continue by describing the evidence that archaeologists have dug up which shows what happened to some of the villas in Britain at this time. This is an opportunity to discuss how archaeologists reach their conclusions, for example why certain items survive in the ground while others may disappear without trace (see Chapter 2, pages 18–19).

Ask the whole class to make a personal response to the situation of a Romano-British villa owner being invaded. They can imagine that they managed to escape and can write a response in the form of a letter describing the invasion and how they felt. The spaces in the villa wall can now be painted in showing, longboats coming up the river.

Suggestion(s) for extension

More able pupils could be referred to the archaeological evidence on the photocopiable sheet and asked to make a list of all the things that archaeologists might have dug up at this villa which would give them clues that it was attacked in an invasion.

Suggestion(s) for support

Children can make pictures of themselves as a Romano-British person who has received news of attack on a nearby villa. Tell them to use a speech bubble to express their feelings and what they intend to do.

Assessment opportunities

Observe how the children use the word invasion in their accounts. Children will by now have studied both the Roman invasion and the first arrival of Germanic invaders. Get them to write about the differences between the Roman invasion (large scale planned expedition, elephants etc.) and the Saxon settlers (small bands of seafarers, sailing up rivers, sacking villas etc.).

Opportunities for IT

Use a word processor to write and draft a letter describing the invasion. Experiment with different types of fonts to give the letter a more authentic feel.

Children could also use a simulation package such as *Arcventure I The Romans* to give them experience of investigating an archaeological site. Such work needs to be a central part of the work in history so that pupils have enough time to explore the software fully and that activities at the computer are linked to other class activities. Teachers also need to talk to pupils about their use of such software, identifying the kind of model that the software is using; its limitations and children's understanding of how they interact with the model.

Display ideas

The villa interior described above should make an attractive display. It should be completed by including pictures of the completed villa wall showing the advancing invaders as seen from the window(s).

Produce a large-scale outline map of your local area and record on it, using an appropriate key, all the evidence for Roman settlement which you know about. Further investigation could then be undertaken with the help of the local museum and books about the early history of your locality (for example Ordnance Survey Maps, and more recent surveys by archaeological groups), this will enable a more comprehensive record of local Roman settlements to be made. (See also *Curriculum Bank History: II* (Scholastic)).

Reference to photocopiable sheet

The photocopiable sheet on page 123 shows an account from a Roman historian on the state of the Roman Empire between 367 and 368 which could be helpful for children writing about their villa invasions.

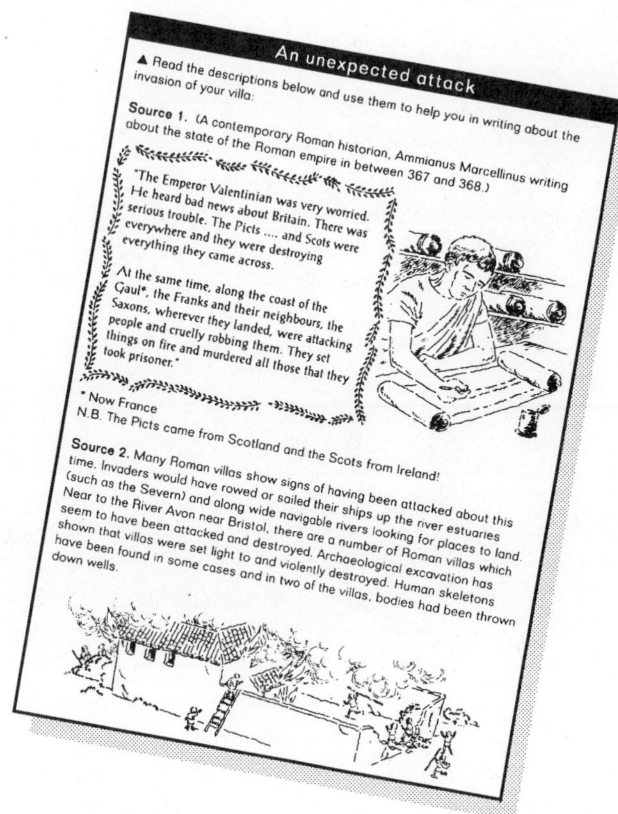

An unexpected attack

▲ Read the descriptions below and use them to help you in writing about the invasion of your villa:

Source 1. (A contemporary Roman historian, Ammianus Marcellinus writing about the state of the Roman empire in between 367 and 368.)

"The Emperor Valentinian was very worried. He heard bad news about Britain. There was serious trouble. The Picts .... and Scots were everywhere and they were destroying everything they came across.

At the same time, along the coast of the Gaul*, the Franks and their neighbours, the Saxons, wherever they landed, were attacking people and cruelly robbing them. They set things on fire and murdered all those that they took prisoner."

* Now France

N.B. The Picts came from Scotland and the Scots from Ireland!

Source 2. Many Roman villas show signs of having been attacked about this time. Invaders would have rowed or sailed their ships up the river estuaries (such as the Severn) and along wide navigable rivers looking for places to land. Near to the River Avon near Bristol, there are a number of Roman villas which seem to have been attacked and destroyed. Archaeological excavation has shown that villas were set light to and violently destroyed. Human skeletons have been found in some cases and in two of the villas, bodies had been thrown down wells.

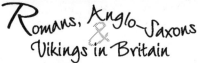

EARLY ANGLE AND SAXON SETTLERS

To find out about the early Anglo-Saxon settlers using documents and artefacts.

Whole class followed by individual/paired/small group work.

60 minutes with opportunities for follow-up work.

Previous skills/knowledge needed

The activities could build on work undertaken in the previous activity, the end of Roman Britain, page 44.

Key background information

Evidence about the early settlers in the fifth and sixth centuries results largely from the work of archaeologists. Extensive study of the pottery vessels in which these people buried the ashes of their dead suggests close connections with the continental homelands from which these people came. Bede, writing in the eighth century, tells us that they came from three very powerful German nations, the Saxons, the Angles and the Jutes.

The people of Kent and the Isle of Wight are descended from the Jutes; the East Saxons, South Saxons and West Saxons are descended from the Saxons; the East Angles, the Middle Angles, the Mercians and all the Northumbrians (north of the river Humber), are descended from the Angles, that is to say, from the country called Angulus (Angeln in Schleswig, North Germany). Their first leaders, it is said, were two brothers, Hengest and Horsa.

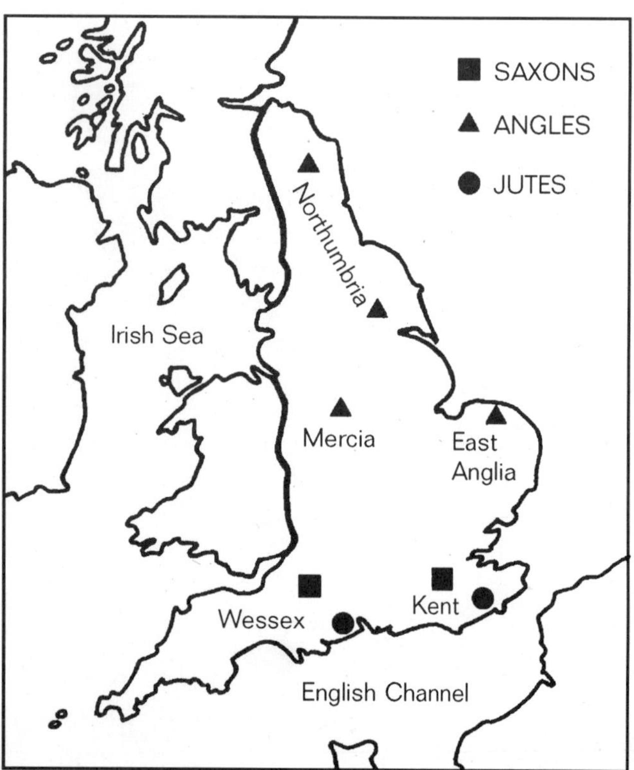

The areas referred to by Bede as settled by Saxons correspond to the ancient kingdom of Wessex and to the modern counties of Essex and Sussex. The term East Anglia is still used to denote the eastern counties of England. The Middle Angles settled around the Peterborough area, whilst Mercia embraced a wide area of the Midlands. A study of the pottery evidence linking places on the continent and the new settlers of eastern Britain during the fifth and sixth centuries suggests that the picture described by Bede in the eighth century was more complicated in reality. In fact two of the examples shown on the photocopiable sheet (page 124), show links between Saxony and areas credited by Bede as being Anglian.

Later Anglo-Saxon rulers claimed that their dynasties had been founded by successful invaders leading war-bands carried in a small number of ships during the fifth century. The use of place name evidence as an attempt to locate the earliest settlements of Germanic settlers in Britain has been the subject of much controversy. However, it is useful to note that there are many place names in England with the syllable -ing, the Old English *-ingas* means 'dependants' of or 'people of', so that the place name Hastings means the people of Haesta (*Haestingas*), with Haesta apparently being the leader of a group of settlers. Similarly Reading derives from the *Readingas* - the people of Reada.

Preparation

Have available a large map of Britain and Northern Europe which the whole class can see. Prepare to use information on this map to explain the early movement of Germanic settlers. Make sure that each child has access to a modern map of England. Copy photocopiable page 124, one per child.

Resources needed

Atlases showing the map of modern England, blank outline maps of Britain, large map of Britain and Northern Europe. Photocopiable page 124.

What to do

Introduce to the whole class the concept of Germanic invasions. You may like to use the account of Bede to give the activity a little excitement and colour. These invasions appear to have been invariably small scale, each led by a warlord. If the class has already undertaken the activity on page 44, the idea will already be clear otherwise the important change here is from invasion to settlement. By the time that the Romans no longer regarded Britain as part of their Empire – Roman legions had long since been withdrawn and in fact, the city of Rome itself had been captured by the 'Barbarians' – Britain was prey to large scale settlement by the new invaders.

Give the children the photocopied sheet and ask them to use arrows to match up the pots on the left hand side with those on the right. They can then use the index of an atlas

of Britain and make a list of all the place names which include the syllable -ing. Tell the children to include place names which end in -ingham and -ington as well as those ending in -ing(s). They can use a blank map of Britain to plot the approximate position of each place name using a dot for each place name.

Now tell the children to place large coloured dots on the map to represent the areas in which the pots on the photocopiable sheet were found.

As a whole class discuss the relative value of different kinds of sources: How far do the finds of pots coincide with the areas covered by -ing place names. How far does Bede in his written account of 200 years later agree with this evidence?

The Angle and Saxon settlers came in their boats by sea and river. As a further development discuss the locations of Anglo-Saxon Place names in relation to rivers.

Suggestion(s) for extension

Ask some children to find the name of a river which runs near to one or more places ending in -ing. Extend the exercise on the photocopiable sheet by supplying the children with the following further additional finds of pots from Anglo-Saxon cemeteries:

Nottinghamshire – Anglian pottery
Cambridgeshire – Saxon pottery
Yorkshire – South German pottery
Kent – Jutish pottery.

Suggestion(s) for support

Help children to find the following places on an atlas using an index and co-ordinates: Hastings, Sheringham, Manningtree and Gillingham.

Assessment opportunities

Ask the children to describe how we know about the early Anglo-Saxon settlers. What evidence do we have to go on?

Opportunities for IT

Teachers could use *Arcventure IV The Anglo Saxons* to explore the archaeological excavation of a particular Anglo Saxon site. Such work needs to be a central part of the work in history so that pupils have enough time to explore the software fully and that activities at the computer are linked to other class activities. Teachers also need to talk to pupils about their use of such software, identifying the kind of model that the software is using; its limitations and children's understanding of how they interact with the model.

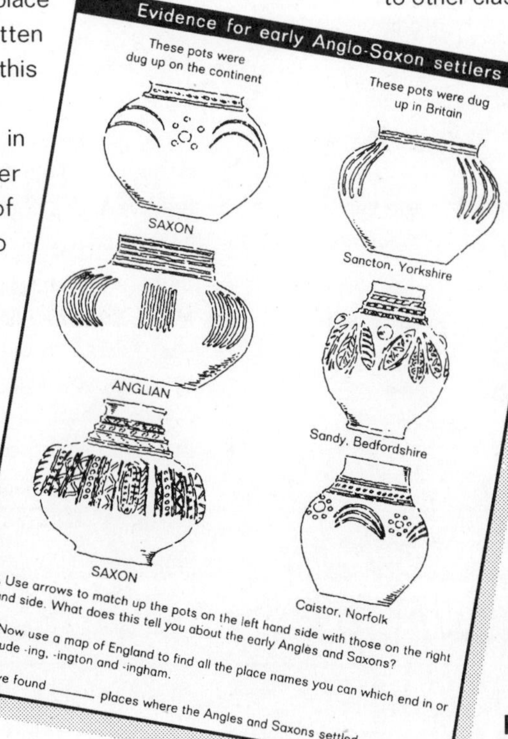

Evidence for early Anglo-Saxon settlers

These pots were dug up on the continent

These pots were dug up in Britain

SAXON

Sancton, Yorkshire

ANGLIAN

Sandy, Bedfordshire

SAXON

Caistor, Norfolk

▲ Use arrows to match up the pots on the left hand side with those on the right hand side. What does this tell you about the early Angles and Saxons?

▲ Now use a map of England to find all the place names you can which end in or include -ing, -ington and -ingham.

I have found ______ places where the Angles and Saxons settled.

Display ideas

A large blank map with place name evidence recorded on it, possibly with each kind of name -ington, -ingham, -ing, etc. separately distinguished. Alternatively a series of maps showing the evidence from Bede, place names and archaeology separately.

Reference to photocopiable sheets

Photocopiable page 124 asks the children to match up pots found on the continent and Britain. It shows how Saxon pots can turn up in normally Anglian areas.

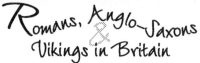

CONVERSION OF ANGLES & SAXONS TO CHRISTIANITY

To introduce the term conversion and to enable children to communicate their knowledge and understanding using structured narrative.

Whole class followed by opportunities for group and individual work.

60 minutes; follow-up.

Previous skills/knowledge needed

The previous activity 'Early Angle and Saxon settlers', page 46, would provide a useful context for this activity, but it is not essential to have worked through it.

Key background information

Although there is widespread evidence for Christianity in Britain in the late Roman Empire, the Angles, Saxons and other settlers brought their own religion with them from Northern Europe. This religion was based upon their worship of the Germanic gods. Unlike the Christians who buried their dead without grave goods, the Angles and Saxons (see previous activity – Early Angle and Saxon settlers) cremated their dead and buried their ashes in urns together with personal objects. 
Meanwhile the Christian church survived in Wales and in Cornwall, Devon, Cumbria as well as in Western Scotland (Strathclyde).

Although attempts at converting the new settlers to Christianity may have been made earlier, the earliest written record of missionary activity appears in the writing of the Venerable Bede, a Northumbrian monk writing in the eighth century. Bede tells us that Pope Gregory sent from Rome a mission under Augustine to the court of the powerful King Ethelbert of Kent in 597. The conversion of Ethelbert, who had married a Christian Frankish princess but was not himself a Christian, is regarded as particularly remarkable, although it was a long time before Christianity was adopted by the English on a large scale. There were significant differences between the practices of the newly converted Christian church of the Anglo-Saxons and that of the Celtic church which had survived in the Western parts of Britain. Accordingly in 664, a conference or Synod was called at Whitby in the kingdom of Northumbria in order to sort out some of these main differences. The Synod, held in 664 was presided over by an important female figure in the Church, the Abbess Hilda of Whitby. Differences in practice between the two Christian churches included a dispute over when Easter should be celebrated.

Preparation

Make sure that you are familiar with the story of Ethelbert's conversion as supplied by Bede on the photocopiable sheet on page 125.

Resources needed

Any available examples of archaeological evidence for early Anglo-Saxon Christianity such as this Anglo-Saxon cross. Photocopiable page 125.

What to do

Begin by talking to the children about religious conversion (people trying to change what other people believe and to accept new beliefs). The mission of the Christian church encouraged this. Being a Christian meant not only living 'good' lives but also persuading others to become Christians. Distribute copies of the photocopiable sheet and read together the story of Augustine's visit to Britain and the conversion of King Ethelbert of Kent to Christianity. Explain that a monk called Bede was interested in telling the story of the Christian church in Britain and its beginnings. The story can be used as a starting point for discussing the concept of religious conversion. Ask the children: what reasons does Bede give for people being converted? Why do you think Ethelbert was persuaded to become a Christian? How did people get to know about Christianity?

Suggestion(s) for extension

Can the children identify the reasons why Ethelbert might have decided to become a Christian?

Ask the children to find out about other examples of early Christian missionaries for example Patrick's mission to convert Ireland (an example of Christianity flourishing in late

Roman Britain) and from stories such as Pope Gregory in the Roman slave market – 'angels not Angles' (Bede Book II Chapter 1) which leads into the Augustines' mission to the English peoples.

Suggestion(s) for support:
Read through the photocopiable sheet with the children. Talk about what happened. Ask them to mime the story. What props will they need to help them do this?

Assessment opportunities
As the children talk through Ethelbert's story listen to what they say. Do they include and use the term conversion correctly? What other ways/terms do they use to explain Ethelbert's conversion?

Opportunities for IT
Children could use a CD-ROM encyclopaedia to find information about other early Christian missionaries; possibly saving the text they find in ASCII format so that it can be used in a word processor. Children could then use the word processor to refine the information they have discovered or to piece together notes and information taken from a variety of sources before writing a short paragraph about a particular missionary. Set a word limit of 400 words to make sure that the children sift the information carefully and include the most important points of the story. Children may be able to add pictures also taken from the CD-ROM or scanned from photographs in other books and resources.

Groups of children could combine their information using a multi-media authoring package to create a presentation about different early Christians. Each group of children could be given three or four linked pages in which they tell the story, using text and pictures and possibly even trying to record their own voices using a microphone connected to the computer.

Display ideas
Display examples of individual cartoon strips made by the children showing the conversion of Ethelbert or a series of pictures showing the story sequence. These could be grouped around an altar with an Anglo Saxon cross.

Reference to photocopiable sheet
The photocopiable sheet on page 125 provides Bede's account of Ethelbert's conversion to Christianity. Children can use this account to draw or write about their own version of the event.

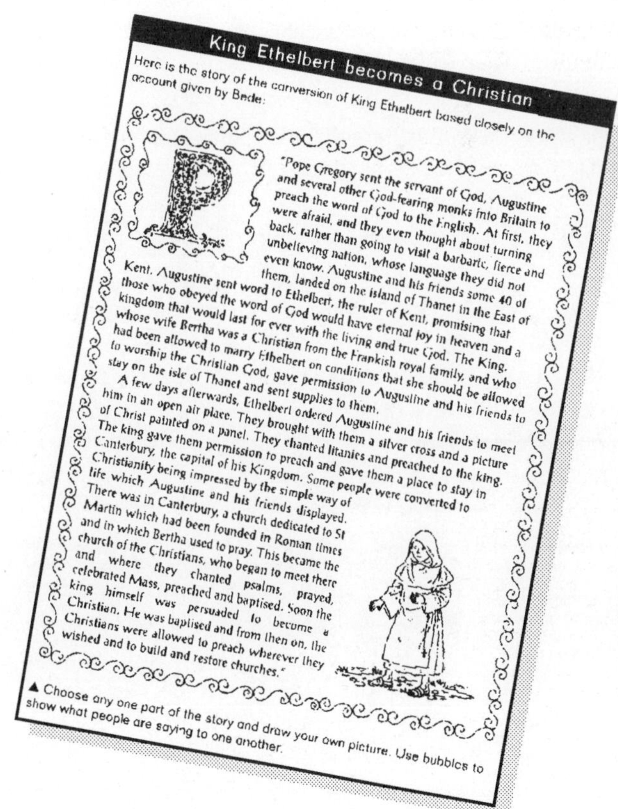

King Ethelbert becomes a Christian

Here is the story of the conversion of King Ethelbert based closely on the account given by Bede:

"Pope Gregory sent the servant of God, Augustine and several other God-fearing monks into Britain to preach the word of God to the English. At first, they were afraid, and they even thought about turning back, rather than going to visit a barbaric, fierce and unbelieving nation, whose language they did not even know. Augustine and his friends some 40 of them, landed on the island of Thanet in the East of Kent. Augustine sent word to Ethelbert, the ruler of Kent, promising that those who obeyed the word of God would have eternal joy in heaven and a kingdom that would last for ever with the living and true God. The King, whose wife Bertha was a Christian from the Frankish royal family, and who had been allowed to marry Ethelbert on conditions that she should be allowed to worship the Christian God, gave permission to Augustine and his friends to stay on the isle of Thanet and sent supplies to them.

A few days afterwards, Ethelbert ordered Augustine and his friends to meet him in an open air place. They brought with them a silver cross and a picture of Christ painted on a panel. They chanted litanies and preached to the king. The king gave them permission to preach and gave them a place to stay in Canterbury, the capital of his Kingdom. Some people were converted to Christianity being impressed by the simple way of life which Augustine and his friends displayed.

There was in Canterbury, a church dedicated to St Martin which had been founded in Roman times and in which Bertha used to pray. This became the church of the Christians, who began to meet there and where they chanted psalms, prayed, celebrated Mass, preached and baptised. Soon the king himself was persuaded to become a Christian. He was baptised and from then on, the Christians were allowed to preach wherever they wished and to build and restore churches."

▲ Choose any one part of the story and draw your own picture. Use bubbles to show what people are saying to one another.

ANGLO-SAXON WRITING

To find out about the Anglo-Saxons using original documents.

Group and individual activities.

60 minutes.

Previous skills/knowledge needed

Any knowledge the children may have of Roman writing would be helpful.

Key background information:

The Anglo-Saxons used an alphabet with 31 characters known as a *futhorc*. It is so called because of the first six characters. The alphabet was partly based on the Roman alphabet but differs in many respects. It was originally designed for cutting letters on hard surfaces such as stone, bone or pottery, and was used to mark personal possessions. The Anglo-Saxons also used tablets which could be covered with wax, for writing on, like those the Romans used. Later on runes were occasionally used on manuscripts, although in surviving Anglo-Saxon texts written on parchment, it is generally the Roman alphabet that is used. The Vikings also used the runic script, but in time the Roman alphabet introduced by the Christian church replaced the less adaptable runic script.

There is a variety of Anglo-Saxon documents which have survived and which are primary sources for this period of British history, for example *The Anglo-Saxon Chronicle*, written in the form of a diary or log. There are many documents written in Latin as well as Anglo-Saxon for example *The History of the English Church* as told by the Venerable Bede. Introduce children to some examples of writing and to illuminated and decorated pages from the surviving biblical works from this period which were the results of lengthy and painstaking workmanship such as the Lindisfarne Gospels.

Preparation

It may be useful to experiment with writing in runic script before the lesson in order to find effective ways of scratching or carving the letters on to a hard surface, such as Plasticine or self–hardening clay. Try shaping a quill with a nib-like end which will enable you to write with ink on paper. If quills are not available use dip-in pens. Copy the photocopiable sheet on page 126; enough for one per child.

Resources needed

Various kinds of paper to write on and implements to write with; either quills cut to make pens or dip-in pens. Implements for scratching letters on hard surfaces such as candle wax. Photocopiable page 126; reference books which include pictures of Anglo Saxon writing including the gospels.

What to do

Introduction

Give the children copies of the photocopiable sheet and ask them to see which of the letters are the same in the modern day (Roman) alphabet. This may generate some discussion about change and continuity, both key concepts in the study of history: what things have stayed the same and which have altered completely.

Development

Ask the children to transcribe the examples of runic script on the photocopiable sheet and then encourage them to use the script to write their own names or to write simple messages to each other using runes.

Using Anglo-Saxon writing

▲ Here is a version of the Runic alphabet for you to use in making your own Anglo-Saxon writing.
▲ Write out your own names using the runic alphabet. What differences do you notice from the Roman alphabet?

▲ This picture was carved in whalebone in the early 700's it shows the story of the three wise men visiting the baby Christ. Can you work out what the runes say? Write the letters below.

Conclusion

It would be a good idea for the children to become familiar with the runic script by first writing with pen and ink, before progressing to carving runes onto a hard surface such as hardened wax or clay.

Suggestion(s) for extension:

Show the children some illuminated Anglo-Saxon documents. What can children find out about the Lindisfarne Gospels. Let them try to reproduce part of the text and illustrations.

Suggestion(s) for support

Read through the photocopiable sheet with the children. Ask them to translate their names into runic script. Write a simple message and let the children try to transcribe it into runic script.

Assessment opportunities:

Ask the children what documents are available to provide information about the Anglo-Saxons.

Opportunities for IT

Some children might like to experiment in creating their own illuminated letter using an art package. The activity could begin by children using an old style font and typing a single letter in with the text facility of the art package. The font size can then be increased so that the letter fills the working page.

Children can then use the art package tools to create their own illuminated letter based on the letter they have written.

Show the children how to use the full range of drawing tools, particularly changing the brush or pencil size to create thin lines, how to copy sections of their work and duplicate them so that they can be used elsewhere in the design. They may need to 'zoom' into the picture to make it much larger to make changes in fine detail. If the software has an 'undo' facility which enables children to unpick their work they may find this useful when things don't work out quite as they planned.

Display ideas

Try making a rubbing of the Frank's Casket shown on the photocopiable sheet. Do this by drawing an outline of the nativity scene on the sheet. Stick string or thin strips of card onto the outline. When this has dried, place a piece of paper over the top and take a rubbing. You can also display the runic versions of the children's names and invite them to guess which rune belongs to which child.

Reference to photocopiable sheet

On photocopiable page 126 there is a list of Saxon runes.

THE SUTTON HOO BURIAL SHIP

To find out about the Anglo-Saxons using sites, artefacts and documents. To discover the characteristic features of Anglo-Saxon England including the beliefs and attitudes of the Anglo-Saxons towards burial and religion.

Whole class, paired, individual and group activities.

60–120 minutes; followed by further session for the final stage.

Previous skills/knowledge needed

Children need to have some knowledge of early Anglo-Saxon Burials, specifically the evidence for early pagan burials (see page 46).

Key background information

In Sutton Hoo in Suffolk a cluster of circular mounds had long been recognised as a possible early burial site. The site lies close to the river Deben a few miles from its mouth. The

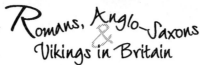

Sutton Hoo burial probably remains the most spectacular archaeological excavation that has ever been made on British soil. The excavation took place in 1939 and extensive work has since been carried out on the artefacts and other evidence taken from the site. The finds are now housed in the British Museum.

Excavations have revealed the burial of a timber-built ship with an interior chamber inside containing a substantial collection of artefacts, many of them spectacular in form. The whole ship has been covered in sand, and the ship's timbers have decomposed leaving a dark stain in the sand to mark their position. The many rusted iron rivets which held the boat together were still in place.

Here is a list of some of the finds:

▲ Gold objects: included a solid gold buckle with animal interlace decoration and weighing 44.5 gm; a pair of hinged clasps with animal designs showing interlinked boars in cloisonné garnets and millefiori glass items; remains of a purse lid decorated with cloissoné garnets and millefiori glass, showing a bird of prey attacking a duck and a man between two animals; gold objects attached to a sword and other objects of gold including 37 gold coins dating to the early seventh century from (Merovingian) France.

▲ Silver objects included a great decorated dish from the Byzantine empire diameter 71.8 cm and dated 491 to 518; ten bowls with cruciform pattern; two spoons marked Saulos and Paulos.

▲ Armour and weapons: included the remains of a rusted coat of mail; a helmet of iron and bronze with bronze gilt decoration; remains of a shield made of leather- covered wood (diameter 91.4 cm) and decorations including a bird and a dragon made from gilt bronze; an iron, large iron boss; rusted iron sword in a wooden scabbard; spear heads.

▲ Bronze vessels included hanging bowls some of them decorated; cauldrons.

▲ Remains of large wooden tubs and buckets.

▲ Drinking vessels made of horn and wood.

▲ A stone sceptre with a bronze stag mounted on it.

▲ A bottle made of pottery and many fragments of objects made from bone, leather (including shoes) and textiles.

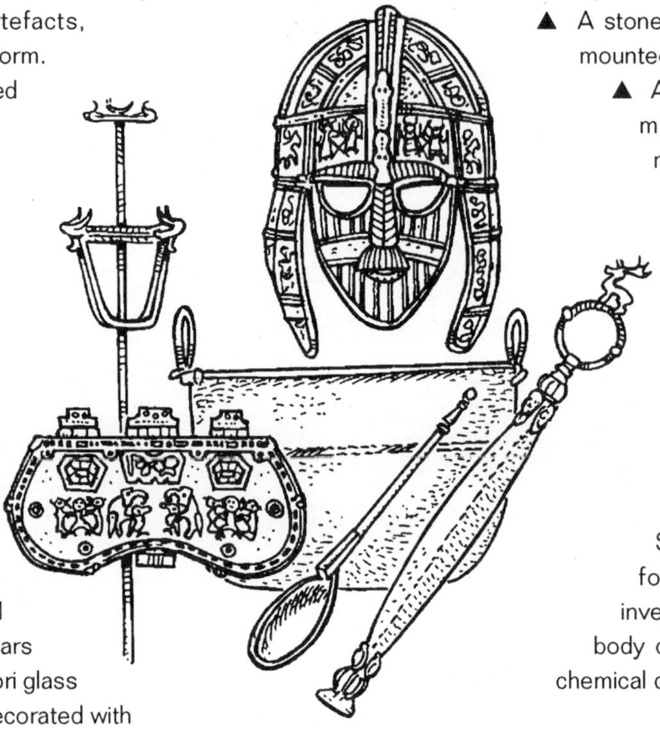

Evidence for human remains – at first, suggestions were made that the burial was without a body. Other people argued that the body might have been cremated. Scientific tests carried out following more recent investigation have shown that the body could be traced by analysing chemical deposits in the soil.

Preparation

Familiarise yourself with the detailed contents of the Sutton Hoo burial ship and choose some of the items for particular mention. Colour slides and postcards can be obtained from the British Museum as well as other sources. Photocopy the sheets on pages 127 and 128, one each per child.

Resources needed

Photocopiable pages 127 and 128.

What to do

Introduce the discovery and excavation by archaeologists of the Sutton Hoo Ship using the information supplied above. Distribute photocopiable page 127 to the class. Explain how the wood from which the boat was built had all rotted away in the sand but that the shape of the ribs of the boat could be clearly traced in the differently coloured soil. The traces of rusted iron rivets could also be clearly identified. At this point it may be useful for the class to read the account of the burial of the Danish King Scyld from the early English poem Beowulf (see photocopiable page 128). Stress that this is a story which the Anglo-Saxons used to tell.

Children can then be asked to suggest what things might have been found inside the ship burial. Having made a list of suggestions, the class can then be invited to consider what

kinds of things might have survived in the ground, bearing in mind what survived of the boat itself (for the survival of organic materials in the ground over long periods see also Chapter 2 pages 18–19).

At this point, because the question is likely to be raised, it may be a good idea to explain that no body was found in the ship and to ask the children for suggestions as to what might have happened to it. What could have happened to the body? They will no doubt come up with some ingenious explanations! The most recent evidence (see page 52) can finally be supplied to the class.

Now present the class with some examples of finds from the ship: use the examples on photocopiable page 128 to begin with. Each item can be introduced with a little of the descriptive material supplied above. Make particular reference to the colours: red garnets and blue and white checked glass. At this point, working in pairs or as individuals, the class can colour in and discuss the pictures on photocopiable page 128. The pictures are numbered from 1-7 and the children should be asked to observe the correct place for each find shown on the ship's plan on page 127. As they complete this, children could also be given a more extensive list of contents from the burial, using the detailed information supplied above and any other reference sources.

Make a list of all the words and phrases you can think of to describe what you think the dead person was like based on the evidence from the burial. Information about the dead person could then be used to compile a large collaborative picture or individual drawings of the person whose burial this is, wearing his armour and using some of the items buried with him. Alternatively ask the children to write an account written by the person describing all his possessions.

Once the whole class has become familiar with the details of the burial ship, it will be possible to move on to the piecing together of the clues in order to find out more about the dead person. The class can be told that the favourite explanation is that this is the burial of the Anglian King Raedwald who died c.625. This will provide an opportunity to discuss the evidence which points to this and how some of the key items could have come to be in Raedwald's burial. Children can be given details of what we know of Raedwald based on our knowledge from Bede. He was apparently converted to Christianity but later put up altars to the Christian God and the devil side by side. This was a traditional pagan form of burial and it was unusual for Christians to be buried with precious objects.

Tell the children that they are going to re-enact the burial of Raedwald. In order to do this the children will have to work on a number of tasks:

▲ Making a set of arms and armour: shield, helmet, sword, buckle, shoulder clasps.

▲ Making jewellery using the gold and garnet cloisonné style.

▲ Preparing food, cakes and honey drink (to represent mead).

▲ Working on prayers and music (Archaeologica Musica) for the procession. Raedwald became a Christian and then reverted to his ancestral gods; will his burial be in the Germanic tradition (prayers to Thunor etc.) or will his Christian relations insist on some aspect of a Christian ceremony? (such as a Gregorian chant.) Perhaps a mixture of traditions would be appropriate.

Once the children have completed these tasks let them re-enact Raedwald's funeral.

Suggestion(s) for extension

A challenging activity for able pupils would be to present them with a recent alternative explanation as to who the burial belonged to and invite them to list in two columns the reasons for and against each identification.

Some people have suggested that this is the burial of King Saeberht King of the East Saxons. He was nephew of Ethelbert of Kent and was baptised as a Christian in 604. He died in about 616. The burial is in East Saxon territory and none of the goods buried in the ship are specifically Anglian, though there are objects which are Saxon in style (Ref. *Anglo-Saxon England* 22 1993).

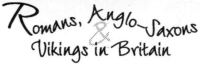

Suggestion(s) for support:

Read the account on photocopiable page 128 with the children or pair less able children with good readers. There will be too many objects included on sheet 128 for some children to cope with so limit the number by selecting just two or three objects. Encourage children to draw the ship with the dead king and his belongings inside.

Assessment opportunities

Can children explain what sources of information they have used to learn about Anglo-Saxon beliefs and ship burials?

Display ideas

Make a large frieze of the burial ship. Use sponge painting to give the effect of planks marked in the sand or string printing to show grains of wood on the planks. Members of the class can all contribute drawings of items to be cut out and added as belongings of the king.

Reference to photocopiable sheets

The photocopiable sheet on page 127 provides a plan of the boat with numbers to indicate the location of the different finds. Photocopiable page 128 contains an extract from the Anglo-Saxon poem *Beowulf*, which dates from the eighth century and gives an account of the Danish King Scyld. It also shows some of the items found on the Sutton Hoo ship for children to colour in and discuss.

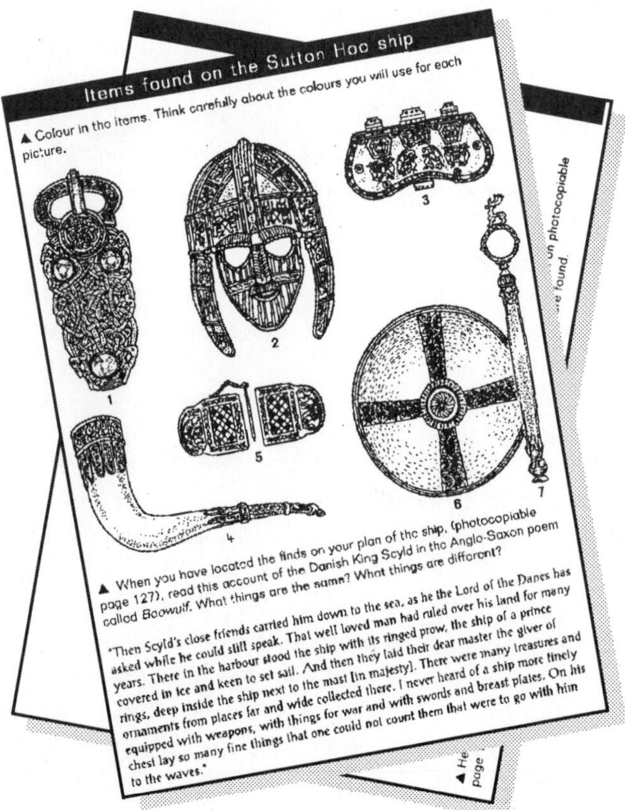

Items found on the Sutton Hoo ship

▲ Colour in the items. Think carefully about the colours you will use for each picture.

1 2 3 4 5 6 7

▲ When you have located the finds on your plan of the ship, (photocopiable page 127), read this account of the Danish King Scyld in the Anglo-Saxon poem called *Beowulf*. What things are the same? What things are different?

"Then Scyld's close friends carried him down to the sea, as he the Lord of the Danes has asked while he could still speak. That well loved man had ruled over his land for many years. There in the harbour stood the ship with its ringed prow, the ship of a prince covered in ice and keen to set sail. And then they laid their dear master the giver of rings, deep inside the ship next to the mast [in majesty]. There were many treasures and ornaments from places far and wide collected there. I never heard of a ship more finely equipped with weapons, with things for war and with swords and breast plates. On his chest lay so many fine things that one could not count them that were to go with him to the waves."

ENGLAND AT THE TIME OF ALFRED THE GREAT

To find out historical facts from documents and discover that there are different ways in which the past is represented.

Whole class.

60 minutes.

Previous skills/knowledge needed

Children will need to have experienced working on documents.

Key background information

Important information about Alfred's life and reign comes from the *Anglo-Saxon Chronicle* which was begun in Wessex itself during Alfred's reign. Other sources such as a document known as the *Burghal Hideage* which attests to Alfred's organisation of the defences in the towns of Wessex are used to support Alfred's reputation.

Alfred was born in 849. He succeeded his older brothers who died early and did not survive long on the throne. He became King of Wessex in 871. After a great deal of fighting against the Danes, referred to in the extracts on photocopiable page 129, Alfred beat them at the battle of Edington in 878 and he came to an agreement with their leader Guthrum, who promised to leave Alfred's kingdom of

Wessex alone. In 886 Alfred and Guthrum agreed to divide England, with Alfred ruling over the south and the Danish, the north and east of the country. It was during his difficult time referred to in the *Anglo–Saxon Chronicle* for the year 878 (photocopiable page 129) in the fens of Somerset that the story of burning the cakes is supposed to have taken place. However, this story did not in fact appear in writing until the next century.

Although Alfred was referred to in later times as 'The Great', there is no evidence that in the Anglo-Saxon period, Alfred was regarded more highly than some of his fellow Anglo-Saxon rulers. In the view of one modern scholar, Alfred was just one of a series of extremely capable kings in the ninth and tenth centuries who helped to turn the Kingdom of Wessex into the unified kingdom of England.

Preparation

Collect any reference books which refer to the life of Alfred. Prepare the photocopiable sheet on page129, one per child.

Resources needed:

Children's books about Alfred the Great, picture of his statue in Winchester, photocopiable page 129.

What to do

Distribute copies of the photocopiable sheet and use the two extracts to introduce the idea of documents as evidence. Get the children to talk about the idea of a chronicle, setting out events year by year (only the details of two years are included in this extract). How would it be set out? Why might someone want to make a chronicle? Use the information on the sheets to discuss some of Alfred's achievements. List the points made by the first source on the board or flip-chart. Point out to the children that this source is sympathetic to Alfred and came from the Anglo-Saxon Kingdom of Wessex where he was the King. Do they think that the Danes whom he fought and kept out of Wessex would have written or spoken about Alfred in the same way? What might they have thought about Alfred? Was Alfred's success against the Danes the main reason for his popularity? Mention the information we have from other sources such as the *Burghal Hideage* that we have about Alfred's organisation of the defences of the towns of Wessex.

Invite the children to imagine they were fighting either on the side of Alfred or the Danes and ask them to describe their experiences month by month (working individually), during the campaigns referred to in the *Anglo-Saxon Chronicle*.

Suggestion(s) for extension

Children can look at other ways Alfred is commemorated. Consider other reasons why Alfred might have been seen as an important king, using information from any other documentary sources, consider for example his contribution to the making of English Laws, his contribution to English literature (translating texts from Latin into Anglo-Saxon) and education. Does the second document add anything or is it just a good story? Look at other accounts about Alfred from history books. Ask the children to read the information and say what is the author's opinion of Alfred and what is likely to have actually happened.

Suggestion(s) for support

Carry out a role-play based on the story of Alfred and the cakes. The children could make a cartoon strip showing a sequence of events to tell the story. Different groups could role-play the story of Alfred to develop children's awareness of how different versions of the same story can be created.

Assessment opportunities

Ask the children how we know about Alfred. Which sources of evidence do we have? To what extent are these sources reliable?

Opportunities for IT

Children could use a CD-ROM to search for information for a class *Anglo–Saxon Chronicle*. The children could then use a word processor or desk top publishing package to write their own chronicle. They could experiment with different fonts to create a more historic-looking document.

Children could also use a multi-media authoring package to create a more modern-style chronicle. The children could work in groups to search and present information on a set number of years in the period. They could include pictures taken from clip art or CD-ROM collections, scanned images

from photographs or their own line drawings. Children could even add snatches of suitable music, either taken from recorded music or created themselves and recorded using a microphone linked to the computer. Set up an initial structure in advance with a front page showing the different periods in the presentation, so that by clicking on a date the user would be taken to the chronicle for that time. This is a fairly ambitious project and children using the software for the first time will need individual support.

Display ideas

Create a wall display based on Alfred the Great. Children can display their own chronicles of Alfred.

Reference to photocopiable sheet

Photocopiable page 129 provides two extracts from separate years in the *Anglo–Saxon Chronicle* and also the later story of 'Alfred and the cakes'.

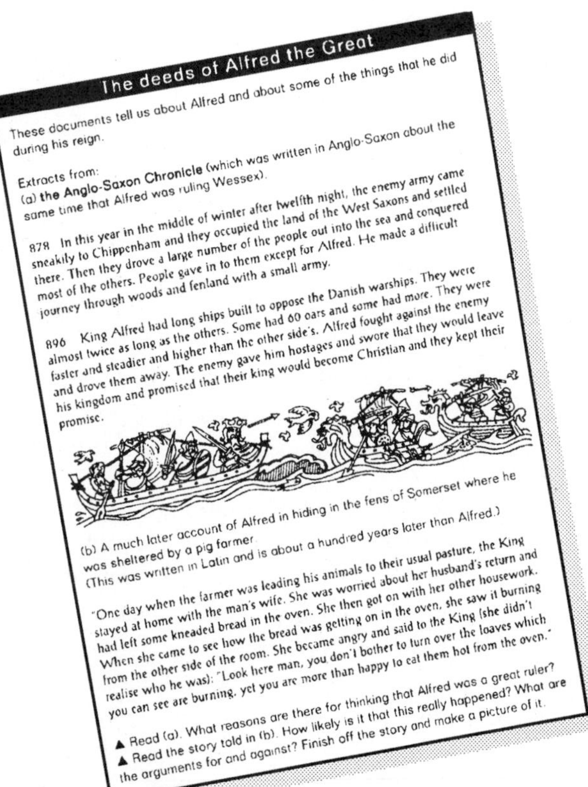

The deeds of Alfred the Great

These documents tell us about Alfred and about some of the things that he did during his reign.

Extracts from:
(a) **the Anglo-Saxon Chronicle** (which was written in Anglo-Saxon about the same time that Alfred was ruling Wessex).

878 In this year in the middle of winter after twelfth night, the enemy army came sneakily to Chippenham and they occupied the land of the West Saxons and settled there. Then they drove a large number of the people out into the sea and conquered most of the others. People gave in to them except for Alfred. He made a difficult journey through woods and fenland with a small army.

896 King Alfred had long ships built to oppose the Danish warships. They were almost twice as long as the others. Some had 60 oars and some had more. They were faster and steadier and higher than the other side's. Alfred fought against the enemy and drove them away. The enemy gave him hostages and swore that they would leave his kingdom and promised that their king would become Christian and they kept their promise.

(b) A much later account of Alfred in hiding in the fens of Somerset where he was sheltered by a pig farmer
(This was written in Latin and is about a hundred years later than Alfred.)

"One day when the farmer was leading his animals to their usual pasture, the King stayed at home with the man's wife. She was worried about her husband's return and had left some kneaded bread in the oven. She then got on with her other housework. When she came to see how the bread was getting on in the oven, she saw it burning from the other side of the room. She became angry and said to the King (she didn't realise who he was): "Look here man, you don't bother to turn over the loaves which you can see are burning, yet you are more than happy to eat them hot from the oven."

▲ Read (a). What reasons are there for thinking that Alfred was a great ruler?
▲ Read the story told in (b). How likely is it that this really happened? What are the arguments for and against? Finish off the story and make a picture of it.

VIKING RAIDS

To find historical details using documents and artefacts and to identify and give reasons for the different ways in which the Viking raids are represented and interpreted. To use appropriate terms to describe a topic studied.

Whole class followed by individual and group work.

60 minutes; and follow-up time.

Previous skills/knowledge needed

Children will need to be able to compare the Viking invasion with other invasions (especially that of Claudius).

Key background information

The term 'Vikings' is generally used to describe the raiders (and later) settlers who first began to make their impact on the shores of Britain from the late eighth century. Early raids by the Vikings have often been portrayed in the most lurid terms in the illustrations which adorn children's history books and it will be helpful to focus during these activities on the actual evidence that survives.

The Vikings were seafarers whose homelands were in Scandinavia (notably Norway, Sweden and Denmark) but they had colonised the Shetland and Orkney Islands to the north east of Britain as well as Ireland and the Isle of Man to the west. (See also activities on pages 58 and 61). Their proximity to Britain now made the island an obvious and alluring target for Viking investigation and exploration. They were at this stage not Christians but worshipped their traditional Scandinavian gods (corresponding to the gods of the earlier Germanic settlers). The *Anglo-Saxon Chronicle* refers to them both as 'heathens' and people from the north (Northmen). Their contact with the British Isles began as piratical raids, but later they became more interested in colonising Britain.

Our major source for the Viking raids and early settlements in Britain is the *Anglo-Saxon Chronicle* (see also the previous activity, page 54). The *Anglo-Saxon Chronicle* for the year 793 refers to attacks by heathens who were wretchedly destroying God's church in Lindisfarne with robberies and killings. Following the attack the Archbishop of York, in whose diocese Lindisfarne was, wrote letters of commiseration to the King of Northumbria and to Higbald and his monks at Lindisfarne. Here is an extract from one of Alcuin's letters:

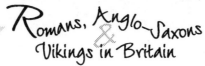

(To Ethelred, King of Northumbria) *'It is now nearly 350 years since we and our forefathers have inhabited this beautiful land and never before have such terrible things happened as we have suffered from pagan people. We did not even think that such an attack from the sea was possible. Just think of it, the church of St Cuthbert spattered with the blood of God's priests and all its ornaments stolen!.'*

Alcuin attributed this attack and others notably on the monasteries at Jarrow and Monkwearmouth, also in Northumbria; to the degenerate state of the English people. The attacks by 'pagan' invaders are seen as divine retribution.

Preparation

Try to familiarise yourself with the actual sources which survive and which are quoted here. Photocopy page 130 one copy per child.

Resources needed

A variety of pictures in books showing artist's reconstructions of the Viking attack on Lindisfarne, photocopiable page 130.

What to do

Introduce the activity by going through the account of the Viking attack on Lindisfarne on the photocopiable page with the children. Contrast this piece of visual evidence with the usual modern artist's impression of a Viking attack. Contrast the simplicity of the carved detail with the fanciful version

shown in the modern art work. Why do they think the pictorial representations are so different? Is there any justification for showing the Viking warriors wearing twin-horned helmets? How could they find out? (See the following activity on page 58). Why might the modern artist have drawn the picture in this way?

Next look together at the documentary sources from Simeon of Durham and also the Bishop's letter. Then encourage the children to role-play the scene inside the monastery as the raiders approach and arrive on the island. The island is connected to the mainland at low tide. Would this provide a possible escape route or would the monks feel that their duty was to defend their church against the invaders?

Suggestion(s) for extension

Look at the book illustrations in the light of the source on the photocopiable sheet. Do the children think the picture gives an accurate representation? What features has the modern artist added that are not in the original sources?

Suggestion(s) for support

At a simpler level, ask the children to write a verbal response to the situation entitled a 'Viking invasion'. This kind of presentation could also form the basis for an activity by a small group of children, in which they create their own step-by-step account of what might have happened, using available sources. Children will need help with new and unfamiliar words for example monastery, pagan and heathen.

Assessment opportunities

Can the children describe the Viking attack in their own words using the sources that survive from earlier times? How did this invasion differ from that made by the Romans in AD 43?

Opportunities for IT

Evidence of the portents and an account of the arrival of the Viking raiders could be presented to the class (who represent the monks of Lindisfarne) either using the computer software *Extra* or a multi-media authoring package set up by the teacher in advance. Most of these packages have a carousel option where information can be presented every few minutes to the user. Each page of the presentation could contain a different item of news, and the time option set so that they are staggered throughout the work. As the 'invasion' builds into a climax the children can be asked to respond in a number of ways to the news. Their responses could be recorded in the form of a series of visual images which could subsequently form the basis of a classroom display.

Display ideas

Make cardboard cut-outs of the figures on the stone carving. Stick them onto a piece of card and make a series of rubbings to give a gravestone effect.

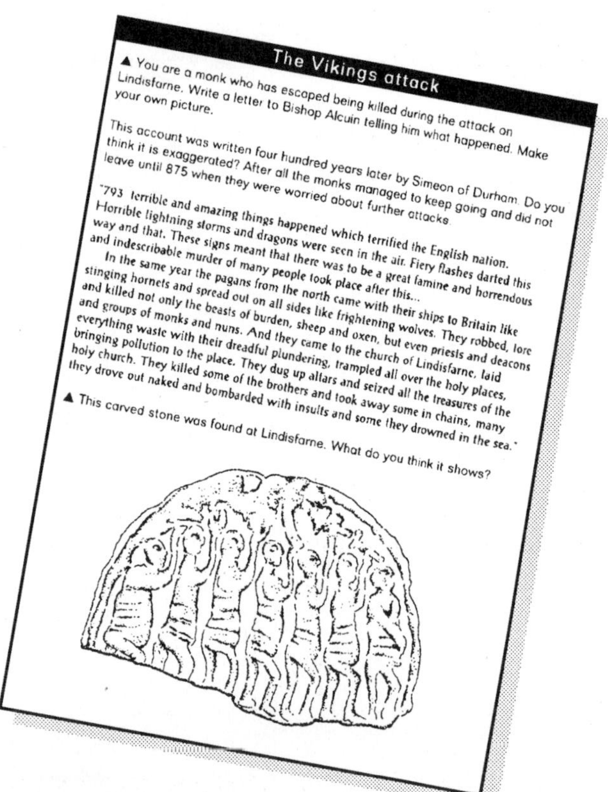

The Vikings attack

▲ You are a monk who has escaped being killed during the attack on Lindisfarne. Write a letter to Bishop Alcuin telling him what happened. Make your own picture.

This account was written four hundred years later by Simeon of Durham. Do you think it is exaggerated? After all the monks managed to keep going and did not leave until 875 when they were worried about further attacks.

'793 terrible and amazing things happened which terrified the English nation. Horrible lightning storms and dragons were seen in the air. Fiery flashes darted this way and that. These signs meant that there was to be a great famine and horrendous and indescribable murder of many people took place after this...

In the same year the pagans from the north came with their ships to Britain like stinging hornets and spread out on all sides like frightening wolves. They robbed, tore and killed not only the beasts of burden, sheep and oxen, but even priests and deacons and groups of monks and nuns. And they came to the church of Lindisfarne, laid everything waste with their dreadful plundering, trampled all over the holy places, bringing pollution to the place. They dug up altars and seized all the treasures of the holy church. They killed some of the brothers and took away some in chains, many they drove out naked and bombarded with insults and some they drowned in the sea.'

▲ This carved stone was found at Lindisfarne. What do you think it shows?

Reference to photocopiable sheet

The drawing on photocopiable sheet 130 is based on a grave marker found at the off-shore Northumbrian island of Lindisfarne. Lindisfarne was a tiny unprotected island where St Cuthbert had been abbot at an earlier date. The stone carving shows a procession of seven figures moving from left to right. They are wearing short clothes which have cross-hatching. Five of the figures are brandishing swords or axes. This ancient carving has often been assumed to represent the Viking attack on the monastery of Lindisfarne in 793. On the other side is a Saxon cross.

There is also a copy of a letter written by Simeon of Durham for the children to consider.

THE VIKING WAY OF LIFE

To study some of the characteristic features of Viking times and the experiences of men and women.

Group work.

60 minutes.

Previous skills/knowledge needed

Children will need to be able to use reference books.

Key background information

The excavations in recent years at York (Jorvik) and in the homelands of the Vikings themselves reveal a contrasting picture to that presented in the previous activity. There is much evidence of peaceful trading and of vigorous commercial activity. This lesson provides an opportunity for children to explore this aspect of Viking life in Danelaw. The picture of Danes we have from our written sources such as the *Anglo-Saxon Chronicle* concentrates on the military actions of the Danes. Archaeological evidence presents a much wider picture. There is abundant evidence for the making of clothes, jewellery and the crafts such as leather making and wood turning. There is evidence of widespread trading connections between northern Britain and far-flung places: they are fragments of silk from the Mediterranean, mill stones from Germany and jewellery and pottery from the continent. York, Lincoln and the other towns of Danelaw were important centres of commercial activity.

Preparation

Prepare a display of visual evidence of arms and armour of the Vikings. Assemble as many resources as possible which include illustrations of Viking artefacts. Prepare photocopiable page 131 sufficient for one per child.

Resources needed

Books, postcards and other resources which have information about the Vikings and in particular artefacts that have been excavated. Maps showing the places to which Viking seafarers travelled (see also page 59 on 'Alfred, the Danes and Danelaw'). Photocopiable page 131.

What to do

The picture of the Vikings presented by Anglo-Saxon sources (see Viking raids, page 56) is very negative and represents the Vikings as pagan raiders hell-bent on destroying and looting. Discuss with the class what other ways there might be that can help us to learn about the Vikings. Excavations in Britain especially at York (Jorvik) and elsewhere notably in the lands they came from give a very different picture. Archaeological evidence has been found relating to a whole range of domestic activities – the manufacturing of foods and trading and leisure activities. Children can use the photocopiable sheet at this point, to match the artefacts found with the trading activities.

Divide the class into groups to investigate the different aspects of Viking life. This investigation work could be used as an opportunity for tackling some of the practical activities suggested in Chapter 2 pages 21–23. For example cloth-making (spinning, dyeing and weaving), making pots or imitation jewellery, arms and armour and so on.

Suggestion(s) for extension

Invite children to write down what they think particular artefacts tell us about life in the Viking Age.

Suggestion(s) for support

Choose just one activity from the pictures on the photocopiable sheet and ask the children to describe what is happening.

Assessment opportunities

Use photocopiable page 131 to test children's knowledge about the Vikings. Ask them to write or talk about what they see in the pictures. What other kinds of traders could they add? Use their responses as a guide for planning future activities and developing their knowledge of the Vikings.

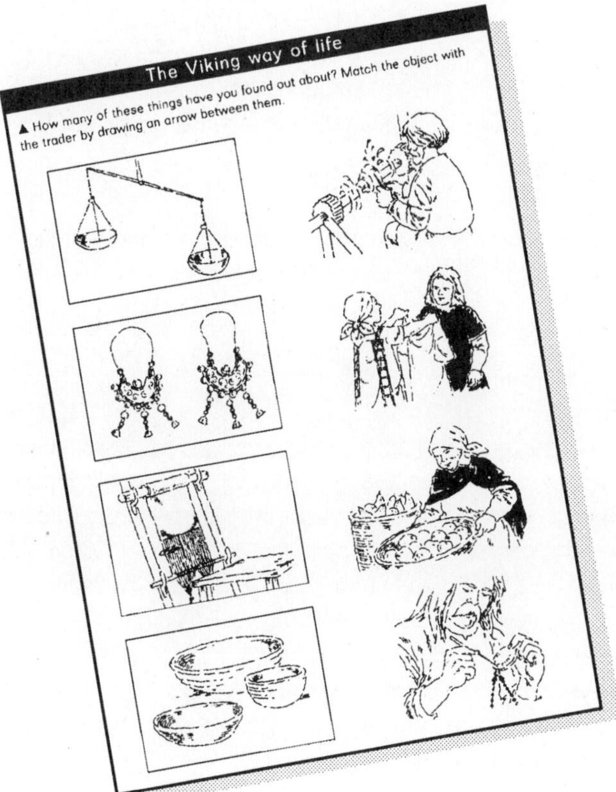
The Viking way of life

▲ How many of these things have you found out about? Match the object with the trader by drawing an arrow between them.

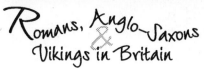

Opportunities for IT

Children could use a word processor to write labels for the class display of Viking artefacts. Experiment with different fonts and layouts to make the labels interesting to look at and easy to read from a distance.

Display ideas

Pin up some of the children's drawings of Viking artefacts that have been excavated. Beside each artefact display an explanation to say what it is, what it is made of and what it tells us about the Vikings. The children could work together to make a collaborative drawing of a market scene. What other kinds of stall might there have been in a port such as Jorvik?

Reference to photocopiable sheet

The photocopiable sheet on page 131 shows a selection of artefacts which have been excavated and some of the traders and market stalls which may have existed in the Viking town of Jorvik for children to match up.

ALFRED, THE DANES AND DANELAW

To ask and answer questions about the extent of the Danish settlement in England. To select and record relevant information. To find out information using maps.

Working in pairs.

60 minutes.

Previous skills/knowledge needed

Previous work on place names of Roman and Anglo-Saxon origin could be helpful.

Key background information

The boundary of Danelaw is recorded in the treaty made shortly before 890 between King Alfred and Guthrum, leader of the East Anglian Danish settlers. The boundary of Danelaw (see map) runs along the Essex side of the River Thames as far as the River Lea. It runs then northwards along the River Lea to its source near Dunstable and on in a straight line to Bedford. From there, the boundary runs along the River Ouse to Watling Street, with Watling Street as its western boundary. Everything to the north of this line as far as the river Tees comprised Danelaw. Within this area was the Danish kingdom (later earldom) of East Anglia, the Danish Confederation of Five boroughs (Stamford, Leicester, Derby, Nottingham and Lincoln) and, to the north the kingdom of York, centred on Jorvik (the Danish name for York). Jorvik remained the seat of a series of Danish Kings until Eric Bloodaxe was expelled in 954.

During the period of Danish rule in the east and north of England, the impact of foreign rule was significant. Today we can measure this impact in terms of the large number of Danish place names which correspond to this area of England. There is also evidence for the survival of Old Danish words in the rural dialects of this part of England.

There are two particular place names of Danish origin which contain the elements: *thorpe* (hamlet or outlying farm) and *toft* (site of a house or homestead) which can be found in profusion within the area which once was Danelaw. There are also very large numbers of place names which contain the ending *-by*. This has the meaning of farmstead or village and is found not only in areas settled by the Danes but in other areas which were settled by Norwegian settlers too. Thus names of this type will be found in the far North West of England, notably in Cumbria and North Yorkshire.

Here is a list of place name elements which correspond to the areas settled by peoples of Scandinavian origin in the ninth, tenth and eleventh centuries:

Old Danish

- Thorpe – farm
- Toft – site of a house, homestead
- Hulme – an island

Old Norse

- Beck – stream
- Breck– hill, slope
- Scale – hut
- Thwaite – clearing
- Rigg – ridge
- Slack – valley
- Holme – island
- Carr – marsh

Both Old Norse and Old Danish

- By – farmstead or village
- Booth – shelter

Preparation

Using photocopiable page 132 prepare a large map to show the boundary of Danelaw. Photocopy the sheet for the children to use, one per child.

Resources needed

Atlases and Ordnance Survey sheets, photocopiable sheet on page 132.

What to do

Introduce the class to the idea of Danelaw using a large map. (It may be useful to make links with 'England at the time of Alfred the Great', page 54.) Talk with the children about boundaries. What makes a recognisable and identifiable boundary that is indisputable? What do they think might happen within those boundaries once the line is drawn and firmly held to?

Give the children the photocopiable sheet and ask them to work in pairs to identify place names of Scandinavian origin. This can be tackled in a number of ways.

Firstly, concentrate on the settlement by the Danes within the area defined as Danelaw using the photocopiable sheet. Children can be asked to plot all those names which are particularly prevalent in the area of Danelaw on their map using a dot to correspond to the approximate position of each place. Remind the children that they can include *thorpe* and *by* as well as *toft(s)* and *booth*.

Another approach is for a group to look particularly at evidence for Norwegian names in north west England, plotting the names which include *carr, beck, how, breck, scale, rigg and slack*.

Suggestion(s) for extension

Transparent overlays showing Viking settlements could be made. Consider what the Vikings would look for in searching for a good settlement place: water supply, defensive site, raw materials and communication for example.

Suggestion(s) for support

Some children might have difficulty in locating places in atlases. In this case, make your own outline map with some Viking place names for children to work with. Also children could draw in small Viking ships and use arrows to show them crossing the sea from their homelands.

Assessment opportunities

Can the children recognise key features of places where the Vikings settled or do they recognise why place names are helpful evidence for where the Vikings settled?

Opportunities for IT

The children could use a commerically created database to look for patterns in the location of place names ending with Viking suffixes such as 'thorpe' or 'by'.

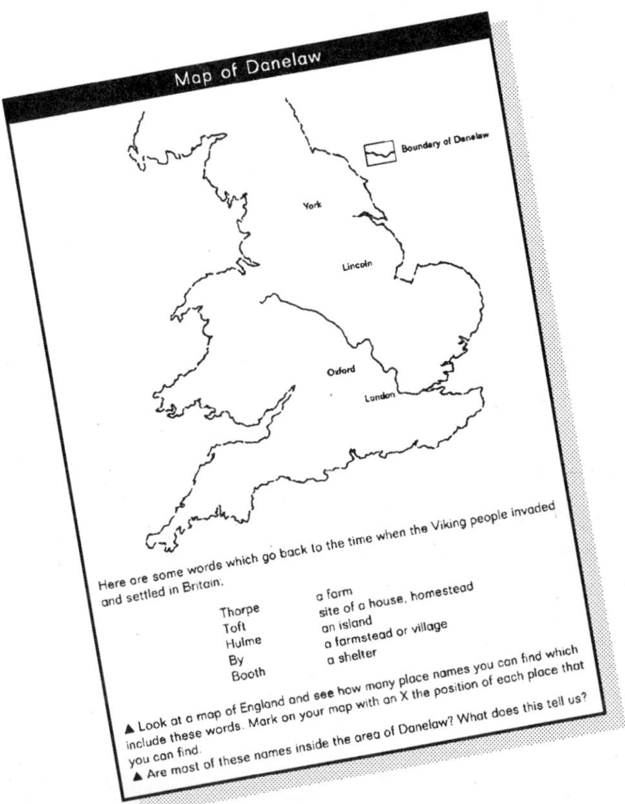
Map of Danelaw

Here are some words which go back to the time when the Viking people invaded and settled in Britain.

Thorpe	a farm
Toft	site of a house, homestead
Hulme	an island
By	a farmstead or village
Booth	a shelter

▲ Look at a map of England and see how many place names you can find which include these words. Mark on your map with an X the position of each place that you can find.

▲ Are most of these names inside the area of Danelaw? What does this tell us?

Display ideas

A large map showing the place name evidence for Viking settlements.

Reference to photocopiable sheet

The photocopiable page 132 shows a map of Danelaw for the children to mark on the position of relevant place names.

VIKING SHIPS FROM ARCHAEOLOGY AND SAGA

To find out about cultural and religious diversity in Viking times. To find out information about their geographical spread, using a Norse saga.

Whole class followed by group, paired and individual activities.

60 minutes and follow-up time.

Previous skills/knowledge needed

Children may already need to have done some work on the Vikings for example Viking raids on Northern monasteries.

Key background information

The Vikings' seafaring activities took them to many parts of the Northern Hemisphere. They settled in Iceland and Greenland. In about AD 1000 evidence from the Vinland Saga suggests that they reached the coast of America almost 500 years before Columbus! They were also active in parts of western Russia. This story of Authen (reproduced here) taken from a Viking saga, gives an insight into the ease with which the Vikings travelled around the seas of Europe and beyond.

Authen and the polar bear

Once upon a time there was a man called Authen. He came from Iceland and he was not well off. He worked for a man called Thorir who was captain of a ship. Most of the money he had earned he left behind in Iceland. It was enough to keep his mother for three years. He sailed with Thorir to Norway where he owned a farm. Then he went to Greenland where he spent the winter. There he bought a polar bear, an absolute treasure, giving every penny he had for it. Next summer, so the story goes, he took his bear with him to Norway and planned to go south to give it as a present to King Svein of Denmark.

When he reached southern Norway to get a night's lodging. He left the ship taking his bear with him. The King of Norway, King Harald got to hear about the bear and sent for Authen.

"I believe you have a bear, an absolute treasure," said the King. "Would you sell it to me for twice the price you paid?"

"I am on my way to Denmark to give it to King Svein" said Authen.

"You foolish man, do you realise that we are at war with Denmark?" cried the King.

"I have made up my mind" said Authen.

"Well" said the king, "Get on your way! But call back and let me know how King Svein rewards you."

Authen reached Denmark and gave his present to the King. King Svein was pleased with his present and wanted to reward Authen, so he gave him a large amount of silver to

go on a pilgrimage to Rome. On his way back from Rome Authen fell very sick, but he reached Denmark at Easter and arrived where the King lived just as he was going into church for evensong. The King did not recognise him at first, but afterwards he heaped him with presents. First he offered to make him his cup bearer, but Authen by now wanted to return home as the money he had left for his mother would soon run out. The King then gave him a fine ship in return for the bear. He gave him another leather purse full of silver and a ring. He told him never to give away the ring unless he found himself under obligation to a very great man.

Authen left Denmark and sailed as he had promised to Norway, to see King Harald. King Harald entertained him but wanted to know how King Svein had rewarded him for the bear. Authen told the King how he had been rewarded by the offer to become the king's cup bearer, by a purse of silver and by the gift of a ship. When the King asked Authen whether he had received anything else, Authen replied that he had been given the ring which he was never to part with unless one day he should find himself under obligation to some great man.

"Now I have found him," said Authen, "for you had the chance to take away both my bear and my life, but you let me go away in peace when others might not have done so."

The King accepted the gift and gave Authen many presents. Authen used the money to help pay for his journey back and so he returned home to Iceland.

Preparation

Read up the story of Authen given here ready to tell the children.

Resources needed

A globe and maps showing the Northern Hemisphere (especially Iceland, Greenland, Scandinavia and Italy), pictures of Viking ships.

What to do

First tell the story of Authen to the class. Discuss what the story tells us about people in Authen's time and their ability to travel long distances. Ask the children to retell the story of Authen. They can make a story board or cartoon strip or retell it orally.

As a whole class, look at and discuss any images of the Vikings which the children may have already gained from the lurid accounts of Viking raids on Britain. What kind of people do the characters in this story turn out to be? How do we know that by this date these Vikings have become converted to Christianity? Is this story likely to be true? Encourage the children to give their reasons believing that it is and is not true.

Finish by asking the children to write a log describing Authen's journey.

Suggestion(s) for extension

Ask the children to try and find evidence to support aspects of the story of Authen. How far is it possible to believe the story?

Suggestion(s) for support

Children can retell the story of Authen by making a drawing of Authen or act out the story rather than having to write it all down.

Assessment opportunities

Can children identify the differences between the Christian Vikings and other information they may have met earlier on? Can children identify on a map the different countries which the Vikings settled or explored?

Opportunities for IT

Children could use a simulation package such as *Arcventure III The Anglo Saxons* to give them experience of investigating an archaeological site. Such work needs to be a central part of the work in history so that pupils have enough time to explore the software fully and that activities at the computer are linked to other class activities; possibly keeping a diary of their finds and experiences with the software. Teachers also need to talk to pupils about their use of such software, identifying the kind of model that the software is using; its limitations and children's understanding of how they interact with the model.

Display ideas

Display a labelled map of the Northern Hemisphere showing where the Vikings travelled to. Make a model of a Viking ship or concentrate on the prow of a ship using papier mâché and black felt-tipped pens to decorate the prow when dry.

Ancient Greece

This chapter provides the basis for studying a European civilisation which existed at a considerable distance from the present but one which has been seminal in the history of the western world. There are a number of aspects of ancient Greek society which have influenced past generations through time and which continue to be relevant in the modern world for example, myths and legends, drama, architecture, sculpture and painting. It is true that some of the spheres in which the ancient Greeks excelled may be largely beyond the reach of primary school pupils. However, children of this age can certainly gain some form of access to the more concrete aspects of democratic government, historical writing and philosophy. Indeed the earliest known form of democratic government was cradled in ancient Athens in the fifth century BC, a form of history (the Greek word literally means enquiry) was pioneered by the Greeks. Quite apart from the literature and art of the ancient Greeks, the Greek language itself has been very influential on the English language.

KEY FACTS

Key events

Key events in Greek history in the fifth century include the conflict between the Persians and the Greeks, the debilitating and long drawn-out war between Athens and Sparta and their respective allies. The fourth century features the emergence of a strong ruler (Philip of Macedon) who came to dominate and unify the Greeks by force of arms and whose son (Alexander the Great) campaigned and successfully destroyed the might of the Persians. By the time that Alexander died at the age of 32, Greek rule had been established from the Mediterranean to the River Indus. Although some parts of Alexander's conquests were soon given up, the remainder of his newly acquired empire was divided into three sections. The Greek communities of the Mediterranean were gradually to become absorbed and developed throughout the Roman world. One area which Alexander had conquered was the ancient country of Egypt. The last independent ruler of Egypt was Cleopatra VI, who fought hard to remain independent of the Romans, but in 31 BC her navy was defeated in battle with the Romans, she committed suicide and her kingdom passed into the hands of the Romans.

History and the ancient Greeks

The study of historical ancient Greece will inevitably be concentrated upon the fifth and sixth centuries BC, the so-called 'classical period', since our literary sources are richest during this period. However, the bulk of what survives either originated from Athenian writers or was produced in the city of Athens. Almost the whole of the literary evidence that we have was written by upper class Athenian men. We have precious little from the pens of writers who were native to other great cities of the ancient Greek world for example, Sparta or Corinth. Most of our literary sources have survived by the process of manuscript transmission which is described in Chapter 2 (page 17). However, fragments of texts have survived as papyri, retrieved from the sands of Egypt, notably at the Greek city of Oxyrhynchus. From time to time fresh texts have come to light even in the modern world.

The themes of the Persian Wars and of the Peloponnesian War loom large in the surviving historical writing of the ancient Greeks. These accounts were written by near contemporaries. Other writers, for example, the biographer Plutarch, writing in the first century AD, drew on much earlier sources for their material. Other written evidence largely in the form of inscriptions (mainly cut on stone) has been found either by chance or through the excavation of archaeological sites. Archaeology has an important part to play in the study of ancient Greece and can be used in conjunction with the written sources that we have for this period of history. Archaeologists can sometimes help to fill out detail in cases where the written sources are either thin or non-existent.

Also of great importance to any study of the ancient Greeks and an area of great appeal to children will be the world of myth and legends which precedes the historical Greece and which derives in part from the late Bronze and early Iron ages. The Trojan War and its various sequels including the wanderings of Odysseus and the sequence of events which afflicted the ill-fated household of Agamemnon are all recurrent themes in the art and literature of the ancient world as well as being influential in later centuries. The first two of these provided the epic poet Homer with raw material for his *Iliad* and *Odyssey* respectively, and all provided inspiration for the fifth century Athenian tragedians. Some of the great stories the ancient Greeks told are preserved in the writings of later Greek authors (for example the story of Jason and the Argonauts) or in Roman literature (for example the story of the wooden horse of Troy in Virgil's *Aeneid* and exploits of gods and heroes in Ovid's *Metamorphoses*). Greek myths and legends made a central contribution to ancient Greek education and they continue to provide a powerful stimulus to children in the later twentieth century.

ANCIENT GREEK TIMELINE

To place events and people in a chronological framework and to use dates which are BC. To understand and use the terms decade, century, settlement and conquest.

In pairs or small groups followed by whole class feedback.

Approximately 60 minutes.

Previous skills/knowledge needed

This will depend on whether children have already studied BC dates. If a topic like the Romans has already been studied, it will be useful to make chronological links. If ancient Egypt has been studied, it will similarly be useful to make cross-connections with the ancient Greeks.

Key background information

Listed below are some key dates in the history of the ancient Greeks:

776 BC The first recorded Olympic Games.

750–700 BC Greek alphabet created and spread around the Greek-speaking world.

750–550 BC Greek colonies established around the Mediterranean.

499 BC The Ionian Revolt of Greek cities in Asia Minor (now part of Turkey) against the Persians; this attracts support from Athens.

490 BC The expedition of the Persian King Darius to punish Athens for her part in the Ionian Revolt; Greeks win the Battle of Marathon.

482 BC Silver discovered in Attica, used to build a navy.

480 BC The second Persian expedition against Greece; the battles of Thermopylae and Salamis.

431 BC Start of the Great Peloponnesian War between Athens and Sparta.

404 BC End of the Peloponnesian War.

336 BC Alexander becomes ruler of Greece.

331 BC Egypt conquered by the Greeks.

323 BC Death of Alexander the Great.

146 BC Greece becomes part of the Roman Empire.

30 BC Following the death of Cleopatra VI, Egypt becomes part of the Roman Empire.

NB: The Trojan War has not been included in this list of historical events as the precise dating of this event is hedged with difficulties. If such an event took place, the war would have happened in the late Bronze Age around 1200 BC or shortly before.

What is important to understand when studying the ancient Greeks is that a rich body of myth and legend precedes the historical events listed above and that many of the stories of the Greek heroes, in part, owe their origin to the Bronze Age Mycenaean period or to the 'Dark Age' which followed. The Homeric poems with their rich and colourful stories relating to the siege of Troy (the *Iliad*) and of the wanderings of Odysseus (the *Odyssey*), the internecine rivalries of the sons of Atreus at Mycenae (which inspired the Greek dramatists) the activities of Heracles and Theseus all owe their origins to this hazy period.

Preparation

Arrange for children to work in small groups. A wall map of ancient Greece would be useful, together with a more detailed timeline for ancient Greek history for adding extra events to the children's time line. It would be helpful if you could familiarise yourself with some details relevant to each of the events listed on the sheet. Photocopy the sheet on page 133, sufficient for one per group.

Resources needed

A large map of the ancient Greek world, scissors, adhesive, sugar paper, felt-tipped pens, photocopiable page 133.

What to do

Invite each group to make a timeline for the ancient Greeks using the photocopiable sheet and a sheet of sugar paper. First draw a straight line on the sugar paper, making it as long as possible. Then the children can mark it into at least ten equal sections to represent the centuries from the eighth to first century BC. Next they can cut up the photocopiable sheet into the separate events and paste them on to the appropriate part of the timeline.

Encourage the children to discuss the events as they order them using the terms conquest and settlement as they sequence the events of Greek history. As each pair/group of children completes the timeline they can colour in some of the detail until everyone has finished.

When the whole class is ready go through the main events with them all together either using one example of a time line made by a group or by making a large timeline of your own using two or three sheets of sugar paper joined together.

Make sure that all the children appreciate that the BC dates run in reverse from the normal, and that the eighth century BC means 799 to 700, the seventh century 699 to 600 and so on. Use the words decade and century.

Things that happened in ancient Greece

All dates are BC

▲ Cut carefully along the dotted lines and arrange the pictures in the order that they happened.

First recorded Olympic Games 776

Greek alphabet invented about 750

Cleopatra dies: the Romans conquer Egypt 30

Greek settlements in the Mediterranean 750 to 550

Pericles makes Athens more democratic 462

Peloponnesian War 431 to 404

The Parthenon is being built about 440

The Ionian Greeks rebel against the Persians 499

The Battle of Salamis (second Persian War) 480

The Battle of Marathon (first Persian War) 490

Alexander the Great's conquests and settlements 336 to 323

Pericles makes Athens more democratic 462

Suggestion(s) for extension

Children who finish early or who appear to find this activity straightforward can use reference books to find additional events to include on the timeline.

Suggestion(s) for support

Concentrate on a smaller number of events for example the Persian War battles. Limit events to the fifth century and make an enlarged time chart to cover just the decades of the fifth century.

Assessment opportunities

The timeline exercise *could* be used (with the dates deleted from the pictures) for summative assessment at the end of the topic. At this stage it may be useful to check the children's understanding of the terms century and decade as well as the conventional use of 'reverse dating' before proceeding.

Listen out for the ways in which children seek to order the events and the language they use.

Opportunities for IT

Children could use a CD-ROM encyclopaedia, or specific Greek CD-ROM to search for extra information for the timeline. They may need to be shown how to make a search for a particular date or event.

Children could then use a word processor to present labels for a class timeline displayed on the classroom wall using the information they have researched. They could add relevant pictures taken from a CD-ROM, clip art or scanned from their own drawings or pictures taken from books.

Display ideas

Timelines can all be displayed on your classroom wall, or the content could be transferred to one large timeline which can be extended as the study of the topic develops.

Reference to photocopiable sheet

Photocopiable page 133 lists a series of jumbled events in Greek history. The dates are given so that most children will be able to arrange the events in the correct sequence.

GODS AND GODDESSES

To find out about some of the characteristic features of Greek religious beliefs and attitudes.

Whole class followed by individual and group activity.

60 minutes; opportunities for follow-up.

Previous skills/knowledge needed

It would be helpful if children already had some knowledge of Roman gods and goddesses (names, function and attributes). Children should also have had experience of finding information from books.

Key background information

The writings of the Roman poet Ovid are a particularly rich source of story material about the exploits of the gods of Mount Olympus. Other material is also available from original Greek sources including Homer. You could research some of the following stories:

▲ Zeus and Hera and their stormy relationships and arguments among the gods;

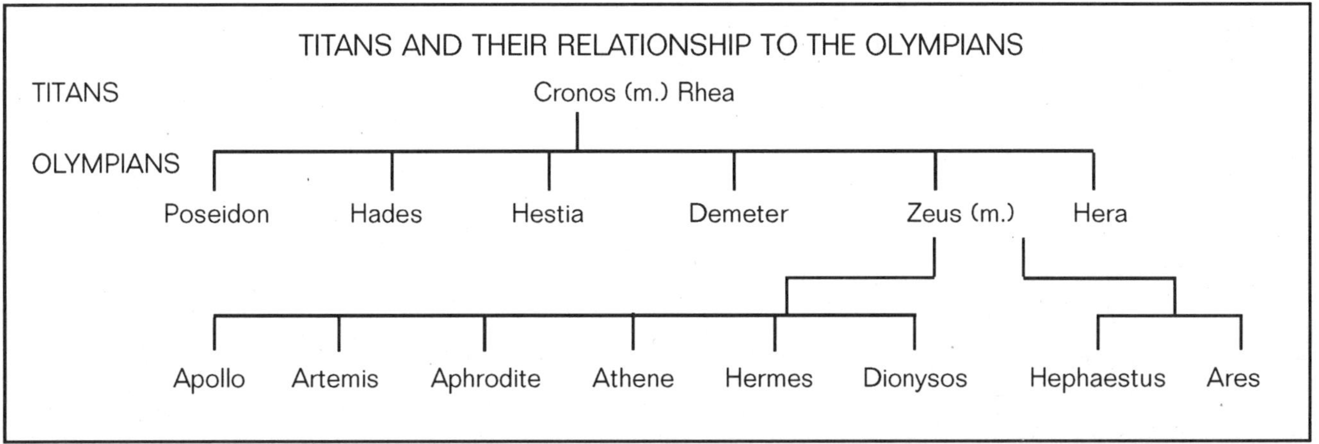

▲ Aphrodite winning the contest for the Apple of Discord;
▲ The competition between Poseidon and Athene for who should be patron of Athens;
▲ Hephaestus forging the shield of Achilles;
▲ Ares enjoying seeing cities captured and men killed in battles;
▲ Hermes playfully stealing Apollo's lyre;
▲ Demeter causing famine on the earth;
▲ Apollo and Artemis bringing sudden death and illness with their bows and arrows;
▲ Dionysus giving King Midas the gift of the golden touch;
▲ Hades and the theft of Demeter's daughter, Persephone.

Hephaestus forging the shield of Achilles

Preparation

Decide which story or stories you are going to use to introduce this lesson together with any visual sources, for example pictures of vase paintings, statues etc. Have materials available for follow-up display as appropriate.

Resources needed

Story books and other sources of information about the gods and goddesses of ancient Greece.

What to do

Present to the class some key information about the gods of Mount Olympus and about the Greek Underworld in the form of stories. Choose any one of the examples given above as a starting point. The subject matter from these stories and also from that given under the following activity is extremely rich and could form the basis of a continuing strand of story material running through the whole Study Unit. Children enjoy these stories, many of which are timeless and it is too good an opportunity to miss! At the very least this activity should place the Gods of Mount Olympus and also the Greek concept of the underworld with its associated stories 'on the map'. Once established, this can provide the basis of a small project that the children can work on in subsequent sessions.

Children will have varying amounts of general knowledge already. If the class has already studied the Romans, some use can be made of their brief acquaintance with the official Roman gods in Roman Britain, since these all had equivalents in ancient Greece (see chart below). Decide on the gods to study and allocate one or two of them to each small group of children. Ask each group to find out as much information as they can about the gods which they have been allocated. Tell them they can use general reference books, books on Greek mythology or use material drawn from texts based on the references cited above. Once each group has found out about their particular god ask them to write out an entry for a class biographical dictionary of all the gods and goddesses studied.

GREEK GODS AND THEIR ROMAN EQUIVALENTS

Zeus = Jupiter	Hermes = Mercury
Hera = Juno	Demeter = Ceres
Athene = Minerva	Dionysus = Liber
Aphrodite = Venus	Hades = Dis
Hephaestus = Vulcan	Poseidon = Neptune
Hestia = Vesta	Apollo = Apollo
Ares = Mars	Artemis = Diana

Suggestion(s) for extension

Using a telephone directory (Yellow Pages) or local trades directory, children can look for names of firms which use the names of Greek gods and goddesses, for example: Apollo Sports; Athena Galleries; Hermes Travel; Olympic Airways; Olympic Sport, travel etc. (NB Olympian Zeus was the god in whose honour the Olympic games were held at Olympia in southern Greece).

Suggestion(s) for support

Children can be asked to draw one god or goddess and to write underneath all the things they know about this particular god or goddess. They could be paired with more able members of the class for their research on a particular god or goddess.

Assessment opportunities

Ask the children to work in pairs and compile a quiz to test each other's knowledge of the Greek gods and goddesses.

Opportunities for IT

Children could use a CD-ROM encyclopedia to research information, and could then present their work using a word processor or desktop publishing package. Create a template in advance and each group of children can load the template and design their own page, including information and pictures of the chosen god. The page can then be formatted to get the best arrangement of text and pictures, font styles and sizes. Older children could also add page numbers, an index and contents page. Each page can be printed out to form a class book of gods and goddesses. Children could also use a drawing package to create a family tree of the gods.

An alternative approach would be to use an authoring package to create a multi-media presentation. The groups could search and present information on their selected gods and goddesses. They could include pictures taken from clip art or CD-ROM collections or scanned images from photographs or their own line drawings. Children could even add their own voices recorded using a microphone linked to the computer. The initial structure could be set up in advance with a front page showing the different gods, or an alphabetic index, so that by clicking on a letter the user would be taken to a page showing all the gods beginning with that letter. This is a fairly ambitious project and children using the software for the first time will need help and support.

Children could also make a simple database of the gods and goddesses, including information about their name, what they were god of, their children, and famous exploits. They could also use software to create a branching database which other children could use to identify a particular god. In this type of software children have to create a series of questions which can only be answered with a 'yes' or 'no' to differentiate between the various gods. The process of framing such questions makes it an excellent language activity as well as a test of children's knowledge about the various gods.

Display ideas

Prepare one classroom wall with crinkled brown wrapping paper to represent Mount Olympus; remember to surround its summit in clouds. Each group in the class or designated individuals can be asked to supply figures of the gods for attaching to the mountain, accompanied by biographical details (using a word processor if required). A similar display could be developed to represent the Underworld, including representation of the associated gods and their exploits and the punishment of the wicked, or Poseidon's underwater palace. Opportunities for drama could develop from all these examples.

An alternative display to Mount Olympus would be for the class to incorporate cardboard figures of the gods into a series of mobiles which can be suspended from the classroom ceiling. A biographical dictionary (see page 67) could be presented as a 'big book'.

HEROES AND HEROINES

To communicate knowledge and understanding of history using narrative and descriptions and to identify and give reasons for different ways in which the past is represented and interpreted.

Whole class followed by group and individual activity.

A session of 120 minutes with time for follow-up work or, if an episodic story such as the Odyssey *or the* Voyage of Argo *has been selected, this would be better handled as a sequence of shorter lessons, with opportunities for follow-up work.*

Previous skills and knowledge

Children will need to have a small amount of general knowledge about the Greek heroes such as names of some heroes and possibly knowledge of some stories. If possible, they need to have already worked with story boards.

Key background information

Like the stories of the gods and goddesses of the ancient Greeks, the stories of heroes and heroines are rich, since we have a number of literary sources which describe these exploits at length and in great detail. Principal sources which children should be introduced to are the two great Homeric epics: the *Odyssey* and the *Iliad*. These two narrative poems are both lengthy (although the 24 'books' which each comprises are more like chapters) and have traditionally been assigned to the poet Homer. They represent some of the earliest literature to be set down in writing. The episodic form into which both stories were cast by their author offers an appropriate basis for serialisation. A number of other heroic stories have been handed down to us from ancient Greece which follow a similar structure, although most do not survive in a single ancient source. Published versions of these stories tend to draw on a variety of sources to provide the necessary richness of detail.

Some Greek stories which appeal to children include:

▲ The siege and fall of Troy (Homer, *The Iliad* (episodes 1–4); Virgil, *The Aeneid*, Book 2 (The Wooden Horse).
▲ The Wanderings of Odysseus (Homer, *The Odyssey*).
▲ The *Voyage of Argo* (Apollonius of Rhodes, *The Voyage of Argo*).
▲ Theseus and the Minotaur (many sources but some material is in Plutarch *Life of Thesus*).
▲ Perseus and the gorgon's head (many sources but some material is in Ovid's *Metamorphoses*, Book V).

Translations of these are also available as Penguin Classics.

Preparation

Research stories from ancient Greece and decide which ones to use. If you decide to use the ones on photocopiable pages 134 and 135, photocopy enough sheets for each child. Also photocopy sheet 136 so that you have one for each child.

Resources needed

Versions of stories specially written for children and/or translated versions of the stories to be used on photocopiable pages 134 and 135, reference books which contain tellings of some of these stories, colour pictures of Greek stories as depicted on Greek vases, photocopiable page 136.

What to do

The story of 'Daedalus and Icarus' is just one of many examples that could be chosen from the abundant literary sources available. The extract from the 'Labours of Heracles' is again only one example of an episodic story. (This is where the original source material is scattered and the extract on photocopiable page 135 is drawn from many sources.)

Use either photocopiable page 134 or page 135 or another source to tell a story the ancient Greeks told.

If the children have not worked with a story board before, you will need to introduce this concept to them. Discuss with them which episodes they will wish to separate out.

Work with the class to think about the number of pictures they will need to tell the story. From the whole-class discussion, individuals can work on their own photocopied story boards.

If a longer story such as the story of 'Jason and the Golden Fleece' or the *Odyssey* has been used it might be a good idea to encourage the children to tell the story through the eyes of, for example, someone on board ship. This could be done in the form of a ship's log book or personal diary, or as a series of letters sent home to Greece. The story boarding and retelling can best be undertaken after a number of episodes have already been covered, or the story is complete.

Photocopiable page 136 provides an opportunity to consider ways in which Greek artists have represented stories using the media of pottery painting and clay modelling. Children can be asked to consider ways in which the same pictures (made by ancient artists) differ from pictures drawn by modern artists, or even from their own drawings. This will provide an opportunity to tackle the Key Element 3a and to consider why these representations are different. The photocopiable sheet could be used in a variety of ways. If it has been possible to tell a number of legends to the class, the sheet could be used as a kind of quiz at the end of the Study Unit, in which individual members of the class are asked to describe which story the picture refers to and what each picture depicts. Alternatively the sheet could be used as a trigger for children to find out more for themselves about those items they do not recognise.

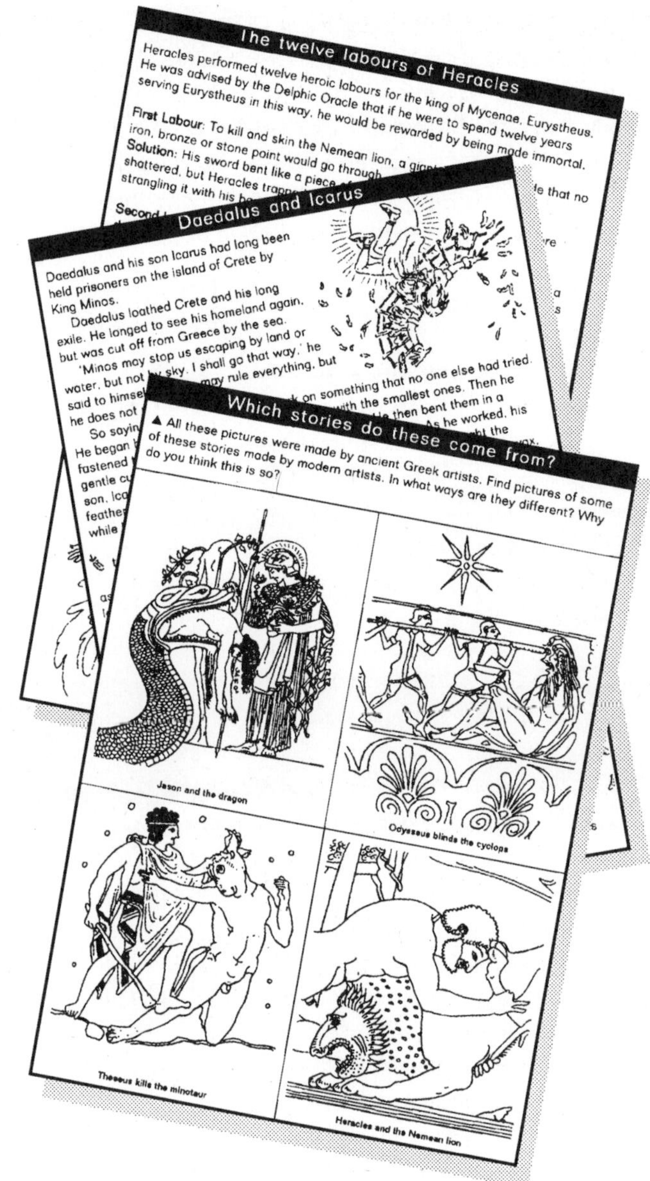

The twelve labours of Heracles

Heracles performed twelve heroic labours for the king of Mycenae, Eurystheus. He was advised by the Delphic Oracle that if he were to spend twelve years serving Eurystheus in this way, he would be rewarded by being made immortal.

Daedalus and Icarus

Daedalus and his son Icarus had long been held prisoners on the island of Crete by King Minos.

Daedalus loathed Crete and his long exile. He longed to see his homeland again, but was cut off from Greece by the sea.

Which stories do these come from?

▲ All these pictures were made by ancient Greek artists. Find pictures of some of these stories made by modern artists. In what ways are they different? Why do you think this is so?

Jason and the dragon

Odysseus blinds the cyclops

Theseus kills the minotaur

Heracles and the Nemean lion

Suggestion(s) for extension
What features can they use to give their story an appropriate Greek flavour? Experiment with the style of writing or decorative friezes taken from vase paintings as borders for their pages.

Suggestion(s) for support
Provide children with a series of sentences and/or words to use in telling a simple version of the story.

Assessment opportunities
Use photocopiable page 136 to see what the children have learned about each of the stories represented. Can they identify what is shown in this picture? Does the picture (made by a Greek artist) differ from pictures they have made (or other pictures they have seen) of the same story?

Opportunities for IT
Children could present their stories or diaries using a word processor. They can use the 'cut and paste' or 'drag and drop' facilities of the word processor to help organise the story so that the sequence of events is correct. The stories could be printed out and bound as a class book. Pictures could be added, taken from clip art or CD-ROM collections, scanned images from photographs or the children's own line drawings.

Display ideas
Try making a papier mâché table-top model of the Mediterranean. Make a large frieze of one or more stories in the style of a black figure vase painting, using black figures on an orange background, (see activity on page 82).

Reference to photocopiable sheets
Photocopiable page 134 'Daedalus and Icarus' and page 135 'The Labours of Heracles' provide stories suitable for this activity. The sheet on page 136 provides scope for extending children's structured narratives, it offers a chance to consider how some ancient artists portrayed the Greek heroes and offers a point of comparison with modern representation or with the children's own art work.

EVERYDAY LIFE FOR THE ANCIENT ATHENIANS

To learn about everyday experiences in Attica and the jobs the people did. To learn about Athenian society.

Whole class followed by individual and paired activity.

90–120 minutes.

Previous skills and knowledge

Children will need to know where Athens/Attica is and be able to locate it on a map of mainland Greece before using the map on photocopiable sheet 137.

Key background information

A central feature of ancient Greek society was the concept of the city state or *polis*. Although children will find it difficult to appreciate the complexities of what this term implies, it will be useful for them to at least appreciate that the people of Athens were not solely confined to the urban area of Athens and its port Piraeus, but in fact inhabited a large area of the surrounding countryside, known as Attica. Attica also included certain off-shore islands, notably the island of Salamis. To the Greeks, the city state was a community consisting of citizens (adult males), citizens without rights (women and children) and non-citizens (resident foreigners and slaves) who lived within a defined area and who were independent of outside people. The size of city states varied enormously, but each included a city centre (usually fortified), a market place or *agora*, a place where the people could hold meetings and centre of government. In the case of Athens, the Agora together with associated official buildings and the Acropolis (see 'Greek Temples' on page 84) have both been extensively studied by archaeologists.

Free men and women

The Greek family was monogamous and was basically composed of husband, wife and their children. Any dependent relatives and domestic slaves may have also formed part of the household.

There was a tendency for marriage to take place within a close circle of relatives in order to keep family property from being widely dispersed. In Athens women were of citizen status as far as being mothers and wives was concerned and they could take part in certain religious cults, but otherwise they had no political rights of the kind enjoyed by their husbands. They could not own property except for their own clothes, jewellery and personal slaves. They were under the protection of a man, either their father (before marriage), or their husband. Marriage depended upon the giving and receiving of a dowry which was passed from one man to another. Once this had been handed over, the marriage was regarded as having taken place.

Slavery

It has been estimated that there were as many slaves in Attica as free inhabitants (about 100,000 in all). Slavery was widespread throughout the ancient Mediterranean and the Greek philosophers such as Aristotle saw no difficulty in justifying slavery as a natural state. Slaves were a class apart in ancient Greek society and they did not enjoy any political rights. A slave was the property of his or her master. Like any piece of property, a slave should not be maltreated and anyone harming the slave of another was liable to pay compensation.

Although the very poor were not in a position to afford slaves, it appears that most families aspired to owning at least one slave. Every soldier on active campaign had a slave with him. It is thought that the average peasant working his own land would have had no more than one or two slaves. On larger farm estates there would be a supervising slave with a team of at least four or five other slaves working under him. A rich man could have as many as 50 slaves in his household. To judge from the jobs that household slaves were expected to do, we can assume that a large wealthy household would have been rather like that of a Victorian household, but with slaves rather than domestic servants as porters, nurses, cooks, maids and tutors.

In most situations, slaves worked either on their own or in small numbers alongside their owner, whether in the house or in the fields or in the workshop. The one exception in the case of Athens, was the silver mines at Laurium, where there was massive exploitation. This major source of Athenian wealth had been discovered early in the fifth century BC.

The state leased out parts of the mines to individuals such as Nicias with his gang of 1,000 slaves. Recently, British archaeologists have excavated the mines at Laurium and have shown evidence of child labour and appalling conditions under which the slaves were expected to live and work.

Preparation

Copy pages 137 and 138 sufficient for one each per child.

Resources needed

Information about everyday life in ancient Greece and Athens, also maps showing location of Athens and Attica, photocopiable sheets 137 and 138.

What to do

Introduction

Introduce to the class the outline map of Attica using photocopiable page 137. Explain that the urban area of Athens was only part of the land which belonged to the Athenians. The city state of Athens in fact covered the whole area known as Attica. Athenian people included country people as well as town dwellers. The kind of job that a person did could vary according to whereabouts they lived in Attica.

Ask the children to work through the list of occupations on sheet 138, ticking appropriate column(s) to indicate where they would expect to find different occupations in Attica.

Development

Ask the children to choose some of the occupations and to record them onto their map of Attica using writing or their own symbols.

Conclusion

Children could then go on to look at the position of slaves in the Athenian economy. Explain that slaves might do a variety of jobs depending upon their owner's occupation. Let them choose one occupation that they have already considered (farmer, sculptor etc.) and write down what jobs these slaves would have been expected to do for their master.

Suggestion(s) for extension

Ask the children to make a list of all the things in their own homes which today depend upon electricity (or gas) for their operation. Ask them to consider which of these would represent jobs done by slaves in ancient Greece.

Suggestion(s) for support

Make a list of things that we use electricity for today. Which of these things would a slave have done?

Assessment opportunities

Invite the children to list from memory all the jobs that people would have done in ancient Athens and in which parts of Attica they might be found.

Display ideas

A large scale map or table-top model of Attica showing occupations and economic activity of various kinds.

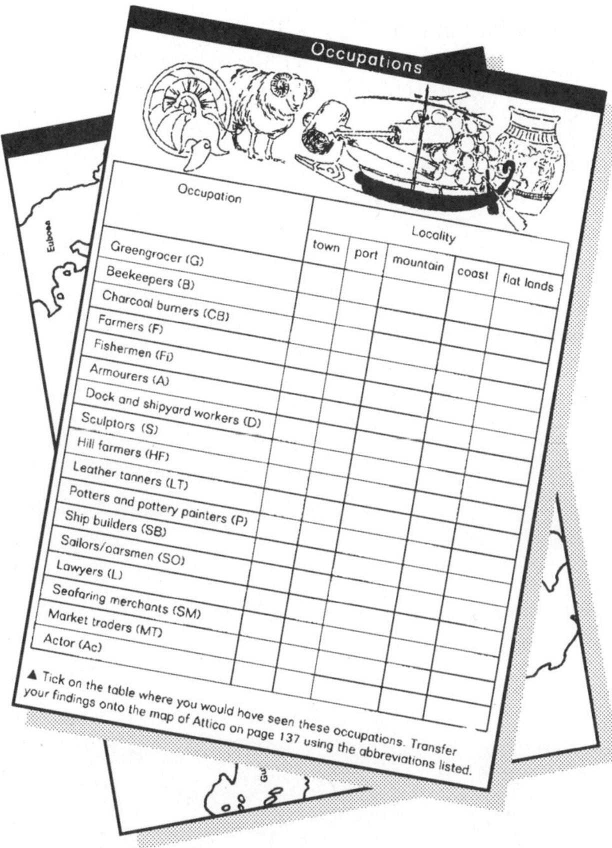

Occupations

Occupation	Locality: town	port	mountain	coast	flat lands
Greengrocer (G)					
Beekeepers (B)					
Charcoal burners (CB)					
Farmers (F)					
Fishermen (Fi)					
Armourers (A)					
Dock and shipyard workers (D)					
Sculptors (S)					
Hill farmers (HF)					
Leather tanners (LT)					
Potters and pottery painters (P)					
Ship builders (SB)					
Sailors/oarsmen (SO)					
Lawyers (L)					
Seafaring merchants (SM)					
Market traders (MT)					
Actor (Ac)					

▲ Tick on the table where you would have seen these occupations. Transfer your findings onto the map of Attica on page 137 using the abbreviations listed.

Reference to photocopiable sheet

The photocopiable sheet on page 137 provides a map of Attica showing the rural areas as well as the urban centre of Athens and its port the Piraeus. The map also makes clear the areas in which different kinds of occupations would have been found: the sea coast, the port, the coastal plain, the mountain country. The list of occupations on photocopiable page 138 is not exhaustive and can be extended but columns are provided for children to indicate where in Attica they think their occupation would have been found.

ATHENIAN GOVERNMENT

To learn about the form of government developed by the ancient Athenians and to use the term 'democracy' as relevant to understanding the term 'Parliament'.

One session with the whole class/followed by individual work. A second session involving the whole class.

One short introductory session of 20 minutes/ followed by a second session of about 60 minutes after children have had the opportunity to work on individual tasks.

Previous skills and knowledge needed

It would be helpful if children had some knowledge of the buildings on the Acropolis (see Greek Temples and the Athenian Acropolis on page 84 if necessary).

Key background information

The Athenian democracy as it operated in the fifth and fourth centuries BC (from 462) consisted of several parts. The assembly, comprising all adult male citizens, the jury courts, the Council of Five Hundred and the Council of Areopagus. There were also officials called archons and generals. Together these bodies and officials had responsibility for running the business of the stage. This included financial matters, law making, running the law courts, religious matters, foreign relations and the organisation of elections.

The Assembly

Decisions were made by all the citizens meeting together in the assembly. Voting on resolutions was by show of hands. All free male adults were eligible to attend meetings. Manual workers had the same voting rights as aristocrats. But women, slaves and foreigners who lived in Athens had no right to take part in the government of their city. Meetings took place in a large hollow on a hill in the middle of Athens called the Pnyx.

The Council of Five Hundred

The Council was selected by lot (fifty from each of ten tribes). Council members took it in turns to form a committee which convened the Council and the Assembly. The Council met in a special building which stood next to the agora.

The Council of the Areopagus

In 462 BC, Pericles and Ephialtes removed most of the powers of this old aristocratic body, making the Council of Five Hundred the governing council.

The archons

These were originally chosen by election from the aristocrats and the wealthy, but later on they were selected by lot from all classes.

The generals

These were chosen by election and were leaders of the people as well as commanders of the armed forces.

Preparation

Make a diagram for presentation on the board or on sugar paper to show the elements of Athenian democracy.

What to do

Tell the children that they are going to participate in a form of Athenian assembly. Explain to them how the assembly worked and who was entitled to attend. Tell them that they are going to debate an important issue from the time and after the debate is over, they will be able to vote on it.

One issue which concerned the people of Athens was the proposal of the general Pericles to rebuild the temples on the Acropolis at Athens which had been destroyed by the

invading Persians in 480 BC (see page 78 The Greeks and the Persians). The proposal went through and work on the Parthenon began in 447 but the proposal was a controversial one, because it involved spending huge sums of money which had been collected from Athens' allies in order to fight the Persians and as a safeguard against the Persians invading Greece again.

Now that the threat of an invasion had gone for ever, the proposal was to use some of the money collected to rebuild the city which had taken the brunt of the attack at the time of the Battle of Salamis.

Allocate a few children specific roles, for example, Pericles (author of the proposal), Thucydides son of Melesias (chief opponent), a herald who introduces the assembly and who invites members to speak with the words: 'Who wishes to address the assembly?'. Next ask the children to prepare a speech setting out arguments for or against the proposal. It may be a good idea to allocate the children to one side or the other and to ensure that Pericles' proposal wins the day (as happened in reality!).

The following arguments can be used by the children:

FOR
The Persians are no longer a danger.
There is plenty of money in the coffers.
The building works will provide lots of jobs.
The city of Athens needs its great temple to Athena.
Athens can look smart once more.
The Acropolis has been derelict for thirty years.
Athens was abandoned at the time of Salamis so the rest of Greece could be saved.
Athene will be pleased.

AGAINST
It is not right to use money given for other purposes.
We ought to consult our allies first.
Can we be sure that the Persians will not strike again?
The money should be spent on other things that the city needs.
We should keep the money in the treasury just in case.

Once the children have prepared their arguments the debate can be held. Afterwards, the herald should invite children to contribute to this debate allowing those 'For' and 'Against' to alternate. All citizens present can vote – by show of hands.

Once the debate is over and voting has taken place it would be helpful to relate the experience the children have had to 'democracy' as they may have seen it in the British Parliament today (for example on the television news).

Suggestion(s) for extension
If you feel it is appropriate, make the procedure a little more complicated, by letting some of the children act as the Council members. These members can hold a preliminary meeting before bringing the matter to the full assembly for its decision.

Suggestion(s) for support
An assembly could be held with a more contemporary theme such as motions for 'improvements to the school' on which the whole class could deliberate and then vote.

Assessment opportunities
What do children understand by the term 'democracy'. How did the Athenian voting differ from democratic government in Britain today?

Display ideas
Make a large drawing of the Pnyx and everyone can contribute human figures to give an impression of an assembly meeting.

SPARTA

To learn about some of the characteristic features of ancient Sparta and to consider the reliability of our written sources.

Whole class followed by individual activity/drama; follow-up once the children's accounts have been written.

60 minutes.

Previous skills and knowledge needed

Any study that the class has already made of Athens will be helpful especially involving attitudes to women, military achievements and the Government.

Key background information

The town of Sparta lies in the southern part of mainland Greece called the Peloponnese. It is hemmed in by high mountains. About 700 BC the Spartans conquered the neighbouring land of Messenia and turned the population of that country into slaves who farmed the fertile land for their Spartan masters. It is difficult to know what life was really like in ancient Sparta as the Spartans wrote very little about themselves. Therefore, the accounts of life in Sparta that survive need to be read with caution.

Spartan women enjoyed much greater freedom than their counterparts in Athens. Girls were given some athletic training and Spartan women could inherit property in their own right.

One thing that comes through strongly from the sources is the militaristic way of life lead by the Spartans. The Spartan army of heavily armed soldiers (hoplites) was very well trained and well equipped.

Preparation

Copy photocopiable page 139 for every member of the class.

Resources needed

Photocopied sheets, page 139. Pictures of Sparta and Spartan soldiers if possible.

What to do

Tell the children about what life was like for Spartan boys; and also for Spartan girls. Give each child a copy of the photocopiable sheet and consider together what life might have been like for a boy in a military unit.

Ask the children to think:

▲ How would you have felt being taken away from your parents at the age of seven?

▲ What tasks might you have been given to do?

Sparta was in many ways very different from Athens. Sparta had two kings and a Council of Elders (28 men who were aged over 60 and were members for life). There was an assembly at which all full citizens over the age of 30 could vote, but they could not put forward proposals of their own. They could only vote on proposals put forward by the Council of Elders. Some matters such as education, finance and law and order were controlled by five magistrates called *ephors* who were elected for one year only.

In addition to those who were full citizens, there were two other classes of people. There were the Perioikoi who were farmers and who could be called on to fight for Sparta in times of war. There were also the Helots who were slaves and had no political rights and no freedom. Every Spartan soldier had a Helot as an attendant, although the Helots also fought in battle sometimes.

▲ What thoughts might you have had when you were allowed to go hungry?

Once the children have looked at what the author of the quote was saying move on to consider together the nature of this source and how it reflects life in Sparta. Tell the children that this source was not written from first-hand knowledge but by the writer Plutarch a long time after the events described. What do children feel about this? How might a Spartan have viewed the training of children through military discipline? Can they suggest reasons why the Spartans went to these lengths?

All the children can use the photocopiable sheet to help them to write their own letter home describing a day in their life at a military camp. When the accounts have been written, invite some of the children to read out their accounts to the rest of the class.

Spartan soldiers

The Spartans were prevented from bringing up their sons in their own way. Lycurgus ordered all boys aged seven to be taken away from their families and to be put into 'military units' where they would be brought up and looked after together. They had a very basic training in reading and writing. The rest of their education was concerned with making them obey orders, putting up with hardship and winning battles.

'A young man aged 20 is in charge of each unit of boys. It is his job to supervise mock battles and the boys have to serve him his meals indoors. He makes the bigger boys fetch firewood while the smaller ones have to gather herbs. The boys steal from what they fetch and anyone who is caught stealing is given several lashes with a whip, either because he has been careless or because he is not a clever enough thief. They also steal what food they can and learn how to be good at attacking people who are asleep or not paying attention.

There is a story that once upon a time a boy who had stolen a fox was carrying the animal under his cloak. Rather than let himself be found out he let the animal tear out his insides with its teeth and claws.'

Suggestion(s) for extension

Ask some children to find out more about what a hoplite soldier wore in battle. Can they find out how we use the word 'Spartan' in English?

Suggestion(s) for support

Rather than write an account of life in a military camp some children may find it easier to act out a series of scenes from daily life in a military camp.

Assessment opportunities

Ask the children to describe the main features of Spartan society and the differences between the Spartans and Athenians to ascertain whether they have learned and understood the key facts. What have they learned about written historical sources?

Opportunities for IT

Children could use an encyclopaedia CD-ROM to help them search for other information on Sparta. Groups of children could present their information on different aspects of Spartan life using a word processor or desktop publishing package and the printed copies used in a class display or book on Sparta. Children could also use a word processor to write and draft their letter home.

Display ideas

Make a display of letters and drawings about camp life.

Reference to photocopiable sheet

The photocopiable sheet on page 139 shows Greek Hoplite (heavily armed) soldiers. The text is taken from Plutarch's biography of an early Spartan king called Lycurgus.

SHIPS AND SEAFARERS

To find out about Greek traders using documents and artefacts and to use the terms 'settlement' and 'trade'.

Whole class introduction/individual activities.

30 minutes introduction/open-ended individual activities.

Previous skills/knowledge needed

Any knowledge that the children already have of Greek legends about the sea especially the *Odyssey*, Jason and the Argo would be useful.

Key background information

Greek ships

The earliest ships we hear about are those which Homer describes in his stories about the Trojan War and the wanderings of Odysseus. He describes ships as they were in his own time, probably around the eighth century. These ships were galleys with 30 oars or galleys with 50 oars. The oarsmen sat on both sides of the ship in a double row. Each oar had a leather strap fixed to it which was looped around an upright wooden peg in the side of the ship, this gave the oarsmen something to pull against. The ship had a special steering oar at the rear. The oarsmen were not slaves but were usually the friends and companions of the ship's captain. The ships also had a sail which was square in shape, and made of patches of linen, fixed to a mast. When the wind was from the right direction the sail was used and the oarsmen were allowed to rest. When the ship was being rowed the mast was lowered on to the deck.

Navigation

In early times, sailors had no compasses, reliable maps or lighthouses to guide them as they journeyed by sea. Therefore, most sailing was done in daylight hours and confined to the spring and summer months. When sailors were forced to travel by night, they relied on the stars. No sailor ever got out of sight of land if he could help it. He hugged the shore all the way or hopped from island to island, even though he might have to go out of his way to do so. In the *Odyssey*, King Nestor describes how he returned home from the Trojan War. He sailed to the nearby island of Tenedos. Then he sailed to the island of Lesbos and then went in one huge hop to Euboea where he held a great sacrifice to Zeus as a thanks offering for his safe arrival. This story well illustrates the caution with which early mariners approached sea journeys.

Greek colonies

Between 750 and 550 BC the Greeks on the mainland became more outward looking; bands of adventurers from many Greek cities set out from their homelands and settled in more distant parts of the Mediterranean. Their motives must have been mixed: land hunger (mainland Greece has a shortage of flat arable land), desire to expand trade, seeking raw materials such as gold and silver, or a sheer spirit of adventure!

These new Greek cities were not colonies in the sense we recognise, for example under the British Empire. They became independent cities in their own right and provided important trading outposts for their founding mother cities. For example, the Greeks colonised the Black Sea area, Sicily and southern Italy. There were Greek cities in southern France (Gaul in ancient times) from which the Greeks were able to trade with the Celts.

Preparation

Photocopy page 140 so that all the children have the map.

Resources needed

Photocopiable sheet on page 140, other maps of Greece and the Mediterranean, pictures of Greek ships.

What to do

Introduction

Use a large map of the Mediterranean, if available, to introduce to the children the idea that the ancient Greeks did not just inhabit the mainland of Greece, but that their settlements were widely scattered. If a large map is not available, distribute the photocopiable sheets and use this map. Draw the children's attention to places such as Naples (Neapolis) and Marseilles (Massilia) and Nice (Nike). These were originally Greek settlements or 'colonies' and their modern names are similar to their ancient Greek names. Explain that many Greeks left their native cities in search of a new home, where they built cities such as the places referred to above, in Sicily, Italy, along the shores of the Black Sea and in Gaul. Discuss with the children the reasons which might have led the Greeks to want to settle in strange lands

far away from home (see Key background information, page 76). Now distribute the photocopied map, if this has not already been done.

Invite children to highlight or underline all the colonies that have been marked on their map. They could shade in lightly in one colour on the map all the areas of the Mediterranean that were occupied by Greeks.

Development

Explain the difficulties faced by early mariners in the Mediterranean. Tell them about Nestor's return home from the siege of Troy. You may like to look at this route on a map. Now introduce the idea of trade. This was one of the reasons why the Greeks were keen to explore more distant places in the Mediterranean. Ask the children to identify on their map some of the items that the Greeks would have been interested in obtaining. What items would the people of the hinterland (regarded by the Greeks as 'barbarians') have hoped for from the Greeks?

Invite the children to draw in trade routes using coloured pens or pencils between the cities of mainland Greece and the new cities or colonies. They will need to think about the exchange of goods that would take place. Read to them Hesiod's advice to sailors:

'Never set sail at the end of October or the beginning of November. The storms are terrible then, so you would be wise to keep yourself and your boat safely on dry land. Bring your boat well up onto the beach and pack stones round it to protect it from the rain. Then put all your equipment and other things inside the house and hang up your rudder near the fire to keep it dry.

The best time of year to go sailing is July or August. You won't wreck your ship or drown your sailors at that time of year. That is of course, unless the gods decide to drown any of them as a punishment. There is nothing you can do about that. As a rule, in mid-summer the sea is calm and the breezes are gentle. Set sail then if you wish, but don't forget to return before the autumn, when the fierce North wind makes the sea dangerous.' (written in the eighth century BC).

Conclusion

In order to consolidate the idea of trade, children could be divided into groups of four: two children in each group to be Greek traders; two children to be Celtic traders. Write on slips of paper the various goods that would have been traded between the Celts and the Greeks and distribute them to the children accordingly. Ask them to imagine that they were actually trading these goods with strangers who did not speak their own language, and to develop a dialogue, in the first instance using sign language and gradually introducing words to explain their transactions.

Suggestion(s) for extension

Children could use reference books to extend their knowledge of trading. They could try to answer questions such as; 'How do we know?'; 'What evidence do we have?'.

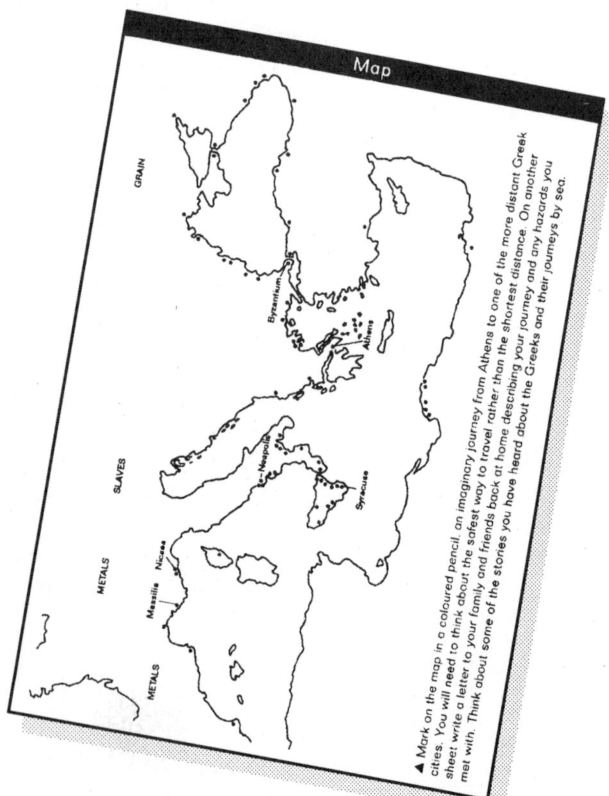

Map
GRAIN
SLAVES
METALS
METALS
Byzantium
Athens
Neapolis
Syracuse
Nicaea
Massilia
▲ Mark on the map in a coloured pencil, an imaginary journey from Athens to one of the more distant Greek cities. You will need to think about the safest way to travel rather than the shortest distance. On another sheet write a letter to your family and friends back at home describing your journey and any hazards you met with. Think about some of the stories you have heard about the Greeks and their journeys by sea.

Suggestion(s) for support

Children could make cut-out shapes with written labels to represent the different items to be traded between the Greeks and the Celts.

Assessment opportunities

Watch and listen to the children as they perform their trading role-play. Have they understood what was involved in these exchanges? (Trade). Have they shaded in their map correctly? (Settlement).

Display ideas

Make a display of trading ships and trade routes between the Greek cities of the mainland and the Greek cities elsewhere. If this is done on a flat surface small boats could be made from balsa wood or matchboxes using spent matches as oars.

Reference to photocopiable sheets

The photocopiable sheet on page 140 shows the extent of Greek colonisation.

THE GREEKS AND PERSIANS

To learn about the reasons for the wars between the Greeks and Persians (between 490 and 480 BC) and to place events in a (relative) chronological framework.
To use the terms invasion and conquest correctly.
Whole class followed by paired activity.
60 minutes/follow-up time. Alternatively break the work down into two separate sessions.

Previous skills/knowledge needed

Geographical knowledge based on the Greeks in the Mediterranean.

Key background information

The Greek historian Herodotus is the main informant on the causes of the war between the Persians and the Greek city States. We have little other documentary evidence, therefore it is important to remember that the account which we have of the Persian Wars is somewhat one-sided and from a Greek perspective. It may well be worth obtaining a copy of the *Histories* by Herodotus (Penguin Classics). Alternatively, children's versions of Herodotus are available and may be obtainable from your local library:

The Lion in the Gateway by M. Renault and *Stories from Herodotus* by B Wilson and D J D Miller (both out of print).

Here are a few details of the Persian Wars largely based on Herodotus' account:

The Ionian Revolt

The map below shows the situation in the years leading up to the Persian Wars after the Persians had overrun Lydia, following the defeat of Croesus in battle. Pro-Persian rulers (tyrants) were installed in all the Greek cities. The word tyrant in Greek means king and does not necessarily carry oppressive connotations. By 499 BC, the Greek cities on the Western coast of Asia Minor, which were heavily involved in trade, revolted against the Persians who were making increasing financial demands, threatening their commercial activities. The leaders of the revolt appealed to the cities of mainland Greece to help. Only two responded positively, one of which was Athens, who sent 20 ships to help.

During the campaign which followed, the city of Sardis was sacked and set on fire. After the revolt of the Greek cities had been put down by the Persians, leading to even greater loss of freedom for the Greek cities along the Western seaboard, the Persian king, Darius, planned revenge on the Greek cities of the mainland who had helped their fellow Greeks.

Herodotus tells us:

'The first thing Darius did was to ask who the Athenians were. When he was told, he ordered that his bow be handed to him, then he put an arrow on the string, shot it up into the air and cried out: "O God, let me punish the Athenians". He then told one of his servants to repeat three times whenever he sat down to dinner, "Sir, remember the Athenians" '.

The 1st Persian War and the Battle of Marathon 490 BC

Eventually, Darius came with an expedition by sea to the mainland of Greece. The city of Eretria which also had sent help was destroyed. Then the Persians set sail for Attica. The best place for the manoeuvring of cavalry was the plain of Marathon. This was also the nearest part of Athenian territory to Eretria. The Athenian army, both cavalry and heavy armed foot soldiers (hoplites), set out for Marathon. Before they left the city, they sent a messenger called Pheidippides, who was a trained runner, with a message to Sparta. He returned to Athens with the news that the Spartans were celebrating a festival and could not set out with their army until the moon was full. The Persians disembarked and camped in the plain of Marathon. After waiting in vain for the Spartans to complete their religious activities, the Athenian army eventually moved down into the plain and confronted the enemy. The result was an Athenian victory which left 192 Athenian dead and 6,400 Persian losses.

The running race which we know as the 'marathon' in fact commemorates the 26 miles by the shortest route from Marathon to Athens, rather than the full journey from Athens to Marathon via Sparta!

The 2nd Persian War 480 BC

(The Hellespont bridge) By 480 BC Darius had been succeeded by his son Xerxes. The second Persian expedition against the Greeks this time seemed intent on invading and conquering the whole mainland. According to Herodotus, it took seven days and seven nights for his troops, their animals and wagon loads of baggage to march on their way to Greece from Asia. In addition an armada of more than 1,000 ships sailed towards Greece. On reaching the Hellespont, the bridge which Xerxes' engineers had constructed in advance, was smashed to pieces in a violent storm. Xerxes ordered the sea to be given 300 lashes and to have chains thrown into the water as a punishment.

(The canal at Mt Athos) Herodotus also describes in detail the canal which Xerxes had built in advance, through the peninsula of Mt Athos. Darius' expedition had suffered disastrously in a storm off the coast of this headland.

(Earth and water) The mighty Persian army marched into northern Greece through the mountains. One by one as the army came southwards, the cities of Greece surrendered, giving the Persians offerings of earth and water as tokens of submission by both land and sea. Not all the cities of the mainland surrendered. Xerxes did not send a request for surrender to Athens and Sparta.

(The battle of Thermopylae) At the narrow defile between the sea and the steep mountains, the Greeks decided to make a stand. Fighting in relays, they threw back the Persian invaders, until a route through the mountains was betrayed to the Persians. The Persians were shown how to reach the pathway through the mountains and Xerxes crack troops, 'The immortals', marched through the night along its course and down to the other side of the narrow pass. Leonidas, the Spartan King was trapped and forced into defending the impossible. He and his troops together with their slaves (Helots) all died.

(The battle of Salamis) Meanwhile the Greek fleet sailed at the Athenians' request to the island of Salamis in Attica. The Athenians planned to evacuate the city of Athens and much of the population moved onto the island thus enabling the Persians (once they had won at Thermopylae) to invade most of Attica including the city of Athens itself. The Greek navy by this time consisted of about 300 ships and lay at anchor in the straits between Salamis and the mainland of Attica. The Spartans and Corinthians wanted to make a stand further south, abandoning Athens to the Persians. When the news came through of the Greek defeat at Thermopylae, work began on building a wall at the Isthmus of Corinth. But the Athenian General Themistocles had other ideas, for he did not wish to see the people of Athens who were currently stationed on the island of Salamis to be abandoned and he saw it as crucial that a showdown with the Persians should take place in the straits between Salamis and the mainland. He used the following stratagem to force the Persians into fighting with the Greek navy while they were still stationed in the straits. He sent one of his slaves, with the following message:

'I have brought you a secret message from the Athenian admiral, who wishes your king well and is hoping for a Persian victory. He has told me to let you know that the Greeks do not think they stand a chance and they are planning to withdraw from here quickly to save their skins. All you have to do is to prevent them escaping and victory will be yours for the asking.'

The slave, having passed on the message, made a quick get away. The Persians believed him and proceeded at the dead of night to seal off the far exit to the straits with some of their ships. The Greek fleet was now hemmed in completely and was forced to join in a battle with the Persians. Xerxes watched the battle from the mainland. Despite the vast superiority in numbers, the Greek navy achieved an outstanding victory. The Greeks are said to have destroyed 200 ships and lost only 40 themselves.

This is Aeschylus' eye-witness account of the Battle of Salamis. The words are put in the mouth of a Persian messenger in his play called 'The Persians':

'At first we were able to hold our own. Then somehow our ships were gradually driven back into the narrowest space between the rocks. We were jammed helplessly against each other, our oars and rams smashing into each other with disastrous results.

The Greeks straightaway took their chance. They made it impossible for us to escape and then they attacked us hard on every side. Many of our ships were overturned and we could hardly see the surface of the water because of the wreckage and drowned sailors. Soon every beach nearby was dark with the bodies of dead Persians.

By this time we had only a few ships still left afloat and they began to try to escape. The Greeks were still not satisfied. They hacked without mercy at any Persian they could find, alive or dead. The whole place was full of the screams of dying men and the sea was a mass of bloodstained bodies'.

Preparation
For a fuller account than is possible here, obtain a copy of Herodotus' *The Histories* (Penguin classics) if possible, or any longer versions of the stories referred to on page 79. Photocopy pages 141 and 142, sufficient for children working in pairs.

Resources needed
Large maps of the Mediterranean, photocopiable pages 141 and 142.

What to do
Tell the story of the Persian invasions beginning at any point in the summarised narrative that you find personally interesting. If available, refer to the text of Herodotus' account to provide more detail. Use the example of the first invasion under Darius and the second invasion by Xerxes to highlight the idea of invasion. The term conquest is also relevant to both (see captions to the maps on photocopiable page 141). The maps can be used at this point to emphasise the difference between the two terms.

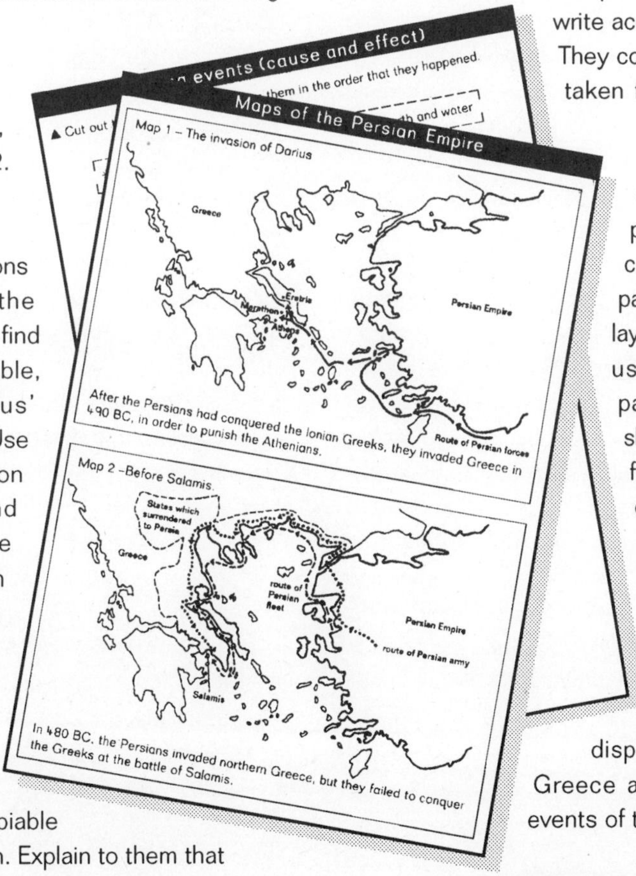

Hand out copies of photocopiable sheet 142 to each pair of children. Explain to them that the sentences show how a chain of events led to the wars between the Greeks and Persians and that they should sort the sentences so that they can link the issues of cause and effect.

As a result of undertaking this sequencing activity it should be possible for the children to identify the reasons for the wars between the Persians and the Greeks drawing a distinction between the first and second expeditions.

Suggestion(s) for extension
Children could work on a radio/TV/newspaper report (for example News at Ten 'From our war correspondent...') explaining why war has broken out in either the first or second Persian war.

Suggestion(s) for support
Some children may need to concentrate on either the first or the second expedition or you could break down the Persian Wars into two separate sessions for them.

Assessment opportunities
As the children work, how well can they recall the sequence of events and how far are they able to link them through cause and effect?

Opportunities for IT
Children could use a desktop publishing package to create a magazine-style presentation on the Persian wars. Groups of children could research and write accounts of the different battles. They could include pictures and maps taken from books or scanned from other books, their own drawings or those drawn by using an art or drawing package. The different groups could each be given two or three pages and asked to design the layout for their section. If they are using a desktop publishing package they will need to be shown how to create and re-size frames, add the graphics and create format text using appropriate styles and fonts.

Display ideas
Choose one of the battles between the Greeks and Persians to make a wall display or make a large map of Greece and Asia Minor to show the events of the Persian Wars.

Reference to photocopiable sheets
Both the photocopiable sheets cover the first and second Persian expeditions against Greece. Page 141 provides maps as a resource for the activity. The sentences on photocopiable page 142 marked with an asterisk refer to the second expedition, those without refer to the first.

PAINTED POTTERY

To find out about ancient Greek painted pottery and to ask and answer questions relevant to pottery as a source.

Whole class and individual activity.

120 minutes/individual follow-up time.

Previous skills/knowledge needed

Children should be familiar with some Greek myths and legends that were often used to decorate vases (see Heroes and heroines page 69).

Key background information

Three categories of Greek painted pottery will be of particular relevance here: these are *geometric*, *black figure* and *red figure* vase painting.

The *geometric* uses abstract patterns and some figure representations. This style was in use down to the eighth century BC. The evolution of the so called *black figure* style in the hands of Corinthian potters can be traced from the late eighth century BC onwards. The Athenian potters took on the *black figure* style and developed their own excellence in this particular medium. However, the Athenians soon developed their own *red figure* style of painting. This style was a major feature of pottery manufacture in Athens during the fifth century. When Athens went into decline following the Peloponnesian War at the end of the fifth century BC, potters migrated to southern Italy taking their style of red figured pottery with them. However, the quality of representation was never as high as in the fifth century.

Black figure ware involved the presentation of silhouettes in paint which fires black in the kiln and which have details incised on them with a sharp instrument. *Red figure* ware on the other hand, involves painting the pot with black paint but leaving 'islands' of lighter coloured pottery which fires an orange-red colour in the kiln onto which details have been painted with a black firing paint.

Favourite motifs were stories from Greek myths and legends, and large numbers of pots also bear themes from everyday Athenian life. Even the mythological paintings reflect contemporary costume and artefacts. All vase paintings are therefore an excellent source for everyday life in Ancient Greece, since it may be assumed that the artist painted those things with which he was most familiar. Since the painted pots represent high quality pottery, the designs they bear may be assumed to be those which appealed to their affluent purchaser. The bulk of vases which survive intact were not used for domestic purposes but were used as burial objects, hence their survival over such a long period.

The purposes for which these painted pots were used is many and varied. Vessels range from domestic drinking cups and dishes to those associated with wine, water and oil. Rituals associated with the dead involved the pouring of libations and the making of offerings.

One further point is that because of the distinctiveness of design and the fact that the names of some actual artists are known to us by name, these pots can often be dated to within a few years of when they were actually being produced and therefore provide invaluable dating evidence for archaeologists.

Preparation

Collect together pictures of vase paintings which represent the three categories referred to above, for the children to study. Refer to the relevant sections of the *Odyssey* story in a full version, translated by E. V. Rieu (Penguin Classics), if necessary. Copy the sheet on page 143, one per child.

Resources needed

Picture books with a range of vase paintings representing *geometric*, *black figure* and *red figure* vases. Try to include examples of mythological as well as everyday life themes. Materials for making pictures of pots and for decorative

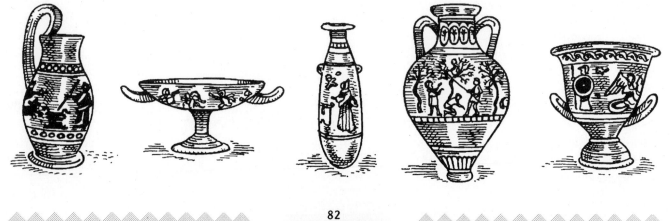

friezes including wax crayons, orange card and sharp instruments for scratching detail. Photocopiable page 143.

What to do

Give each child a copy of the photocopiable page and ask them to read the story of Odysseus and the Sirens as described in the extract from Homer's *Odyssey*.

Discuss with them how much of the story is included in the picture. What aspects *could* the artist have included but has not? The story is a legend but can we rely on the picture to tell us what Greek ships were really like? Would an Athenian pottery painter have painted ships which could be seen everyday in the port at Athens?

Encourage the whole class to look at the themes represented in vase painting. Ask them to make lists of subjects they can find. How many are stories from Greek mythology and how many are from everyday life? Discuss why the painters might have chosen these particular themes.

Next use orange card and black wax crayons (to represent the colours in black and red figure vases) to make drawings which could be seen on vases. *Black figure* vase paintings can be effectively simulated by making black silhouette figures with black crayon on orange coloured card. Detail can then be scratched on the silhouette figures by using a sharp instrument. *Red figure* vase paintings can be effectively simulated by drawing a picture onto orange card in outline. The background can then be filled in using black crayon. This leaves the outline shape of the figures as 'islands' of orange which can have the detailed features added using black crayon. Alternatively, you could use black poster paint on orange card.

Suggestion(s) for extension

Make a collection of pictures taken from Greek geometric painted pottery. What other kinds of design were in use down to the eighth century BC and what kind of information can you gather by studying them? Try reproducing the decorative patterns on these pots.

Suggestion(s) for support

Using crayons or paint, children can concentrate on reproducing, in a continuous line, the frieze patterns found on the Greek vase on the photocopiable sheet. This activity could be extended to include looking at friezes on other pots.

Assessment opportunities

Encourage the children to retell the story of the Sirens and to identify stories from vase paintings and other visual sources.

Opportunities for IT

Some children could design their story vase using an art package, perhaps being given a vase template as a starting point. They could be limited to just the orange and black colours. Children could also use framework software like *My World 2* and the *Greeks* resources file to design their own Greek vase.

Children could use an art or drawing package to create a continuous line geometric frieze pattern in a Greek style. Show them how to mark a section of the pattern, duplicate it and then position it to create a repeating pattern. If the software has a 'snap to grid' option it is useful to turn this on so that sections of the pattern line up with each other automatically.

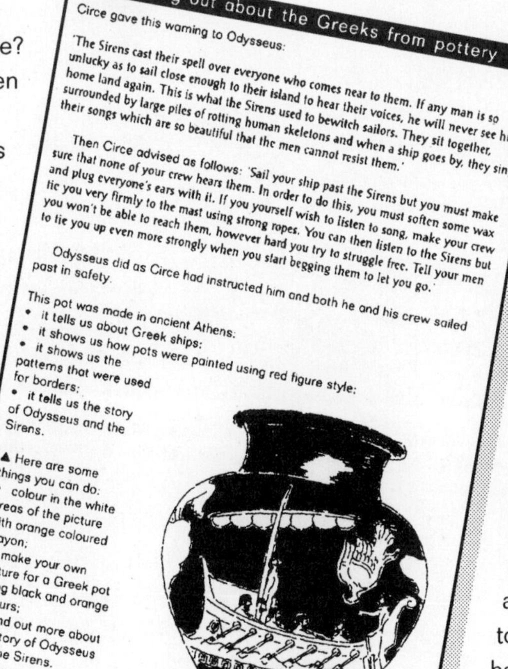

Finding out about the Greeks from pottery

Circe gave this warning to Odysseus:

'The Sirens cast their spell over everyone who comes near to them. If any man is so unlucky as to sail close enough to their island to hear their voices, he will never see his home land again. This is what the Sirens used to bewitch sailors. They sit together, surrounded by large piles of rotting human skeletons and when a ship goes by, they sing their songs which are so beautiful that the men cannot resist them.'

Then Circe advised as follows: 'Sail your ship past the Sirens but you must make sure that none of your crew hears them. In order to do this, you must soften some wax and plug everyone's ears with it. If you yourself wish to listen to song, make your crew tie you very firmly to the mast using strong ropes. You can then listen to the Sirens but you won't be able to reach them, however hard you try to struggle free. Tell your men to tie you up even more strongly when you start begging them to let you go.'

Odysseus did as Circe had instructed him and both he and his crew sailed past in safety.

This pot was made in ancient Athens:
- it tells us about Greek ships;
- it shows us how pots were painted using red figure style;
- it shows us the patterns that were used for borders;
- it tells us the story of Odysseus and the Sirens.

▲ Here are some things you can do:
- colour in the white areas of the picture with orange coloured crayon;
- make your own picture for a Greek pot using black and orange colours;
- find out more about the story of Odysseus and the Sirens.

Display ideas

The pictures of pots, the friezes and decorative patterns which the children make can all be used to decorate the walls in the classroom.

Reference to photocopiable sheet

The red figure illustration on photocopiable page 143 (based on a vase now in the British Museum) shows a galley equipped with both oars and a sail. The passage refers to the story of the Sirens and has been adapted from Homer *The Odyssey* Book XII (Penguin).

GREEK TEMPLES AND THE ATHENIAN ACROPOLIS

To find out about the ancient Greeks and especially their beliefs from temple buildings that survive.

Whole class session followed by group and individual activities.

60 minutes/follow-up as necessary.

Previous skills/knowledge needed

It will be helpful if children have already been introduced to the idea of a society in which, not one, but many gods and goddesses were worshipped (for example see Gods and goddesses, page 66).

Key background information

From earliest times it appears that the ancient Greeks built shrines to particular gods and goddesses. Some of the finest buildings that survive from ancient Greece are its temples, built of fine quality stones such as marble. A temple was a house built for a god or goddess and this was the place which he or she was believed to inhabit. A large statue of the deity was housed in a strong room (*cella*). Within this room offerings including items of value such as jewellery would be placed. As time went by temples became more elaborate (see photocopiable page 144). Painted sculptures were made to decorate the outside of the building which told the stories of Greek myths. Temples stood within an area called a precinct which was regarded as sacred and it was within this precinct (not within the temple itself) that sacrifices took place.

The great temple which stands today on the Acropolis at Athens, was dedicated to Athene, the patron goddess of Athens. It was in the second half of the fifth century BC that the Parthenon and other surviving buildings were built on the Acropolis. Other buildings (see illustration) built at this time included the temple of Erechtheus (Erechtheum). Since the time of the battle of Salamis in 480 BC, the Acropolis stood empty of great buildings for thirty years. The reasons for this were that the Athenians had been forced to abandon their city at the time of the invasion of the Persians and the buildings on the Acropolis had been destroyed (see Athenian government, page 73). Elsewhere in Greece were many other fine temples, for example at Olympia (see The Olympic games, page 87) and Delphi.

Archaeologists have found evidence of the destruction which occurred at the time of the Persian invasion in the burnt deposits which they have excavated on the Acropolis. Pottery and other artefacts from this deposit provide sound dating evidence for the year 480 BC which can be used by archaeologists as dating evidence on other sites.

Preparation

Collect together pictures of the Athenian Acropolis as it is seen today, together with any reconstruction of the buildings as they may have looked in the late fifth century BC. Photocopy the sheet on page 144, one per child.

Resources needed

Pictures of the Acropolis and other surviving temples in Greece. Model-making materials including narrow cardboard tubes, cardboard boxes, brown wrapping paper, PVA adhesive, paints. Photocopiable page 144.

What to do

Start by listing some of the gods and goddesses that the children are already familiar with and the responsibilities that each had. Ask them: Which god was particularly important at Athens? (Athene). Which god might have been particularly important at a seaside place? (Poseidon). To farmers whose livelihood depended on grain growing? (Demeter).

The children will already have seen pictures of statues and figurines made to represent different gods (normally shown in human form). Introduce the idea of shrines being built to house the statue of a god or goddess. Emphasise that religious ceremonies did not take place inside the temple but outside within the area surrounding the temple (precinct), this is also where sacrifices of animals took place. The earliest shrines or temples were built like small houses to protect the statue and to protect any precious gifts that may have

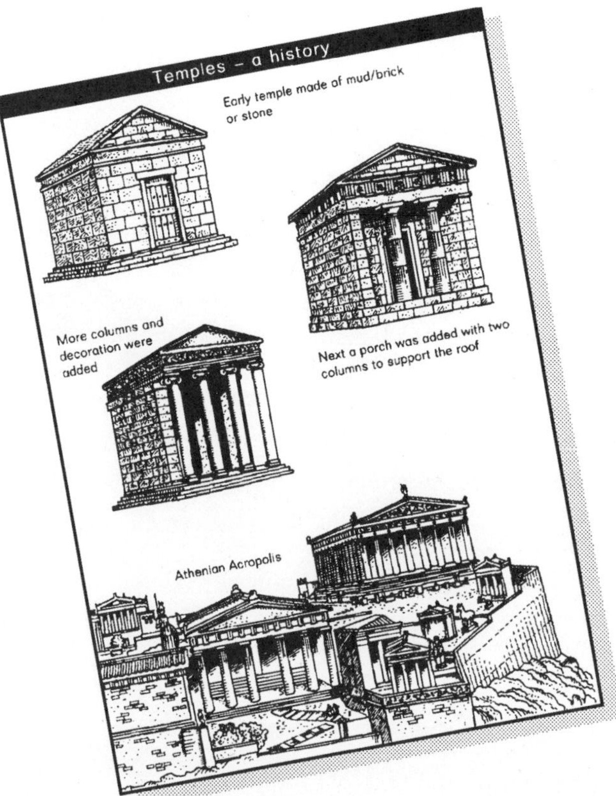
Temples – a history
Early temple made of mud/brick or stone
More columns and decoration were added
Next a porch was added with two columns to support the roof
Athenian Acropolis

been presented to the god or goddess. Discuss the different building materials that might have been used: these would be principally timber, terracotta and stone. Ask: Why would stone be preferable to wood?

Ask the children how they think temples changed over time. Distribute the photocopiable sheet and use it to explore with the children some examples of changes, including the use of sculpture.

Children can now be asked to write their own account of the development of temples from early times using the information supplied. Moving from the general to the particular, attention should now be drawn to the buildings on the Acropolis at Athens. Explain that the Athenians had a nearby quarry (on Mt Pentelicus) of fine quality white marble which they used for these buildings. Finally ask the children to contribute to a model of the Acropolis with all its buildings, made out of reclaimed materials. Suggest that each group of children contributes to a different section.

Suggestion(s) for extension

You may wish to introduce some children to the main features of temple architecture developed by the Greeks and which have been copied by later generations. This could be developed in the classroom as a building-style collage. Some more able children could conduct an investigation into the specialised temples at Delphi and at Epidaurus. What would they have done on a visit to the oracle of Apollo at Delphi and/or of the healing god Asclepius whose shrine was at Epidaurus? How do these places and the things that have been found there help us find out about the ancient Greeks?

Suggestion(s) for support

Using Lego or other construction materials some children could make one of the temple structures depicted on the photocopiable sheet.

Assessment opportunities

Get the children to tell the story of how temples evolved over time. See if they can use the correct terms and explain the sculptures which were used.

Display ideas

Decorate the entrance to your classroom with columns and a decorated pediment. Make a frieze of sculptures to go along the classroom wall like that from the Parthenon, choosing your own Greek myth.

Reference to photocopiable sheet

The photocopiable page 144 is an information sheet and does not involve an activity as such. It contains a visual history of the Greek temple and its development from early times, the final picture shows the buildings on the Acropolis.

THE GREEK ALPHABET AND LANGUAGE

To learn about the language used by the Ancient Greeks by studying their alphabet and documents.

Paired and individual activity.

60 minutes.

Previous skills/knowledge needed

Familiarity with the Roman alphabet for comparison with the Greek names which appear on the photocopiable sheet 145.

Key background information

The alphabet was first used during the eighth century BC and was developed from the Phoenicians with whom the ancient Greeks came into contact through their colonising and trading activities. The earliest Greek literature dates to the end of the eighth century when it first became possible to set down oral poetry in writing.

This activity provides an interesting opportunity for language awareness. Children will be able to see some differences and similarities between ancient Greek and modern English. They should be encouraged to explore the different alphabets and if possible study some specific examples of Greek writing.

Preparation

Photocopy the alphabet and Greek words on the photocopiable sheet on page 145 sufficient for children to work in pairs or as individuals.

Resources needed
Photocopiable page 145, together with any other examples of Greek writing.

What to do
It will not be necessary to introduce the alphabet to the whole class, as this activity can best be undertaken by individuals or pairs of children as and when they complete other tasks. Children enjoy codes and will be able to make a successful attempt at deciphering Greek words that are recognisable. They can also use the alphabet to make their own messages for one another. Distribute the photocopiable sheet to pairs of children and invite them to decipher the names and words on the sheet using the Greek alphabet.

If you have gathered together any other examples of Greek writing you may like to draw the children's attention to the use of 'the'. Children will be curious to know why three forms are used for our word 'the'. (For example the three words Acropolis, the Parthenon and the Erectheum all have different forms for 'the', because Greek has three genders, masculine, feminine and neutral and each form is different.)

Suggestion(s) for extension
Ask the children to transliterate the names of children in the class into Greek letters. They could be asked to prepare flash cards using some of the Greek words included on the photocopiable sheet. Do the children notice any differences between ancient Greek and modern English? For further activities see *Learning about Ancient Greece* (Open School).

Suggestion(s) for support
Children who have difficulty with transliterating letters should be encouraged to concentrate on those letters which are the same as in the Roman alphabet. They can then go on to tackle those which are different including those which combine the letters. Children could be shown Greek words on flash cards and asked to identify them.

Opportunities for IT
Many word processors and desktop publishing packages have access to a 'Greek' font which children can use to make their own Greek words, labels and signs for display in the classroom. It is also possible to purchase a 'Greek' font and add it to those available for the children.

Display ideas
Children can write out signs using Greek letters to describe the different parts of their classroom.

THE OLYMPIC GAMES

To describe the ancient Olympics and to make links between the ancient Olympic Games and their modern day counterpart.

Whole class and individual or group activity.

60 minutes.

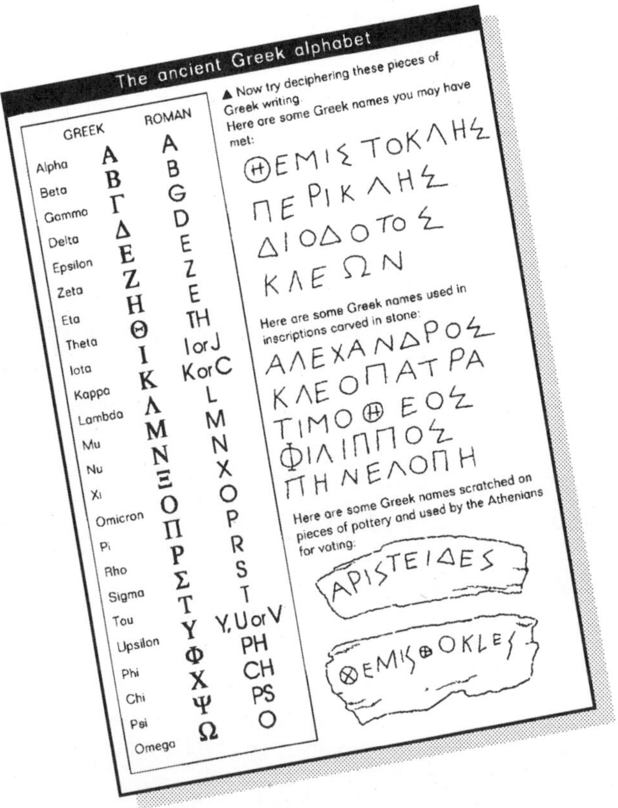

The ancient Greek alphabet

Name	GREEK	ROMAN
Alpha	Α	A
Beta	Β	B
Gamma	Γ	G
Delta	Δ	D
Epsilon	Ε	E
Zeta	Ζ	Z
Eta	Η	E
Theta	Θ	TH
Iota	Ι	I or J
Kappa	Κ	K or C
Lambda	Λ	L
Mu	Μ	M
Nu	Ν	N
Xi	Ξ	X
Omicron	Ο	O
Pi	Π	P
Rho	Ρ	R
Sigma	Σ	S
Tau	Τ	T
Upsilon	Υ	Y, U or V
Phi	Φ	PH
Chi	Χ	CH
Psi	Ψ	PS
Omega	Ω	O

▲ Now try deciphering these pieces of Greek writing.

Here are some Greek names you may have met:

ΘΕΜΙΣΤΟΚΛΗΣ
ΠΕΡΙΚΛΗΣ
ΔΙΟΔΟΤΟΣ
ΚΛΕΩΝ

Here are some Greek names used in inscriptions carved in stone:

ΑΛΕΧΑΝΔΡΟΣ
ΚΛΕΟΠΑΤΡΑ
ΤΙΜΟΘΕΟΣ
ΦΙΛΙΠΠΟΣ
ΠΗΝΕΛΟΠΗ

Here are some Greek names scratched on pieces of pottery and used by the Athenians for voting.

ΑΡΙΣΤΕΙΔΕΣ
ΘΕΜΙΣΘΟΚΛΕΣ

Previous skills/knowledge needed

Gods and goddesses, page 66 and Greek temples, page 84 will both be relevant, as will children's knowledge of the modern Olympics and athletics.

Key background information

The ancient Greek Olympics were held every four years at Olympia in south western Greece. Other games were held on a regular basis at Corinth, Delphi and at Nemea. Special games for women were also held (see Sparta on page 75). An early example of an athletics contest is described in the *Odyssey* before Odysseus finally set sail for Ithaca and in the *Iliad* following the death and burial of King Priam of Troy. The games begin with a religious ceremony in honour of Olympian Zeus, whose temple was at Olympia. Events in the games, included: throwing the discus and the javelin, the long jump, running, the torch race, the pentathlon, boxing and wrestling.

Reference to photocopiable sheet

Photocopiable page 145 contains the capital letters of the ancient Greek alphabet for reference and some examples of Greek names for the children to translate.

Translations are as follows:

1. A selection of Greek names that the children may have already met during their work on the ancient Greeks. The examples on the sheet are:
Themistocles;
Pericles;
Diodotus;
Cleon.
2. Some Greek names used in inscriptions carved in stone. The examples on the sheet are:
Alexander;
Cleopatra;
Timothy;
Philip;
Penelope.
3. Some Greek names that were scratched on pieces of pottery (used by Athenians for voting). The examples on the sheet are:
Aristides:
Themistocles.

Preparation

Photocopy sufficient copies of the photocopiable sheet on page 146, one per child. Collect some posters and reference books containing information about the ancient Olympic games. Try to find pictures of vase paintings and sculptures which show each of the events in the ancient Olympics. Collect pictures of modern athletic activities.

Resources needed

Information about the ancient Olympics. Pictures of modern athletics events from newspapers, photocopiable page 146, writing materials.

What to do

Distribute copies of the photocopiable sheet. Begin by discussing with the children athletics in modern times, including the modern Olympic Games. Use any available newspaper cuttings or pictures of modern day athletic field and track events to get the children thinking about the features of athletic events today. Next introduce the ancient

Olympics using posters and reference books. Compile a list together of events in the ancient Olympics and discuss with the children some of the chief differences that they notice between ancient and modern athletic contests.

Here are some points for comparison with modern day Olympic Games (with modern day features in brackets):

▲ The ancient Olympic games were held in honour of the god Zeus (nowadays no religious connections).

▲ They were held every four years (same today).

▲ The games were always held at Olympia (now they are held in different countries each time).

▲ Only men took part (women as well as men).

▲ Only Greek cities competed (all countries of the world can take part).

▲ Prizes were pottery and wreaths made of olive leaves (medals and flag raising ceremony).

▲ Men are shown naked (full kit worn).

▲ There were 'field' and 'track' events including the pentathlon (continues today but some events differed: jumping with weights and new events added).

▲ Athletes travelled to Olympia by sea and land (land, sea and now by air).

Children can use available reference books to follow up the whole-class discussion by working on their individual photocopied sheet.

Further developments could include a class (or school) Olympic contest and/or writing a sports commentary (for recording onto audio or video tape) of an ancient Olympic games.

The Olympics

▲ Compare the ancient Olympics with today's games. Write/draw in the boxes.

Here are some events that are the same.

Here are some events that are different.

Here are some other things that are the same (for example, prizes).

Here are some other things that are different.

▲ Consider these questions:
- Where did the athletes come from?
- What prizes were there for the winners?
- How often were the games held?
- Did women and men take part?

Suggestion(s) for extension

Find out about the other games that were held, for example, at Delphi. What evidence of sport has been found by archaeologists at Delphi?

Suggestion(s) for support

Choose one ancient athletic event that is the same as today and say what an athlete had to do.

Assessment opportunities

Do the children have a clear idea of the differences and similarities between the ancient Greek and modern Olympic games?

Opportunities for IT

Children could use newspaper software or a desktop publishing package to create their own Olympic games 'Sports Extra'; selecting a range of ancient Greek events and describing them in newspaper style. Pictures could be added by using scanned images taken from books and children's own drawings, or imported from suitable CD-ROM or clip art collections. The class can work in two groups to make a modern and Greek newspaper for comparison between the same events and the whole Olympic Games.

Display ideas

A display could be based upon the children's conclusions as to differences and similarities between the Olympic games, ancient and modern.

Reference to photocopiable sheet

Photocopiable page 146 provides opportunities for the children to draw or write in a series of boxes and spaces, their findings about differences and similarities between the Olympic games in ancient and modern times.

A past non-European society

The topics covered in this chapter cover between them a vast span of centuries and material to study. Two sorts of lesson plans have been devised to cope with the amount of material to be studied. The first four activities in this chapter are as such, 'content-free'. Each of these plans (with a given example) suggests ways in which certain Key Elements can be tackled using any of the non-European societies under study.

The remaining activities are specific to particular civilisations. The teaching suggestions contained in all the lesson plans may be transferred across all the societies under study. In some cases there are clear cultural links between two of the topics, for example the Sumerians flourished in the same geographical region as the later Assyrians and the Gilgamesh story is common to both and can be used with both. There are also important links between the Maya and the later Aztecs.

Egypt is a popular choice of topic (due to the availability of resources). It is, however, worth considering other options. A study of the West African civilisation of Benin is an alternative to Egypt as an example of a flourishing society in Africa, prior to the European colonisation of large parts of the continent. The non-European society Study Unit provides opportunities to study the ancient civilisation on the Indus Valley, an area roughly corresponding to present day Pakistan.

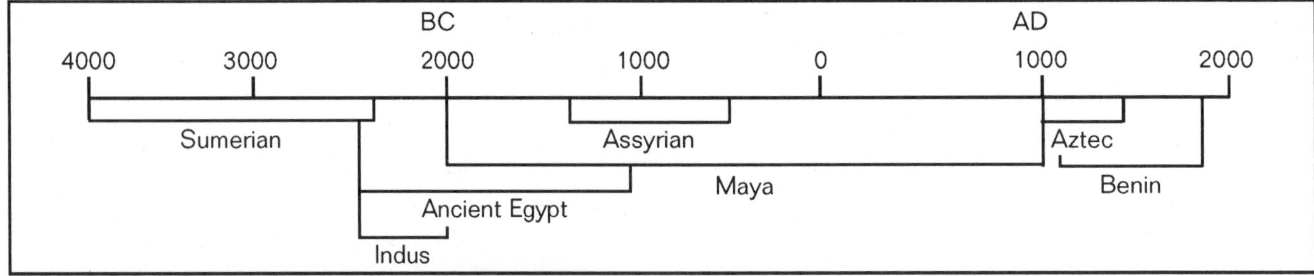

PLACE, TIME AND QUESTIONS TO ASK

To place the major events, people and changes in that society within a chronological framework and to use the terms relating to the passing of time as appropriate (ancient and modern, BC/AD, century and millennium) as well as terms relating to the particular society being studied, for example Mayan, Sumerian. To ask questions about and identify some of the main features of their society.

Individual followed by whole class activity.

90 minutes.

Previous skills/knowledge needed

Cross-referencing to other Study Units that have already been dealt with would be helpful, both in relation to chronology and in relation to identifying different aspects of the society. (How were they governed? Did they use writing? What sort of buildings did they have? etc.)

Key background information

The civilisations in the non-European Study Unit are:

Ancient Egypt (see pages 97-100).

One of the earliest civilisations in the world. The Kingdom of Egypt lasted 3,000 years and its archaeological remains are extensive. Published material on the ancient Egyptians is widespread and readily accessible in many books and museums.

Ancient Sumer (see pages 100-103) and the *Assyrian Empire* (see pages 104-105).

Two phases in the early history of Mesopotamia, (or, in Greek, 'the lands between the rivers'). The rivers Tigris and Euphrates, which flow through modern Iraq, were once at the centre of early civilisations including the Sumerians during the fourth and third millennium BC and the Assyrians from about 1200 BC to the fall of Nineveh to the Medes and Babylonians in 612 BC. The British Museum contains many finds from excavations of ancient Sumer and some fine stone monuments from Assyria.

Indus Valley (see pages 105-107).

One of the world's first great civilisations which may be compared with Ancient Egypt and Mesopotamia. The ancient cities of the Indus Valley which today lies within Pakistan and part of north west India were first investigated during the 1920s. There are large gaps in our knowledge largely as a result of a failure to decipher the writing.

The Maya (see pages 108-109) and *The Aztecs* (see pages 109-111).

Both civilisations belong to a group of early indigenous American cultures which came to an end in the Americas before the arrival of European adventurers from the late fifteenth century AD. Both American Indian civilisations developed in central America. The Maya were the earlier civilisation and span a long period of time stretching back to 2000 BC, although the 'classic' period, identified for study here, is concentrated mainly within the first millennium AD. The Aztecs on the other hand, were relative latecomers. They settled in the area around 1000 AD and built their capital city, Tenochtitlan during the fourteenth century. This is now the site of Mexico City.

Benin (see pages 112-116).

Not to be confused with the modern country of Benin. The civilisation which flourished within part of what today is modern Nigeria began in the eleventh century AD and is the latest of the civilisations included for study within the non-European Study Unit. The civilisation continued until Benin was sacked by the British in 1897, but the civilisation reached its greatest power between the mid 1400s and mid 1600s.

Preparation

Familiarisation with the chronology and geographical location and key events and features of the society to be studied. For example, if the topic is Ancient Egypt it is likely that children will know more information than with the other topics.

One way of compensating for this would be to anticipate the start to the topic by bringing in resources, especially relevant picture books and pictures for display which will arouse interest and curiosity before study of the topic begins in earnest.

Resources needed

Sheets of sugar paper and felt-tipped pens. For concept mapping exercise, one blank sheet of A4 size paper and writing implement for every individual member of the class. Adult and children's reference books, text books, video recorder and other relevant resources.

What to do

Step 1

Begin by asking the children to record on a sheet of blank paper all that they know about ancient Egypt, using writing and or drawing. Allow no more than ten minutes. Collect in the results and store these for future reference. For an example of a 'concept mapping exercise' of this kind, refer to *Humanities in Primary Education,* D. Kimber et al. (see pp 147–8) where our example based on ancient Egypt is discussed.

Step 2

Now invite children to contribute to a whole-class brainstorm, in which you record all the information on a large sheet of sugar paper pinned to the wall. This initial list (depending on its contents) can provide starting points for considering the chronology and location of the society. For Egypt: River Nile, desert, hot sun, palm trees – locate on the African continent, using a globe to show climatic conditions and the length and central significance of the River in Egypt. Pyramids, Cleopatra, Tutankhamun – could all be put into a chronological sequence as starting points for adding in other events in Egypt's early history at a later date.

Step 3

With the help of the class compile a list of questions relating to the society being studied. Here are a number of key questions which could be identified.

▲ How were they ruled/governed?
▲ What social classes were there?
▲ Did men and women live different lives?
▲ Did they have slaves?
▲ What food did they produce? (Hunting/gathering; pastoral; agriculture).
▲ Did they have calendars? how did they tell the time? Did they have clocks?
▲ Did they trade with other people?
▲ What sort of gods did they have?
▲ What was their religion like?
▲ What sort of festivals did they have?
▲ What were their biggest buildings like?
▲ What were people's houses like?
▲ How were children brought up/did they go to school?
▲ Did they use writing?
▲ What kind of land transport did they have?
▲ What kind of sea transport did they have?
▲ What kind of technology (stone/metals) did they use?
▲ What kind of art did they have? (Also music, dance etc.).
▲ What kinds of arms and armour/warfare did they have?
▲ Did they live in towns?

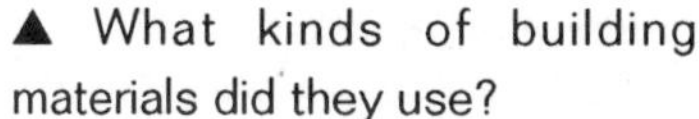

▲ What kinds of building materials did they use?
▲ Did they have running water, drains? Baths and toilets?
▲ What arrangements for medicine/health?

Having identified about twenty or more questions these can be grouped together, for example government, technology or religion, each group of children could then be given one group of questions to answer.

Step 4

(If time permits). Using the information available from a variety of sources, children can begin to list their responses to the questions posed.

Suggestion(s) for extension

Some children who display evidence of having already studied the society in question could be given particular assignments to research on their own, with a view to contributing their findings to the class at a later stage. This would be particularly helpful for tackling areas which you are not likely to be able to cover with the whole class. An alternative project could be for some children to work together to make a wall map or table-top model.

Suggestion(s) for support

Concept mapping – some children may have extreme difficulty in searching their memories for knowledge of the Egyptians but the presence of a few pictures or books may help to get them started and give them one or two ideas to record.

Assessment opportunities

The record of the children's state of knowledge before they begin their study of the topic will provide a valuable benchmark against which to measure their learning once they have completed the study. Use the sheet on which they have recorded their initial knowledge to compare what they have learned while studying this topic. In particular, can they handle the terms century, millennium and BC dates.

Opportunities for IT

Children could either use dedicated timeline software such as Soft Teach Educational's *Timelines*, or create a vertical timeline using a word processor or desktop publishing package. Children should be discouraged from using the spacebar to position the text on the page as changes to other formatting commands can wreak havoc with previously aligned text! Show the children how to set 'tabs' and create a hanging indent so that text 'wraps' at the correct points in the lines.

If a desktop publishing package is used, two vertical columns can be created with the dates in one and the accompanying text in the other.

Children could also use a word processor to create a class list of all the things they know about the civilisation being studied. Different children could add their own line of information which can be printed out and displayed in the classroom and later used as a reference.

Display ideas

A wall display of a chronological framework with the few initial items recorded on it which can be filled out as the topic develops.

Some children could be asked to make a wall map or table-top model (see page 91) on which places can be located as the topic develops.

WHAT DID THEY LOOK LIKE?

To consider how past civilisations and their artefacts are represented and interpreted.

Whole class/follow-up using the photocopiable sheet.

45 minutes.

Previous skills/knowledge needed

General knowledge of other archaeological sites and use of skills developed as a result of looking at pictures and the visual sources on historical evidence. Experience of doing jigsaw puzzles.

Key background information

An ideas brainstorm to provide some preliminary knowledge of the society would be useful. The children will then have some ideas about the kind of sites and the kind of artefacts that we have as evidence of that society.

Preparation

Try to find one or two pictures showing reconstructions by artists (it doesn't matter whether these pictures were made by artists a long time ago or whether they are by modern artists in recent publications). There are likely to be some such pictures in most information books about past non-European societies. Think about the process of translating archaeological sites, that are not very photogenic and which are difficult for the lay person to interpret, into reconstructed pictures. For example, think about how much of the reconstruction will be based on firm evidence and how much will be intelligent guess work. Make copies of photocopiable page 147 for all the children.

Resources needed

Copies of photocopiable page 147 for the class. History books about the society which include an artist's reconstruction of buildingsand everyday life. If there is a shortage of reconstructions relevant to the civilisation being studied, find reconstructions of other sites for example Alan Sorrell's well-known reconstructed drawings of British archaeological sites with their dark cloudy skies are to be found in many children's books about Roman Britain.

It would also be helpful to have some photographs of the original excavations, which may be available in reference books about the non-European society being studied.

What to do

Stage 1

Bring into the classroom a broken flower pot or other inexpensive pottery article and use this to show how archaeologists go about reconstructing incomplete articles from fragments. It may be a good idea to involve several children in putting a real pot together again. This should be attempted step-by-step allowing each join to bond firmly before attempting the next. A sand tray can be used effectively to 'anchor' one of the pieces before glue is applied to make the join with a second piece. If possible obtain an example of a real shard from a pot that has been excavated and allow individuals to handle this and discuss with them what the whole pot might have looked like and how we can work that out. Careful study of the way in which the rest of the pot might be recreated (even though only one piece has been found) can serve as a small scale illustration of what the artist has to do in reconstructing larger scale items. Ask the children what would happen if some pieces were missing?

Stage 2

Present to the class one picture of an artist's reconstruction based on the society you have chosen to study. Discuss with the class what they can identify in the picture, drawing on their knowledge already gained. If other sources of art work can be found, for example from history information books of an earlier date, this will enable you to introduce the idea of interpretation. Discuss with the class the possibility that the most recent artists' drawings might be more accurate because we now have more knowledge, as the result of the work of modem day archaeologists. This may lead on to the question: how does the artist know what things were like? Now introduce the photographs of excavations. These will show just how much the artist has had to reconstruct, attempting to use all the evidence available but sometimes using his/her imagination to fill gaps. It is important to emphasise that some items in the reconstruction are based on hard evidence, but that other things may be based on what we know from the sources or on the artists' imagination. All the class could be invited to do the activity on photocopiable page 147 as a conclusion to this activity.

Suggestion(s) for extension

Look at examples of reconstructions based on other archaeological sites to compare with the one being studied. Get the children to consider: How much can the artist be sure of? How much will be imagined?

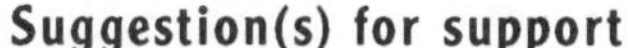

Suggestion(s) for support

Some children may benefit from working closely with a more able child.

Assessment opportunities

How successful are the children at completing the pot on the photocopiable sheet? Let them compare their reconstructions and discuss the differences in interpretation.

Opportunities for IT

Children could use a CD-ROM encyclopaedia or other collection of ancient civilisation clip art and search for pictures which illustrate the period. These could be printed out and used for comparative purposes.

Children could also use a simulation package like *Arcventure II (Egyptians)* to help understand the process of archaeological excavation. Such a package should be used as an integral part of the work and time is needed to introduce the software and for teachers to discuss with children the reality of the model they are using as well as the historical implications of the work.

Display ideas

Display the reconstructed pots and comparative interpretations that children have carried out.

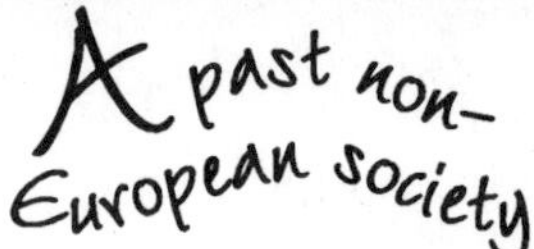

Reconstructing pottery
▲ These pieces all belong to one pot. Cut the pieces out and make it up again. There is a piece missing, see if you can draw it in to complete the pot.

HOW DO WE KNOW?

To find out about aspects of the society using a range of sources: documents, artefacts, buildings and sites. To ask/answer questions about archaeological evidence.

Pairs followed by whole class 'brainstorm'; pairs.

60 minutes.

Previous skills/knowledge needed

Builds on the activities on the previous pages 90-93, in particular although work on other Study Units will also have introduced children to a range of sources and to ways in which they can be studied.

Key background information

Table indicating major items of evidence for the seven societies in question. It will be readily seen from the chart that the non-European societies are extremely varied in the opportunities they offer for studying different kinds of source.

The range of artefacts, and sites/buildings which children can study will vary according to the civilisation studied. Here are some notes on the written records which are available for the civilisations included in Study Unit 6.

Documents:

Egypt hieroglyphic picture writing carved or painted or written in ink on papyrus. **Sumer** cuneiform picture writing using a wedge-shaped tool and its prototypes (not fully deciphered). **Assyrians** cuneiform script. **Indus Valley** undeciphered. **Maya** pictorial glyphs. **Benin** no written records, but powerful oral tradition. **Aztecs** codices bearing glyphs.

Reference to photocopiable sheet

The photocopiable sheet on page 147 shows an incomplete pot from an excavation carried out in Mesopotamia. This gives children the opportunity of attempting to interpret what is missing from broken and incomplete ancient pots. In doing this, they will be going through a similar set of thought processes to an artist who reconstructs archaeological sites. The type of pottery is known as Ninevite V pottery. It was richly painted and probably dates to about 3000 BC.

	Buildings	Government	Religion	Art	Documents	External relations	Technology	Burial
Egypt	Pyramids Tombs Towns	Pharoah	Deities Life after death	Tomb paintings	Hieroglyphs	Crete Syria Hittites	Stone carving Irrigation Glass making	Mummies
Sumer	Ziggurats		Gilgamesh story	Gold and silver inlay	Pictograms Cuneiform	Bible lands	The wheel Copper casts	Death pit
Assyria	Palaces	Powerful and warring kings		Stone relief	Cuneiform			
Indus Valley	Towns Granaries		Origins of Shiva?		Undeciphered script	Mesopotamia	Sanitation Engraving	
Maya	Temples		Ball game Calendar	Reliefs	Glyphs stelae			
Benin	Benin city	Obas	Ancestor worship	Brass sculpture	(Oral history)	Portugal	Brass casting	
Aztec	Tenochtitlan Temples	Montezuma	Human sacrifices Calendar	Mosaics Sculpture	Codices	Spanish conquistadors	Recycled waste, canals	

Preparation

Having previously surveyed in broad terms what is known about the society being studied and having looked at the value and limitations of reconstructing from fragmentary evidence, this lesson is intended to involve the children in looking at the range of sources available for study and for examining them in more detail. The table on page 94 summarises under different headings some of the major pieces of evidence available for study in relation to buildings and sites, artefacts and documents. Build on the previous

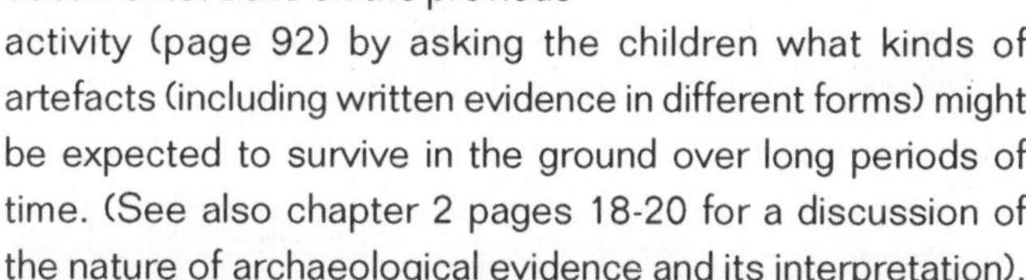

activity (page 92) by asking the children what kinds of artefacts (including written evidence in different forms) might be expected to survive in the ground over long periods of time. (See also chapter 2 pages 18-20 for a discussion of the nature of archaeological evidence and its interpretation).

Resources needed

As many books as possible about the civilisation being studied as well as general reference books for example, children's encyclopaedia, plans of buildings in urban or rural contexts, photographs of locations and surviving structures, artefacts representing a range of activities (for example religion or agriculture), artistic representations and writing (where appropriate).

What to do

Ask the children to work in pairs and give each of them a sheet of paper on which to record their findings. The central task is to answer the questions 'How do we know about the ....?' and 'What kind of evidence do we have?' They will need to list the sources under the following headings:

▲ What are the names of sites/places archaeologists have studied?

▲ What buildings and other places have been found?

▲ What objects have been found?

▲ What evidence of writing has been found?

▲ Are there any things which may not have survived?

When children have had time to consider each heading and there is evidence that most children have made substantial progress in collecting ideas, the whole class can then brainstorm the range and nature of sources that archaeologists have unearthed.

The survey of the range of sources available will then lead into the detailed interrogation of individual sources by children working in pairs. Here is one example of the kind of question that could be asked of an artefact.

Example: Sumerian cylinder seal showing a goddess presenting two people to a seated god (c.2050 BC). Impression of seal as well as the seal itself to show detail. The cylinder would have been rolled in melted wax or soft clay which would set hard.

▲ What does the object in your photograph look like at first sight?

▲ Discuss between you what you can see in the picture.

▲ What might your object be made of?

▲ Both make a detailed drawing. Try to be as accurate as possible.

▲ What kind of person might have used it?

▲ Write out in sentences all the things that you can say about your object, from what you can see.

▲ How do you think it was made?

▲ Can you find other items like this in books about the *Sumerians*?

Suggestion(s) for extension

It will be particularly useful if some children can consider the difference that written records (or the lack of them) might make to our knowledge of a civilisation. What kinds of records survive/fail to survive in the ground over long periods of time. Children could experiment by burying different kinds of written record in the ground. Write messages in a number of different ways: write in ink, pencil, biro and lemon juice onto pieces of paper, punch holes in a piece of paper to make a message, scratch with a sharp point on a piece of flower pot or wood. Press the same message on two pieces of untreated clay (not self–hardening or Plasticine); let one harden either by baking or in another strong heat source. Cover them both with soil and compare what happens to the message.

Bury all these in the ground and leave for at least a week. After an interval the exhumed forms of writing will exhibit different degrees of survival which can be discussed and used to reinforce the points made above.

Suggestion(s) for support

Children could concentrate on the objects by listing what they can find and by drawing some of them. They could also be involved in one or two of the activities suggested for experimenting with written evidence (see suggestions for extension).

Assessment opportunities

Compile a quiz in which children are shown a series of pictures of sources and are asked to consider and describe (a) what their source represents and (b) what it tells us about the people of that time.

Opportunities for IT

Children could use a CD-ROM encyclopaedia to search for information; they can compare the information from different CD-ROMs and discuss how the simplified information may lead to inaccuracies or broad generalisations. Show the children how to print out the information from CD-ROMs and how to save text in ASCII format so that it can be loaded into a word processor and re-organised to pick out the key points of information. Children could work away from the computer to start with using the printed copy and a highlighter pen to identify and mark the most important parts of the information retrieved.

Children may also enjoy using the *Landmarks* series (*Aztecs* or *Project Egypt*) of software where they are guided around an ancient simulated world by a child who will answer their questions (provided the computer simulation knows the answer). This is an interesting way of developing children's understanding of the limitations of computer models and simulations as well as providing useful information for the period under study.

Display ideas

Make a wall display showing a large plan of the site and/or key buildings with a series of strings leading to pictures of some of the artefacts including writing that have been excavated from the site.

MAKING SENSE OF THE EVIDENCE

To communicate knowledge and understanding: by planning and presenting structured narratives, descriptions and displays.

Individual followed by whole class activity.

Several sessions of 45 minutes.

Previous skills/knowledge needed

Experience of studying specific sources in detail and knowledge gained by doing this.

Key background information

Reference to early European excavators of archaeological sites for example Heinrich Schliemann, Sir Arthur Evans and also to archaeologists whose work relates to topics included in this book, Howard Carter and Flinders Petrie (Egypt), Sir Leonard Woolley (Sumer), Sir Mortimer Wheeler (Indus Valley) and to accounts of exploration and discovery which cover the sense of excitement.

Preparation

Refer to any examples of descriptions by archaeologists of excavations and discoveries they have made, copy the photocopiable sheet on page 148, one per child.

Resources needed

Picture books and accounts of excavations by early archaeologists, copies of the sheet on page 148.

What to do

Use the photocopiable sheet to help children to plan their own accounts of what they have learned about the people they have been studying. They will be encouraged to deal with different aspects of the society in turn and to give examples of evidence on which their knowledge is based. They can record their findings in extended writing.

This procedure could be followed by collaborative work between pairs or by groups of children working towards the production of a 'big book' or class record for display. The use of word processing and other IT applications should be considered in this context.

Suggestion(s) for extension

Some children could emphasise modern day differences in interpreting either of artefacts or buildings and their intended purpose or archaeological evidence by different archaeologists over time.

Suggestion(s) for support

Some children will need to concentrate on the more concrete aspects of everyday life. They could choose one (or more) artefact(s) and talk or write about them, saying what their chosen items can tell us about the people who made them.

Assessment opportunities

The photocopiable sheet could be used for summative assessment if so desired. You should look to see whether children have been able to provide a range of aspects and sources, before they present their findings to the class.

Opportunities for IT

Children could use a CD-ROM encyclopaedia to search for information on the archaeologists being studied. They should be shown how to save pictures for later use, and any useful text in ASCII format so that it can be reworked in a word processor.

Children could use a word processor or desktop publishing package to create a class book on the people they have been studying. Different groups or pairs could work together to collect all the information on one archaeologist and then present it on a single or double page spread along with illustrations taken from CD-ROMs, or scanned from pictures in books or the children's own line drawings.

Display ideas

Make a big book or a wall display about an ancient civilisation showing the civilisation located both geographically and chronologically. Children can make drawings and illustrations to show what they have found out.

Reference to photocopiable sheet

The photocopiable page 148 provides opportunities for children to record what they have found out about the society they have been studying and can be used by the children to help them plan their presentation to the rest of the class. They can list different things they have found out using the headings supplied on the left hand side of the sheet. On a separate piece of paper they can record examples of evidence that they have studied in answer to the question: 'How do we know?'.

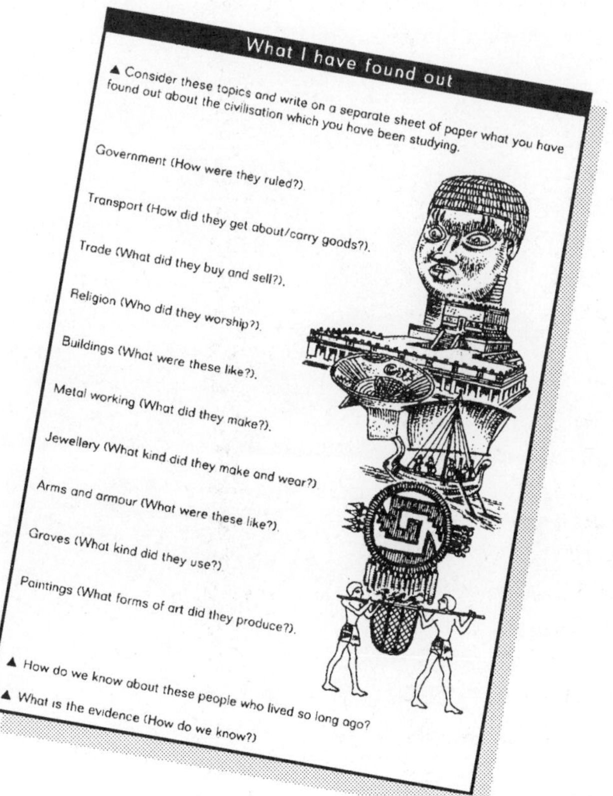

What I have found out

▲ Consider these topics and write on a separate sheet of paper what you have found out about the civilisation which you have been studying.

Government (How were they ruled?)

Transport (How did they get about/carry goods?).

Trade (What did they buy and sell?).

Religion (Who did they worship?).

Buildings (What were these like?).

Metal working (What did they make?).

Jewellery (What kind did they make and wear?)

Arms and armour (What were these like?).

Graves (What kind did they use?)

Paintings (What forms of art did they produce?).

▲ How do we know about these people who lived so long ago?

▲ What is the evidence (How do we know?)

ANCIENT EGYPT

To find out about some of the characteristic features of the ancient Egyptians including their beliefs, using artefacts. To look at the everyday life of an Egyptian king.

Whole class followed by individual activity.

90 minutes.

Previous skills/knowledge needed

Any preliminary consideration of ancient Egypt using the activities on pages 90-97 will be helpful. It is likely that most children will have heard of pyramids and mummies already. They should also be told that the Egyptians took a particular interest in how their dead were buried. Children should be made aware of the geographical location of Egypt and that the period of antiquity being referred to belongs to the second millennium BC.

Key background information

The ancient Egyptians believed that their life in the next world would be just like that which they had left behind. Consequently the dead were buried in tombs which resembled houses, these were painted inside and the body was surrounded by all the person's earthly possessions. This activity will focus upon the discovery of King Tutankhamun's tomb, leading onto a series of possibilities for extension of this topic. The fame surrounding Tutankhamun has more to do with the sensational discovery of a relatively unvandalised tomb (the inner chambers had not previously been discovered) than with his achievements as a ruler. In fact his reign was very short and he died while still in his youth.

Preparation

Assemble as many resources as possible which relate to the rediscovery and opening up of Tutankhamun's tomb by Lord Carnarvon and Howard Carter in the 1920s. Copy the photocopiable sheet on page 149, sufficient for one per child.

Resources needed

Hopefully you will be able to provide pictures and information books about Tutankhamun's tomb. They should show the assembled contents of the tomb, details of the king's burial, his masks etc. A well illustrated summary can be found in *Ancient Egypt* by A.R. David (Phaidon) (pp. 57-64), but many other sources have relevant information. Children undertaking the extension activity will need reference books about Queen Hatshepsut (the only female Pharaoh). Children carrying out the support activity will need craft materials including card, scissors, paints/ felt-tipped pens and adhesive. Photocopiable page 149.

Tutankhamun's tomb

The ancient Egyptians buried their rulers with all their belongings. These tombs had once been full of gold and many other riches. Most of the Egyptian tombs had either been robbed a long time ago or had been found by archaeologists. Howard Carter was an English Egyptologist who explored the area called the Valley of the Kings. In 1922 Carter was about to give up looking, but he decided to look in just one more place.

▲ Here are some of the things which were found in Tutankhamun's tomb. Can you name them?

Beneath some ancient huts, Carter's workmen found first one step cut in the rock, then more steps. Finally, he uncovered 15 steps which led down to a door covered with plaster. They found that someone else had already got there, but they found another room behind, which was still untouched. Inside they saw gold and silver objects, brilliant jewellery, a throne, and other furniture. It took them a very long time to clear out the room, but they found yet another room beyond. In this room they found the buried king who was only 19 when he died. His body was in a stone coffin, but it was covered in no less than four gilded shrines made of wood.

What to do

Hand out the photocopiable sheet and introduce the account of Howard Carter's exploration and rediscovery of the tomb. Ask the children to consider each of the objects that came from the tomb of Tutankhamun. What kinds of object were included in Tutankhamun's tomb? What do these objects tell us about the Egyptians or about the king when he was alive? What would they tell us about the beliefs the Ancient Egyptians held?

A series of activities could be explored with the children working on each in rotation to ensure all children take a turn at each activity. Time availability is crucial here and these extra activities would require more time than the 90 minutes allocated for the initial task.

Ideas for further activities are: **Jewellery**: making necklaces using plastic tubing, drinking straws and assorted beads; **Death Masks**: making model masks; **The gods**: investigate those associated with death and burial (Anubis, Horus and Osiris); **Making a large-scale wall painting**: based on a fresco of Tutankhamun's tomb or other pictures using squaring technique, charcoal rough outline and poster colours; **Pyramids**: what other kinds of royal tomb were there? Use a 'Roamer' to explore the passage ways inside a pyramid. Consider a variety of other forms of mathematics. You may like to refer to knowledge of 3-4-5 triangles *before* the Greek Pythagoras!

Suggestion(s) for extension

More able children can find out about the life of Queen Hatshepsut, the only female pharaoh. See *History Today* (May 1994 (pp23-29) Hatshepsut: the female pharaoh - John Ray).

Suggestion(s) for support

Children could make a copy of Tutankhamun's mask out of card. This could then be stuck onto a card base and the children could use the edges around the mask to write what they know about King Tutankhamun and the discovery of his tomb.

Assessment opportunities

Use the concept mapping exercise referred to on page 90 to compare what the children have learned on an individual basis with the exercise undertaken at the outset.

Opportunities for IT

Children could use *Arcventure II Egypt* or *Landmarks Project Egypt* materials to extend this work. Each of the simulations should be used as an integral part of the work so that there is time for children to record what they do and discuss the limitations of the computer model they are using.

Display ideas

Make a model of either the outer room or the inner room of the tomb using a shoe box with peep holes to show what Carter and his men would have seen. Display the masks or other artefacts which may have been made.

Reference to photocopiable sheet

Photocopiable page 149 contains some information about Howard Carter and his discoveries. The information and illustrations will enable children to study some of the items which Howard Carter found in Tutankhamun's tomb.

INVESTIGATING A DEAD EGYPTIAN

To find out about the characteristic features of people in the past and the experiences of men and women using documents and artefacts.

Whole class activity followed by individual work.

60 minutes introduction/follow-up.

Previous skills/knowledge needed

If the previous activity has been undertaken, (pages 97-98) this session could build on the knowledge children will have acquired about Tutankhamun. They will also have an opportunity to develop and apply skills of handling evidence and using unfamiliar scripts.

Key background information

Not all people in Ancient Egypt were buried like Tutankhamun. This activity provides an opportunity to study the remains of a poor person who, although he was a young man like Tutankhamun, was at the other end of the social scale. The hieroglyphs on photocopiable page 150 tell us about 'The dead weaver of the funeral temple of King User-khaure - NAKHT'. Nakht's body was found in a re-used royal tomb. It dates to the early twelfth century BC. The fact that he was a weaver, probably employed to make shrouds for members of the royal household, suggests that he was much more typical of the population of ancient Egypt than the usual mummified bodies that have been excavated. His family seem to have been able to afford a reasonable quality of coffin though study shows that Nakht had not been given the full treatment and mummified. His body had been washed and wrapped in linen bandages which probably came from old bed sheets and curtains.

A thorough investigation by doctors and scientists found that all the man's organs were present and surprisingly well-preserved. Nakht had acquired a parasite which was found in his liver and also a tapeworm, probably through eating poorly cooked meat. His lungs contained particles of carbon showing a polluted environment and granite dust.

Here are some of the things that the doctors and scientists found out by unwrapping and studying the body of Nakht:

▲ The abdomen was filled with clothing.
▲ Washed but no evidence of embalming.
▲ Organs not taken out, but left in the body.
▲ Analysis of Lungs – carbon and granite dust.
▲ Analysis of Liver – larva of parasites eggs,(which still kill people today in Egypt where there is polluted water or infection).
▲ Analysis of intestine – tapeworm eggs.
▲ X-rays of the leg bones showed signs of malnutrition or infection.

According to the Greek writer, Herodotus, there were three ways in which the Egyptians could have their dead prepared. One was very expensive, the second was less expensive and not so good. The third was the cheapest of all. The full treatment is like this; They take out the insides, wash the body, filling it with sweet smelling spices. Then they pickle it for 70 days and wrap it from head to foot in strips of linen. Next they smear gum underneath. The family have a wooden case made which is shaped like a human being. They do not take out the organs for cheaper burials.

The Egyptians also mummified animals. Herodotus tells us that when a cat died it was mummified and buried in a sacred container. There is archaeological proof of this.

Preparation

Copy sufficient numbers of the photocopiable sheet on page 150 for all the children.

Resources needed

Pictures of mummies including mummified animals. Other evidence of coffins etc., photocopiable page 150.

What to do

Tell the children about Nakht and his burial. If the children have undertaken the activity on Tutankhamun they will have an idea of how a rich person was buried. Hand out the photocopied sheet and see whether the children can identify some of the hieroglyphics which were written on the coffin.

Discuss with the children what they might find inside the coffin. Consider the differences between the tomb of a rich person and a poorer person. Read them the account of mummification from the Greek historian Herodotus, (see Key background information) to help them focus on the different sort of burial that Nakht might have had. Now read them the account of what was found out about Nakht's body and ask them: How might Nakht have got granite dust in his lungs? Why do you think people would want to unwrap bodies that have been buried for so long? What evidence is there to suggest that Nakht was a poor man?

Children can make a replica of a mummified Egyptian together with a painted mummy case. Use newspaper to make the shape of a body and then wrap it in strips of white paper. The outer case could be made of papier mâché, dried and then painted bright colours.

Suggestion(s) for extension

Children could use the hieroglyphic alphabet provided on photocopiable page 150 to transcribe names and words from English into hieroglyphs.

Suggestion(s) for support

After making the model of a mummy in a tomb some children could use hieroglyphs to write a simple message or inscription on the side.

Assessment opportunities

Ask the children to describe how the Egyptians prepared their dead for burial. Can they suggest reasons why they went to all that trouble? What were the differences between a rich person's burial and that of a poor person?

Display ideas

Children may wish to display the differences they have learned about between a rich person and a poor person's burial, alongside the models of the mummy and tomb.

Reference to photocopiable sheet

Photocopiable sheet on page 150 provides a copy of the hieroglyphic inscription from Nakht's tomb and the full hieroglyphic alphabet.

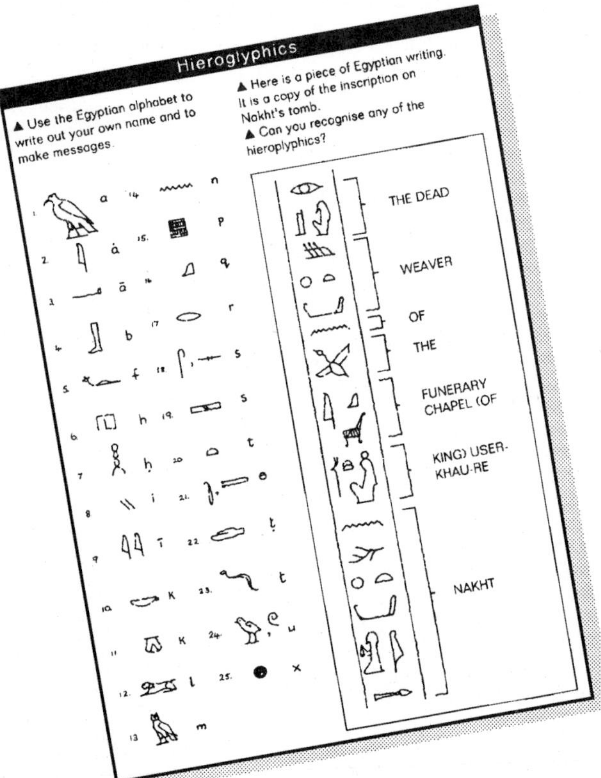

ANCIENT SUMER – THEIR EARLY ACHIEVEMENTS

To find out about the characteristic features of the Sumerians and about the everyday lives of men and women.

Work in small groups of three/four.

Up to 120 minutes.

Previous skills/knowledge needed

Experience of one or more of the activities on pages 90 -97, in particular work using reference books to extend knowledge of specific studies. The children may have located the Sumerians geographically as well as chronologically during their work on the activity on page 90.

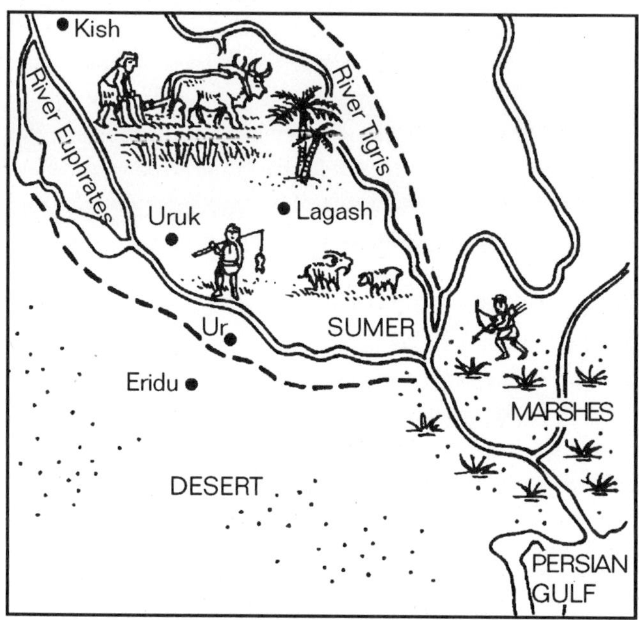

Key background information

The civilisations of both Ancient Sumer and the later Assyrian Empire both flourished in the area of the near East which we call Mesopotamia (from the Greek meaning 'the land between the rivers'). The land is watered by the two great rivers the Tigris and the Euphrates (1,200 and 1,700 miles in length respectively) which flow into the Persian Gulf. In modern times this area is part of Iraq. It is in the land of Mesopotamia where civilisation began thousands of years ago. Farming began in the valleys of the Tigris and Euphrates between 6,000 and 5,000 BC. The fertile soil of the river valleys was tilled with wooden ploughs and crops included wheat and barley as well as dates and vegetables. In addition to agriculture, animals were reared including sheep, donkeys and goats and the people there also hunted and fished.

During the Fourth millennium BC, the people built walled towns containing houses made from bricks of mud, the most important feature of the towns were temples. Trade also developed by the use of the wide rivers as well as by land.

By 3,500 BC the area was dominated by people we call Sumerians. Ancient Sumer was centred on the Southern part of the Tigris and Euphrates valleys where there were a number of cities, including the chief city of Ur, each with its own government and its own gods and priests.

Innovations included the invention of the wheel and its use for transportation purposes; using irrigation to support the increasing population; the creation of a writing system using pictograms and the development of a code of law. The Sumerians also made some important early developments in mathematics. The most famous literary achievement of the Sumerians was the epic of Gilgamesh, a third millennium King of the city of Uruk in Sumer.

The autonomy of the Sumerian cities came to an end around 2,350 when King Sargon from Akkad to the North swallowed up the whole of Sumer into his expanding empire. Although the Sumerians reasserted themselves towards the end of the Millennium, the City of Ur was sacked by invaders from the West around 2,000 BC.

Preparation

Collect together as many information books as possible which include details about the ancient Sumerians. Ensure that you have a globe and a large map of the near East available (this could be a modern atlas which shows the location of modern Iraq and the rivers Tigris and Euphrates).

Resources needed

Information books should include pictures of the following items: Sumerian wheels, a Ziggurat (a temple built on a platform), oval enclosure and arch, house plans, objects made by the *cire perdue* (lost wax) process including the copper goddess and pictographic writing.

What to do

This lesson is concerned with finding out as much as possible about the ancient Sumerians using whatever resources you have. Divide the areas for investigation among five different groups of children. The five main areas are:

Sumerian technology – The wheel; metal working; lost wax casting (copper goddess); silver, bronze.

Sumerian buildings – The ziggurat of Urnammu; the arch used in tombs; the eye temple; oval temple enclosures; private houses.

Sumerian writing – Pictographs then cuneiform; accounts and numbers (base of 60); words we can identify for example * = star, god, heaven; the Gilgamesh story dates back to the Sumerians see Key background information.

Sumerian art – Painted pots and designs; carved stones (especially eye idols); cone mosaics using red, black and white card; jewellery.

Sumerian gods – Death, burial and religion. Burial practices; male gods – Anu (the Sky); Enlil (the Earth); Enki (the Waters); female gods – Inanna (Ishtar) (love, the Great mother); Nanna (the moon).

Other areas for investigation could include: farming, finding out about the Sumerians and their achievements.

Suggestion(s) for extension

Some children could develop their findings about Sumerian mathematics (the Sumerians counted in 60s rather than using a system based upon ten) by devising some simple sums based on the base 60.

Suggestion(s) for support

Children could work in pairs on investigative activities and share the work of recording their findings using words and pictures.

Assessment opportunities

How many things can the children identify as evidence of the Sumerians? What does each item tell us about the way of life then?

Opportunities for IT

Children could use a CD-ROM encyclopaedia to search for information about the Sumerians. They should be shown how to print their findings and save pictures and text to retrieve for later use.

Children could work in groups using a word processor or desktop publishing package to present their findings on the Sumerians. Alternatively the class could create a multi-media presentation using an authoring package. The groups could search and present information on their selected aspect of the Sumerians. They could use pictures taken from clip art or CD-ROM collections, scanned images from photographs or their own line drawings. Children could even add their own voices recorded using a microphone linked to the computer. The initial structure could be set up in advance with a front page showing the different aspects of the civilisation so that by clicking on a title the user would be taken to a page showing the information on that subject which could be spread over several pages. This is a fairly ambitious project and children using the software for the first time will need some support.

Display ideas

Children can display their findings as written work and pictures on the classroom wall and you could mount this alongside a map of Mesopotamia (the land between the rivers).

ANCIENT SUMER – THE PEOPLE OF SUMER

To find out about Sumerian society using artefacts.

Whole class followed by individual activity.

90 minutes.

Previous skills/knowledge needed

Children should already have had experience of working on specific source items including artefacts. Interrogation of pictorial representation of artefacts (see page 96) would also be useful.

Key background information

The Royal Standard of Ur was found in a Royal tomb which had already been plundered before it was carefully excavated by the archaeologist Sir Leonard Woolley in the 1930s. It measures 45cm long and is in the form of an oblong box, which may have been the sounding box of a stringed instrument. The figures are made out of shell and limestone and are set against a background of blue lapis lazuli. The whole decorative cover is fastened to a wooden background by bitumen. The two long panels represent *war* and *peace*, the details are as follows:

The *war panel:* an enemy is defeated by heavy four wheeled chariots drawn by wild asses (bottom row); prisoners of war are being driven by the king's shock troops: they are equipped with short spears, felt cloaks and helmets, possibly made of leather (middle row); the king has climbed out of his chariot and is receiving his captives who are led in by lightly armed troops (top row).

The *peace panel:* servants lead wild asses while others carry heavy bundles on their heads (bottom row); bullocks, rams with thick fleeces and another animal (an oryx?) are led by servants, while a figure carries a fish (middle row); a court banquet is in progress and the king and his courtiers are drinking wine to the accompaniment of a lyre (top row).

The Royal Cemetery at Ur contained up to 74 bodies from the king's household who had been killed and buried with the dead king. This practice, not unknown in some other early societies, is referred to in the epic of Gilgamesh.

Preparation

Make sufficient copies of photocopiable sheet on page 151 for each child.

Next hand out the photocopiable sheet. Invite the children to study the drawings on the sheet and to answer the first two questions on a piece of paper.

When they have all finished this activity, discuss with the class some of the evidence that they have used to identify which panel is which. This provides an important opportunity for you to discuss with the children the built-in bias that such a picture represents. Whose point of view is represented here? The servants/the foreign enemy/the king? Ask the children to consider whether they can see any women. If not, what might be the explanation for this?

This discussion of the different activities shown can then lead to more detailed description of the activities depicted. To finish, the children could make a large-scale class version of the panels for display or make their own class version of a war and a peace panel to reflect modern day times.

Resources needed

If possible, obtain a large colour picture of the Royal Standard, photocopies of page 151, large sheets of paper and paints for a wall display, crayons/felt-tipped pens and cards for the support activity.

What to do

Introduce the picture of the Royal Standard on the photocopiable sheet to the children making reference to the great death-pit. If you have a large colour picture of the whole or part of the Royal Standard use this to show the children more details. Tell the children that the standard is now kept in the British Museum in London.

Use the Key background information to tell the children some of the details about the standard and explain the way in which it was found.

Suggestion(s) for extension

Children could use the information in the illustrations to contemplate this find and the evidence for the way that a king's servants were treated when he died.

Suggestion(s) for support

Rosettes were used to decorate the Sumerian Eye Temple. They looked like this one, (left) and were made of stone in black (shale), red (limestone) and white (marble). Some children could cut out simple card shapes to represent the rosettes and they can then colour them in to show the three colours used.

Royal Standard of Ur

▲ This picture shows the activities of the Sumerian King and his court during peacetime and at war. Can you say which picture is which? Give your reasons why you think so. Write your answers on a piece of paper.
▲ Describe what you can see in each picture.
Whose point of view does this picture show?
The King?....
Servants?....
The enemy?....
▲ Can you see any women? What does this tell you?

Assessment opportunities

To assess what the children have understood ask them to represent different figures who appear on the Royal Standard. They could form a 'tableau' to represent the line up on the Royal Standard (one half of the class to portray *peace* the other to represent *war*). They can then be asked to play in role, to explain what they are doing and to say how they have deduced this from the evidence.

Display ideas

The children could reproduce the Royal Standard on a large scale using different coloured card or other materials such as coloured tin foil to represent the original materials. A number of rosettes could be made using different coloured card and used to decorate the classroom wall at intervals.

Reference to photocopiable sheet

The photocopiable sheet on page 151 shows the illustrations on both sides of the Royal Standard of Ur.

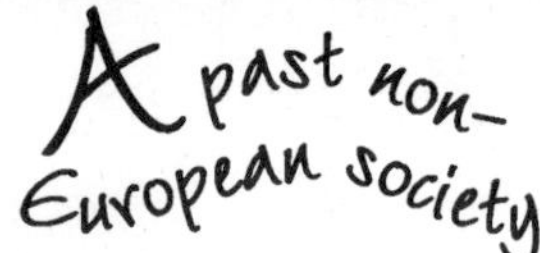

THE ASSYRIAN EMPIRE– RUTHLESS OR NOT?

To study the ways in which the Assyrians have been represented in different sources.

Pairs.

60 minutes.

Previous skills/knowledge needed

Builds on skills achieved from activities on pages 90-97 and on both Ancient Sumer activities.

Key background information

The Assyrians acquired a large empire that included, at its height, the Nile valley in Egypt and which covered the whole of the area previously occupied by the Sumerians. Whereas the Sumerians had been centred on the southern end of the Tigris and Euphrates valleys, the centre of the Assyrian empire lay further north. Major cities of Nineveh (where a royal palace was built) and Nimrud lay in the Tigris valley along with the ancient city of Ashur or Assur (dating from about 2500 BC) which was the heart of Assyria.

By 1200 BC, the three important Bronze Age societies; Egypt, the Hittites (to the north in what is now Turkey) and the Babylonians (in Mesopotamia) were all in decline. The Assyrians took advantage by expanding their own territory northwards, southwards and eastwards.

In the ninth century, two strong kings Ashurnasirpal II (883-859) and Shalmaneser III (858-824) built up the Assyrian army into a formidable fighting force and conquered huge areas of land. As they did so they crushed the people they conquered with enormous violence and savagery. By the middle of the seventh century King Ashurbanipal claimed to have conquered the world. However, the empire did not last long after his death and the city of Nineveh fell to the invading Medes and Babylonians in 612 BC. (See page 78 for information about the Persian Empire which succeeded.)

Assyria is mentioned in the Old Testament, but little was known about the ancient Assyrians until archaeologists began to excavate the ruins of the city of Nimrud, more than one hundred years ago. In the 1840s and 1850s, Henry Layard found the remains of a great palace belonging to King Ashurnasirpal, and excavated huge statues and carved pictures made of stone. Some of the statues tell the story of King Ashurnasirpal's military victories; the pictures would have decorated the palace walls. Carved stone monsters were also found which would have guarded the king's throne room in the palace. These sculptures are now housed in museums around the world including the British Museum.

Another palace was excavated at Nineveh, where the Assyrian King Ashurbanipal had his palace. Excavations found that his palace was decorated with hunting scenes showing the king and his men hunting lions and other beasts.

Preparation

Collect together as many resources as possible that relate to the ancient Assyrians. A principal visual source will be the reliefs from the British Museum showing Assyrian warfare and details of the temple building that certain monarchs engaged in following their military successes against their neighbours. Copy the photocopiable sheet on page 152 sufficient for children to work in pairs.

Resources needed

Books on the Assyrians such as from the British Museum Education Service. Coloured pencils. Copies of page 152.

What to do

Tell the children about one or more of the examples of the reliefs brought from the Assyrian palaces. Use this to introduce Assyrian warfare and wars fought against neighbouring peoples, and also to introduce the King's hunting expeditions. What do these reliefs tell us about the ancient Assyrians? What kind of picture do they give of them? Ask

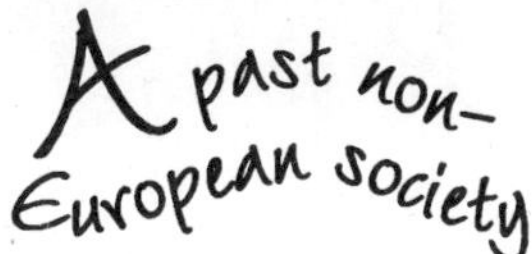

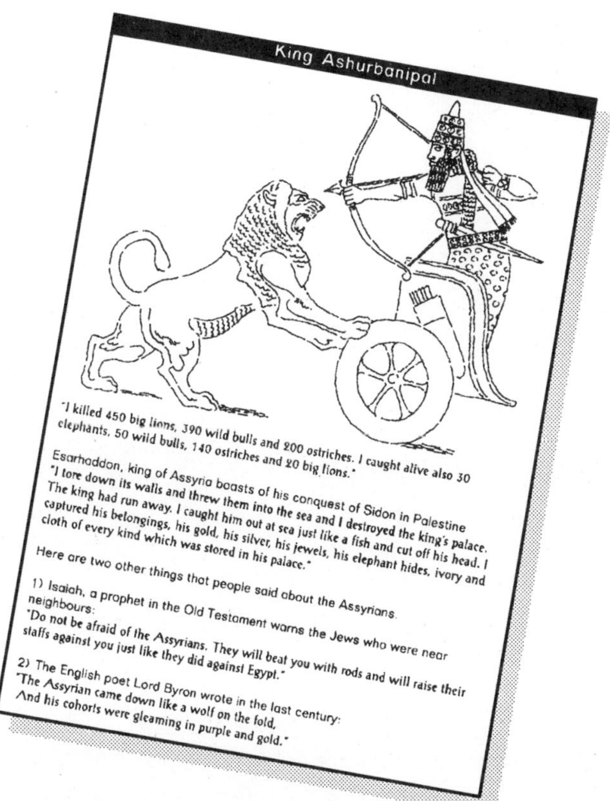

King Ashurbanipal

"I killed 450 big lions, 390 wild bulls and 200 ostriches. I caught alive also 30 elephants, 50 wild bulls, 140 ostriches and 20 big lions."

Esarhaddon, king of Assyria boasts of his conquest of Sidon in Palestine
"I tore down its walls and threw them into the sea and I destroyed the king's palace. The king had run away. I caught him out at sea just like a fish and cut off his head. I captured his belongings, his gold, his silver, his jewels, his elephant hides, ivory and cloth of every kind which was stored in his palace."

Here are two other things that people said about the Assyrians.

1) Isaiah, a prophet in the Old Testament warns the Jews who were near neighbours:
"Do not be afraid of the Assyrians. They will beat you with rods and will raise their staffs against you just like they did against Egypt."

2) The English poet Lord Byron wrote in the last century:
"The Assyrian came down like a wolf on the fold,
And his cohorts were gleaming in purple and gold."

the children to make a list of questions they would like to ask about the Assyrians. They could use the reliefs as a starting point.

Hand out the photocopiable sheet for the children to further consider the image of the Assyrians.

Suggestion(s) for extension

Ask some children to consider what the existence of these large stone reliefs tells us about building operations, especially the Palaces at Nimrud and Nineveh? Some of the reliefs bear cuneiform script and the texts are available to read alongside a study of the pictures.

Use the picture of the reliefs being brought into the British Museum to discuss the motives of the early archaeologists who brought the reliefs all the way to Britain. Why did they go to all that trouble and (no doubt) expense?

Suggestion(s) for support

Children can concentrate on the visual image of Ashurbanipal. Ask them to colour in the picture on the photocopied sheet and then to write a few sentences to describe how the king set about catching the animals.

Assessment opportunities

Invite the children to talk or write about what they have learned about the Assyrians. Give them the following headings: what things do we know the Assyrians did? How do we know? What kind of people were the rulers of Assyria. How far do the sources agree? What other kinds of things is it difficult for us to find out about and why?

Display ideas

Children can make a large version of an Assyrian relief either from the photocopiable sheet or in a familiar style.

Reference to photocopiable sheet

The photocopiable sheet on page 152 shows a picture of King Ashurbanipal and various quotes about the Assyrians for children to consider.

INDUS VALLEY – LIFE IN TOWNS

To find out about the characteristic features of the Indus Valley society and their achievements paying particular attention to their technology including the water supply and sanitation.

Investigation in groups/whole class.

60 minutes.

Previous skills/knowledge needed

Builds on links with approaches on pages 90-97.

Key background information

Much of what we know about the Indus Valley civilisation which flourished between about 2500 and 2000 BC comes from archaeological excavations of the main cities. The civilisation covered a large area of the North West Indian sub-continent, largely within the boundaries of modern Pakistan. The fertile flood plain of the River Indus first attracted communities around 3500 BC.

Archaeologists have shown that the people of the Indus Valley planned their cities very carefully. They contain large public buildings probably used for administration and other features such as an assembly hall, a granary complete with loading bays and a swimming pool, possibly used for religious purposes.

What is remarkable is the sophisticated level of urban planning including the provision of water and sanitation (including brick-built lavatories). Almost every house in the city of Mohenjo-Daro had a bathroom, and waste from the bathrooms emptied through the drains into covered sewers which ran beneath the streets. There were inspection holes at intervals.

Mud bricks of a standard 28 × 14 × 7 cms were used for building, although houses varied in size. The bigger constructions at Mohenjo-Daro were rectangular with rooms arranged round a courtyard and stairs led to an upper storey. Poorer people lived in houses which only had one room.

There is however a great deal that we do not know about the Indus Valley civilisation, as nobody has been able to decipher the script which appears on large numbers of artefacts from this period. A further problem is caused by

the annual flooding of the Indus which has caused the ancient sites to be covered by a very deep layer of silt, accumulated over many centuries. The excavations at Mohenjo-Daro (which began under silt) by Mortimer Wheeler in the 1920s went down about ten metres, but deeper layers are below the water table and are therefore very difficult and dangerous to excavate.

Preparation

Collect as many reference books as possible about the Indus Valley civilisation. Photocopy page 153, one per child.

Resources needed

Information books about the Indus Valley civilisation and the geography of Pakistan, an atlas and a large wall map of modern Pakistan, a globe and photocopied sheets.

What to do

Divide the children into groups, to investigate specific topics. Hand out the photocopied sheet to help the children get started and they can then go on to use other resources which you have available.

Topics for the children to study are:

▲ town planning
▲ sanitation and water supply
▲ houses of the rich and poor
▲ farming
▲ public buildings
▲ religion and burial customs
▲ writing
▲ metal working
▲ jewellery
▲ pottery

Following their independent investigations children can report back to a plenary session on what they have been able to find out. Children who complete their research early can be asked to imagine they were a visitor staying in the Indus Valley for the first time and to describe their impressions.

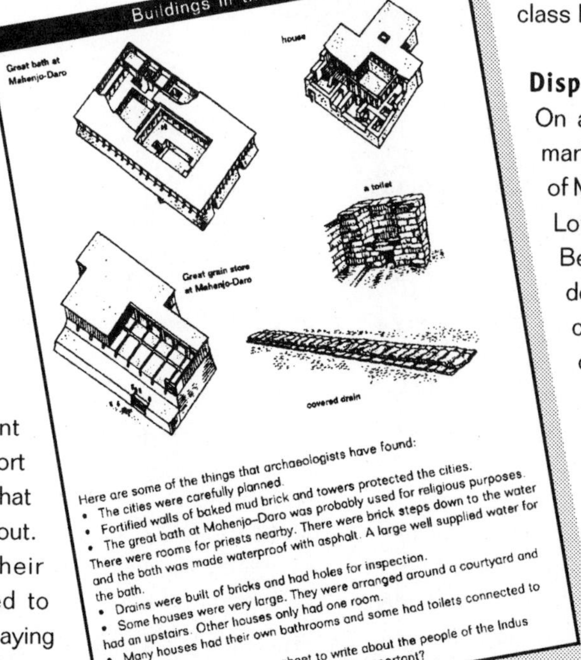

Buildings in the Indus

Here are some of the things that archaeologists have found:

- The cities were carefully planned.
- Fortified walls of baked mud brick and towers protected the cities.
- The great bath at Mohenjo–Daro was probably used for religious purposes. There were rooms for priests nearby. There were brick steps down to the water and the bath was made waterproof with asphalt. A large well supplied water for the bath.
- Drains were built of bricks and had holes for inspection.
- Some houses were very large. They were arranged around a courtyard and had an upstairs. Other houses only had one room.
- Many houses had their own bathrooms and some had toilets connected to sewers.

▲ Use the information on this sheet to write about the people of the Indus Valley. Why was the Indus Valley civilisation important?

Suggestion(s) for extension

Children can compare the ancient civilisation of the Indus Valley with (for example) Victorian towns in the mid-nineteenth century. Ask them to consider what differences there might have been in terms of attention to hygiene.

Suggestion(s) for support

Concentrate on the water supply. Children can make a drawing of the great bath as it might have looked.

Assessment opportunities

How does the Indus Valley compare with any one other society that the children have studied already? Check what terms the children use to describe differences and similarities. What vocabulary do they use?

Opportunities for IT

The children could work in pairs or small groups to present their findings about their particular aspect of the Indus Valley using a word processor or desktop publishing package. If children are able to use a CD-ROM encyclopaedia they may be able to retrieve and organise text and pictures taken from the CD-ROM. The printed versions of the different topics could be put together into a class book or used as part of a display.

Display ideas

On a large wall map of modern Pakistan, mark in the River Indus and the ancient cities of Mohenjo-Daro, Harappa, Kalibanaan and Lothal, as well as any other settlements. Beside the map display the drawings and descriptions of finds from the Indus Valley civilisation that the children have found out about.

Reference to photocopiable sheet

The photocopiable sheet on page 153 shows a street plan indicating the houses, the great bath and the grain store at Mohenjo-Daro, covered drains and a toilet. The captions give background information which will provide a starting point for children's study.

MAKING INDUS VALLEY AMULETS

To find out about the Indus valley people from artefacts.

Individual.

60 minutes.

Previous skills/knowledge needed

Model-making skills.

Key background information

The photocopiable sheet on page 154 shows examples of excavated amulets from the Indus Valley civilisation. Seals carved from stone, engraved with animals and other designs as well as inscribed with written information were used as amulets. It is believed that the script represents the name of the person who owned the amulet and that he/she would wear it round the neck to ward off evil spirits. The seal would be used to place a mark on wet clay in order to seal goods such as belongings. Archaeologists have found 1200 seals suggesting that literacy was fairly widespread. Animals depicted on seals include the rhinoceros, elephant, bull, and a fish-eating crocodile.

Preparation

Have available sufficient copies of photocopiable page 154, one for each child.

Resources needed

Card, adhesive, scissors, colouring materials, photocopied sheets (page 154).

What to do

Invite the children to make their own amulet. To do this they should paste the photocopied sheet onto a sheet of card and then cut it out as indicated. The amulet can then be coloured and cut out with an attachment behind for threading a cord so that it can be worn around the neck.

Suggestion(s) for extension

Invite children to design their own seals or amulets.

Suggestion(s) for support

Some children may need help cutting the amulet out and piercing the hole.

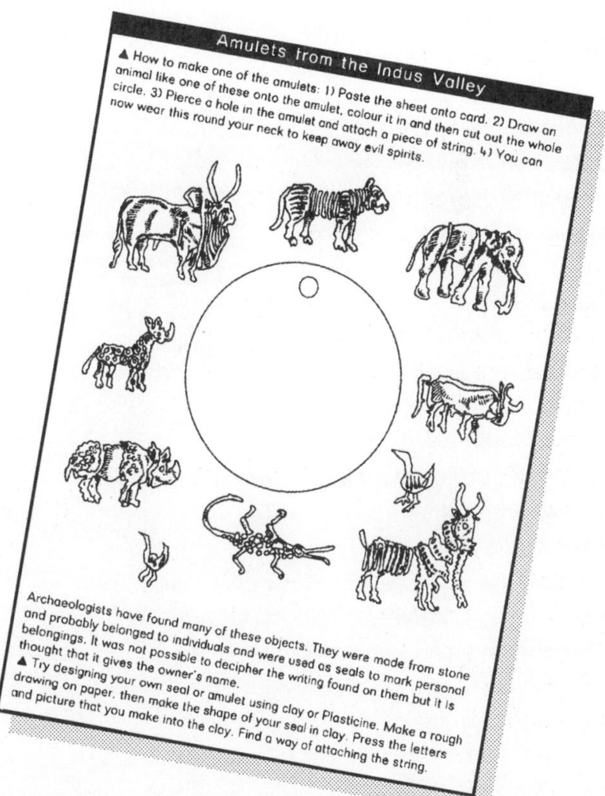

Amulets from the Indus Valley

▲ How to make one of the amulets: 1) Paste the sheet onto card. 2) Draw an animal like one of these onto the amulet, colour it in and then cut out the whole circle. 3) Pierce a hole in the amulet and attach a piece of string. 4) You can now wear this round your neck to keep away evil spirits.

Archaeologists have found many of these objects. They were made from stone and probably belonged to individuals and were used as seals to mark personal belongings. It was not possible to decipher the writing found on them but it is thought that it gives the owner's name.

▲ Try designing your own seal or amulet using clay or Plasticine. Make a rough drawing on paper, then make the shape of your seal in clay. Press the letters and picture that you make into the clay. Find a way of attaching the string.

Assessment opportunities

Ask the children to describe their amulet and how they have made it. Ask them to explain what the object tells us about the ancient people of the Indus Valley.

Display ideas

Children can suspend their finished amulets from the classroom ceiling to bring the whole class good luck.

Reference to photocopiable sheet

The sheet provides a template for an amulet together with details of typical illustrations from those found in excavations.

THE MAYA AND EVERYDAY LIFE

To find out about some of the characteristic features of the ancient Maya including the Mayan ball game, using evidence from artefacts, sites and documents.

Pairs.

60 minutes.

Previous skills/knowledge needed

This activity builds on or links with approaches suggested on pages 90–97.

Key background information

The great majority of our knowledge about the Maya and their buildings comes from Spanish missionaries and from the observations of contemporary Indians who lived 600 to 1,000 years after the time when the Mayan temples were built.

The Maya settled in central America around 2000 BC engaging in a simple agricultural way of life. By about 1000 BC they were also building temple-like buildings on raised platforms. By about 300 BC, a number of major Mayan centres had been developed, each with its own pyramid and platform structure. The Maya also developed a form of writing and made calendars during this period. During the so-called Classic period, (AD 250 to 1000) the Maya carved stone slabs which are known as *stelae*. These record events in their history including such things as observations of the stars, and have pictures and writing on them. No more *stelae* or pyramids appear to have been built after about AD 800 and most of the Mayan centres were abandoned by AD1000. The reasons for the collapse of the Mayan civilisation are unknown.

The Mayan centres seem to have been mainly for religious, administrative and trading purposes. Temples and palaces built on platform structures were often associated with large plazas. Sometimes there was also a ball court in which two teams played a special kind of game (see below). The Mayans worshipped very many gods.

The Mayans were very interested in working out the passage of time mathematically. They used a number system based on the base 20 and involving dots and dashes. Mayan priests recorded their observations of the heavens, they developed two kinds of calendar. One was the sacred year based on 260 days in which each day had its own name and a number between one and 13. Priests used to work out which days were unlucky and which were lucky. The Maya also used a 365 day calendar in which the year was divided up into 18 months each lasting 20 days, with five days left over at the end.

The Mayan ball game was very different from our modern day sporting events. It was a religious and political activity, in which only the elite took part. The game was probably invented by the Olmecs and continued to be played in Mexico for a period of 2,000 years. It was a game in which the chief player on the losing side paid for it with his life!

Preparation

Make photocopies of the account based on archaeological evidence of the Mayan ball game on photocopiable page 155 sufficient for the children to work in pairs.

Resources needed

Drawing paper and coloured crayons, pencils or felt-tipped pens, photocopiable sheets on page 155.

What to do

Introduce the class to the idea of the ball game by using the account on the photocopiable sheet, which can be read or told as a story. Alternatively the details of how the game was played (or rather might have been played) could be left to the children's imagination. Discuss with the children what the account contributes to our knowledge. Is it likely that we would be able to know *exactly* how the ball game was played? Invite the children to draw their own picture of the ball game being played using their knowledge and imagination. Alternatively, they could make a series of pictures to show the sequence of events as described in the account on the photocopiable sheet. Children could be invited to make up their own rules for the game.

Suggestion(s) for extension

Some children could devise their own version of the ball game (though not the sequel!). The game could then be played in a PE lesson.

Suggestion(s) for support

Some children may benefit from working closely with a more able child and may need to be given some support in reading the account.

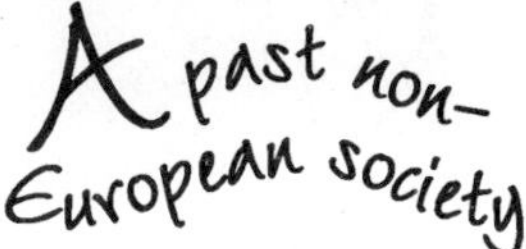

Assessment opportunities

Children could be asked to consider how helpful the account is. How did the children decide on what to draw in their pictures of the game? How much did they have to use their imagination?

Opportunities for IT

Children could use a word processor to write and present the captions for the Mayan buildings. Children could also use an art or drawing package to draw pictures of Mayan buildings.

Children could use a word processor to write and draft the rules for the Mayan ball game. They could look at other rules for similar ball games and organise and present their version of the rules in an appropriate format. This might include the use of features such as 'tabs' and 'indents' to format the text and different font styles such as bold and italics to highlight more important rules. Some children might want to use 'bullets' to highlight lists within the rules.

Display ideas

Make a wall display based upon the picture of a ball court in which the game is being played or a picture showing the winners and the losers. Ask each child to contribute a player for the display and make up a large scale wall display of the game. Use the written evidence on the photocopiable sheet to supply necessary information.

Reference to the photocopiable sheet

The information on the photocopiable sheet on page 155 is a made-up piece of narrative which is based to a large extent upon surviving interpretations by archaeologists of evidence for the ball game.

The Mayan ball game

This account is based on archaeological evidence and on what people wrote after the conquest of Mexico by the Spaniards.

"It is baking hot. The ball player straps on his chunky belt, his hip pads and knee pads made of cotton and leather. This will help to protect the players from the hard rubber ball. The players are from important families.

There is a perfumed smell of resin coming from incense burners. Priests meet the players as they reach the main door of the temple. Prayers are offered up to Tlaloc, the rain god. They pray for lots of rain and a good harvest of maize during the summer ahead. Priests and players together process to the hill where the great palace of the ruler stands. The ruler cuts himself in honour of the gods and then joins the procession. They all go towards the ball court. They cross an area which is covered in white plaster. As they do so they pass buildings that are plastered and painted bright colours. They reach the ball court. The priests and all the important people climb the stairways at the back of the ball court and sit down in a place from which they can watch the game.

Then the players take up their places at opposite ends of the court. The two chief players stand in the alley and the rest of their team stand behind them at the far ends of the court. Then the large hard ball made from the sap of a rubber tree is brought out. The players have to hit the ball through rings which have been arranged high on each side of the court. Each team aims for one of the rings. They can only play in the narrow alley down the middle of the court. The players must use their bodies to hit the ball but they must not use either their hands or their feet. After many tries, one player gets his chance. He makes a beautifully placed shot from his hip. The ball bounces off the wall, goes through one of the rings and the game is over."

This was no ordinary sport. There is evidence that the leader of the winning team was rewarded with a jade necklace. but the leader of the losers was tied up with ropes and dragged to the temple. Here his head was cut off by one of the priests and his body was rolled down the temple steps.

THE AZTECS EVERY-DAY LIFE

To identify and give reasons for the different ways in which the past is represented and interpreted.

Whole class and individual work.

45 minutes.

Previous skills and knowledge

Experience of work on different kinds of historical sources would be helpful.

Key background information

The Aztecs arrived in the geographical area we now call Mexico in about AD 1100 but it was not until about 1325 that their capital of Tenochtitlan was established and they began to expand and to develop an empire. It is likely that the Aztecs were originally a nomadic tribe, wandering in the wilderness for more than a hundred years. The settlement of Tenochtitlan was established on rocky islets among the reed marshes. The name of the settlement means 'place of the prickly pear cactus'. By the time that the Spanish Conquistadors reached Mexico in the early sixteenth century, the city was roughly rectangular in shape and covered an area of about 10 km squared. The main square was dominated by the great temples of Huitzilopochtli (the hummingbird god and god of the sun and of war) and Tlaloc (the rain god).

The first Europeans to enter the capital of the Aztecs were amazed by what they saw. The Spaniard Cortes compared the city to Seville and Corduba in his own country. The passage on photocopiable page 156 is taken from the writings of another Spaniard called Diaz. The eyewitness accounts of these two Spaniards are crucial to our understanding of what life was like among the Aztecs before the conquest by the Spanish.

In 1521 the Aztecs were conquered by the Spanish and the Aztec capital was systematically destroyed. Today it is the site of modern Mexico City. Excavations by archaeologists in recent years have begun to unearth many features of Aztec culture and the records which were set down in writing by captive Aztec people after the conquest provide us with important sources of information. As with the ancient Maya, however, (see page 108) it is difficult to establish, just from accounts written after the conquest, a clear picture of earlier history.

Cortes described the market at Tenochtitlan in a letter to Charles V:

'*The city has many open squares where markets are held all the time and where people buy and sell merchandise. One of the squares in particular is twice as large as that in Salamanca and it is completely surrounded by arcades where more than sixty thousand people come each day to buy and sell. There is every kind of thing there for sale.*'

Written sources dating before the Spanish conquest There are several manuscripts remaining but the Spanish destroyed thousands of books and many more may have perished over time. It is difficult sometimes to interpret fully the symbols and pictures in these texts.

First hand accounts written by Spanish Conquistadors Cortes and Diaz were members of the Spanish expedition which entered Mexico and were among the first Europeans to come into contact with the Aztecs. Their writings provide us with vivid descriptions of what they saw and often their findings were compared with what they already were familiar with in their own country.

First hand accounts by Aztecs written after the conquest These are written in the form of *codices* (singular: *codex*) they are an attempt to describe life before and during the conquest of Mexico by the Spanish, but they do not necessarily tell the whole story.

Archaeological evidence There have been recent excavations in Mexico City and elsewhere which have begun to give us information about the Aztecs before the conquest. Archaeological evidence can tell us about population sizes, agriculture and irrigation techniques used, about the kinds of food eaten and, from human remains, about the age at death and state of health of some of the Aztec population and about religious beliefs and practices. For example, recent excavations at the site of the great temple of Tenochtitlan, where the Aztecs worshipped Huitzilopochtli and Tlaloc, where the first Europeans saw and described human sacrifices taking place, have revealed enormous numbers of other sacrificial offerings.

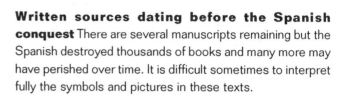

Preparation
Copy the photocopiable sheet on page 156, one per child.

Resources needed
Collect as many reference books with information about the Aztecs as possible, drawing paper and pencils. Photocopiable page 156.

What to do
Explain to the whole class that they are going to look at evidence for the Aztecs. They should be told about the different kinds of source upon which our present day knowledge of the Aztecs is based. Invite the children to consider the advantages and disadvantages of different kinds of evidence. The ideas we have about the Aztecs are bound to be very incomplete.

Distribute the photocopiable sheet and read out the extract from an account written by Diaz of the market at Tenochtitlan. Encourage the children to make a list of all the things that were said to be on sale in the market place.

The children can then be introduced to the pictures which are taken from a *codex* (the Codex Florentinus). Get them to record on their lists of goods mentioned by Diaz the items which are *also* shown in the pictures. Are there any things which are described by Diaz which are not shown in the pictures? Are there any things in the pictures that are not described by Diaz? Which of the two sources might provide us with the better record and why?

Children can make their own drawings of the market place. What plants can they find out about which were first seen by Europeans when they came to America? Children could find out about and include the following fruit and vegetables which were all grown by the Aztecs but which were new to the Europeans: runner beans, melons, peppers, prickly pears, pineapples, pawpaws, avocados, guavas, tomatoes, maize and cocoa beans.

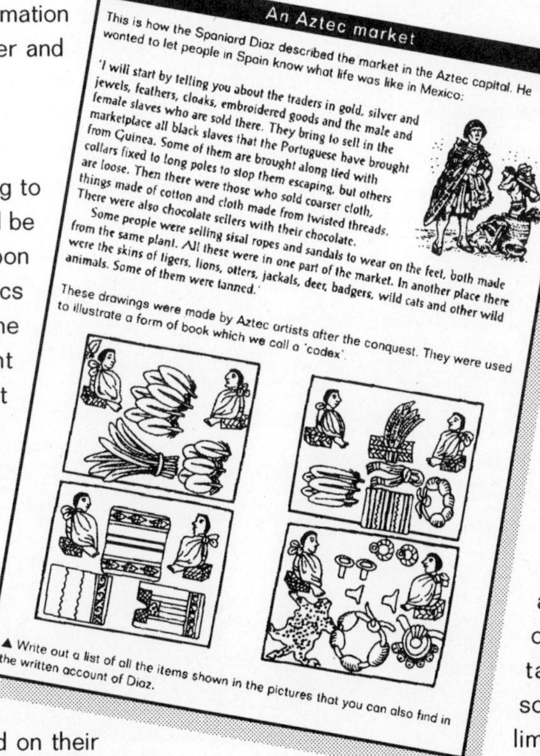

An Aztec market

This is how the Spaniard Diaz described the market in the Aztec capital. He wanted to let people in Spain know what life was like in Mexico:

'I will start by telling you about the traders in gold, silver and jewels, feathers, cloaks, embroidered goods and the male and female slaves who are sold there. They bring to sell in the marketplace all black slaves that the Portuguese have brought from Guinea. Some of them are brought along tied with collars fixed to long poles to stop them escaping, but others are loose. Then there were those who sold coarser cloth, things made of cotton and cloth made from twisted threads. There were also chocolate sellers with their chocolate.

Some people were selling sisal ropes and sandals to wear on the feet, both made from the same plant. All these were in one part of the market. In another place there were the skins of tigers, lions, otters, jackals, deer, badgers, wild cats and other wild animals. Some of them were tanned.'

These drawings were made by Aztec artists after the conquest. They were used to illustrate a form of book which we call a 'codex'.

▲ Write out a list of all the items shown in the pictures that you can also find in the written account of Diaz.

Suggestion(s) for extension
Children can make a codex from folded paper strips.

Suggestion(s) for support
The items for sale in the market could be highlighted in Diaz' account and children could make their own list by copying out each highlighted word in turn and then making a drawing to go with each item.

Assessment opportunities
Choose some examples of source material for the Aztecs. Children could be asked to describe the value and limitations of different kinds of sources.

Opportunities for IT
Children could use the *Landmarks Aztecs* software to help them discover more about everyday life at the time. Children are guided round the Tenochtitlan by a child who answers questions the children type in at the keyboard, provided of course the computer knows the answer. An alternative program to use would be *Time Detectives Aztecs* where children solve a mystery based around the theft of Montezuma's turquoise mask. In both cases the work should form an integral part of the study of Aztecs and time should be taken to introduce the software and talk about the limitations of the simulation and the way that it works.

Display ideas
A large picture of the Aztec market could be made with labels to describe the different commodities.

Reference to photocopiable sheet
The photocopiable sheet on page 156 provides an extract from an account written by Diaz of the market at Tenochtitlan and pictures taken from the Codex Florentinus.

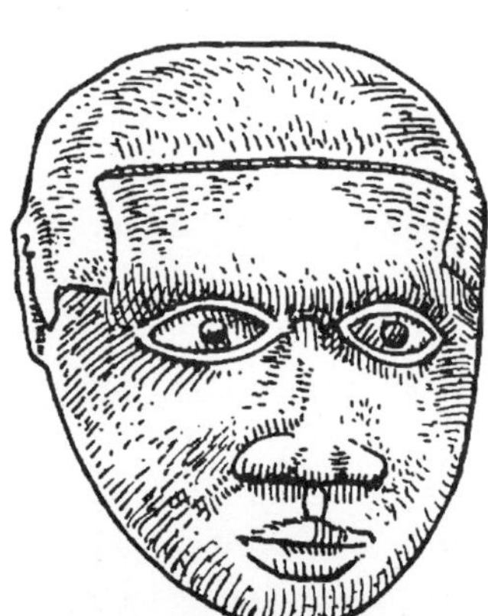

BENIN SOCIETY

To investigate some of the characteristic features of Benin society using a variety of sources.

Whole class;group work;whole class.

120 minutes/extension work for display activity.

Previous skills/knowledge needed

Builds on the activities in pages 90–97 and in particular upon work undertaken using specific items of source material.

Key background information

The powerful kingdom of Benin was situated within the boundaries of the modern country of Nigeria (see map). The civilisation of Benin should not be confused with the modern State of Benin, which is also in West Africa but which used to be known as Dahomey. The people of Benin (Bini) are mainly from the ethnic and linguistic group known as Edo. The environment of Benin was tropical rain forest, although much of the forest has now been cleared to make way for arable farming.

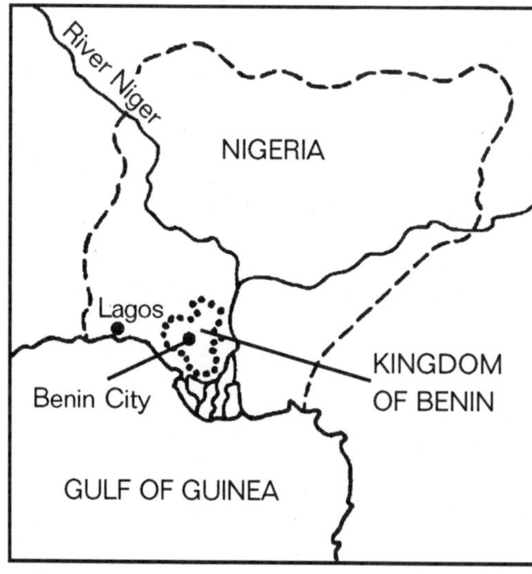

Nigerian archaeologists have excavated some of the defensive earthworks which protected the ancient city of Benin. The inner core was surrounded by a massive circuit of ramparts and ditches 11.5 kms in length. We can learn a great deal about the civilisation from the artefacts that archaeologists have uncovered or which were taken from Benin when the city was captured by the British in the late nineteenth century (see following activity on page 115).

The people of Benin did not use writing but preserved their history orally. Early visitors to the city from Europe are also an important source of information. The Portuguese were the first European visitors to Benin, and their arrival coincided with a great period of political and artistic development which was used to advantage by the Oba who ruled Benin. Portuguese soldiers fought as mercenaries on behalf of the Oba. Traders supplied important luxury goods such as coral beads, cloth for ceremonial occasions and large quantities of brass manillas or bracelets (see illustration on photocopiable page 157) which could be melted down and turned into cast sculptures. In exchange, the people of Benin traded pepper, cloth, ivory and slaves.

A Portuguese visitor in the 1490s is recorded as saying:

'The Kingdom of Benin is about eighty leagues* long and forty wide. The people are usually at war with their neighbours and they take many people prisoner, whom we buy for fifteen brass bracelets each or for copper bracelets which they prefer.'

Another Portuguese visitor speaking in about 1550 said:

'The kings are worshipped by the people. They believe that they come from heaven and they speak of them with great respect. They keep their distance and kneel down before them. Many of these kings never allow themselves to be seen eating food in case people stop thinking that they can live without food.'

Here is a description based on reports of a Dutch visitor in the early seventeenth century:

'The court of the king is square in shape. It is certainly as big as the town of Haarlem and it is completely surrounded by a special wall, like the one which surrounds the town. It is divided into many wonderful palaces, houses and apartments for the king's courtiers. It consists of beautiful long square galleries which are about as big as the Exchange in Amsterdam. It stands on wooden pillars which are covered from top to bottom in cast copper, on which are carved pictures of wars and battles'.

* A league is about three miles in length.

Preparation

Collect together as many sources as possible, including resource packs and children's reference books which relate to Benin. Write out the ten tasks listed below ('What to do') onto cards for the children to refer to.

Resources needed

Information books about Benin, encyclopaedias, postcards and other pictures. It would be helpful to have a globe, world atlas and also a large-scale local map (for example Ordnance Survey) of the area in which the school is situated, information about tropical rain forests and their environment, the Benin creation story. For task 2 children will need a piece of string equivalent to 11.5 kilometres on the map they are given; for task 4 children will need books about the Tudor period.

What to do

Begin by explaining that the children are going to carry out an investigation into the society of ancient Benin. Point out the location of Benin on the globe and/or on a modern map of Africa. Next divide the class into groups of about four children and ask each group to find out about as many of the following topics as possible. They can make notes and draw pictures to record their findings:

1. Make a large map of modern Nigeria and colour in clearly the territory of the ancient Benin people including the city of Benin.
2. Make a tracing of a modern map which includes the town or village where your school is, using as large a scale as possible. Take the piece of string (designed to measure 11.5km on the map) and arrange it in circular formation around the area where your school stands. The area enclosed by the string will be about the same size as the capital of Benin. The string is as long as the boundary of that city. Draw in the boundary on the map so that you can remove the string.
3. Find out about tropical rain forests using children's encyclopaedia and geography reference books. What is the climate like? What kinds of animals live there? What sort of food grows there? Use reference books to find out what the people of Benin used to eat and what part animals including birds played in their lives.
4. Make a timeline which shows the history of Benin on one side and the history of Britain on the other. Include the following: Ewuare the Great about 1440 to about 1480, Portuguese explorers reach Benin 1486, Ozolua the conqueror ruled from about 1480 to about 1504, Oba Esigie 1504 to 1551 and Oba Orhogbua from 1551 to 1578. Try to find out more information about the warrior kings of Benin: Ewuare, Ozolua, Esigie and Orhogbua. Use reference books to help you to find out what was happening in England between 1400 and 1600. Can you suggest reasons why the earlier rulers have dates that say 'about'? You could also add the destruction of Benin City by the British in 1897.
5. Use reference books to find out how Benin was ruled. What jobs did the Oba do? What can you find out about the different groups of people in Benin?
6. What can you find out about the different jobs that people did in Benin? In what ways were the lives of men different from that of the women?
7. Find the Benin story of how the world was created. Compare this with the story in the Old Testament. In what ways were the stories the same? In what ways were they different?
8. What can you find out about Benin religion and festivals?
9. Who were the first Europeans to visit Benin? Describe what happened when the first Europeans came to Benin. What can you find out about the slave trade?
10. Why did Benin come to an end in 1897? Describe what happened.

When all the groups have had a chance to do the tasks they have been given including collecting the information and answering the questions posed, ask each group to give a brief report to the rest of the class on their findings. At this point you can draw attention to the chief ways in which we are able to know about Benin: oral history, archaeology including surviving artefacts and accounts of the early European visitors to Benin.

Suggestion(s) for extension

Some tasks are likely to be more demanding than others, although this will depend upon resources available in the classroom. Children who complete their investigations early could be asked to develop their investigations further or be given extra tasks to complete.

Suggestion(s) for support

Some children could be restricted to the simpler tasks and they could be asked to present their information in picture form with captions.

Assessment opportunities

Children could be asked to recall orally what they have learned about Benin in the next lesson and helped to appreciate that Benin history was communicated by word of mouth and from generation to generation. They could also be asked to explain how the people of Benin passed on their history to the next generation.

Opportunities for IT

A CD-ROM encyclopaedia could be used to provide a source of information for the research activities on Benin and tropical rain forests. Children should be taught how to save text, in ASCII format, and pictures from the CD-ROM so that they can be used in later work on the computer.

All of the information collected could be presented using a desktop publishing package to create a magazine-style format with sections about each of the aspects covered. Alternatively it could be printed out as a part of a class display.

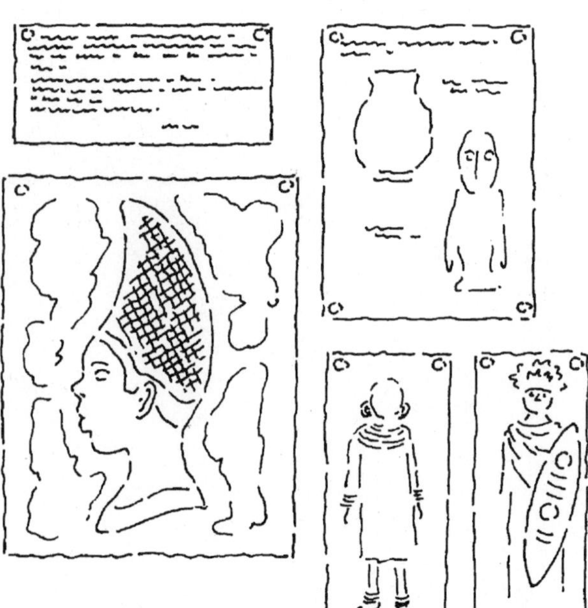

Some Benin artefacts

▲ Can you suggest what these objects are made of? Colour in the pictures with the colour you think should be used:
Brass = green
Ivory = yellow
Terracotta = brown
Wood = black
Coral = orange

▲ Choose one of these objects. Write two sentences to say who you think might have used it.
▲ Try making your own plaque using kitchen foil.

A different approach would be to create a multi-media presentation using an authoring package. The groups could search and present information on their selected aspect of the Benin. They could use pictures taken from clip art or CD-ROM collections, scanned images from photographs or their own line drawings. Children could add their own sound commentary or music recorded using a microphone linked to the computer. The initial structure could be set up in advance with a front page showing the different aspects of the Benin civilisation so that by clicking on a title the user would be taken to a page showing the information on that subject. This could be presented over several pages. Forward and back arrows allow the user to move between the various pages and back to the main index. This is a fairly ambitious project and children using the software for the first time will need some support.

If you have access to Ordnance Survey maps of your own locality in digital format these could be used either in a drawing package or with specific map software such as *Aegis 2* to mark the area of the Benin capital city.

Display ideas

Children can present their findings in the form of a wall display, showing the questions and their answers together with any artwork produced for this activity. If the following activity is also undertaken the display could encompass both pieces of work.

Reference to photocopiable sheet

None for this activity although the photocopiable sheet on page 157 relates to the same topic.

BENIN – ART AND TECHNOLOGY

To learn about Benin art and technology by studying their artefacts.

Individual.

60 minutes.

Previous skills/knowledge needed

This activity could usefully build on Benin society page 112 and upon activities on pages 90-97, which includes the detailed study of specific artefacts.

Key background information

Over 400,000 works of art found their way into foreign museums after the sacking of Benin city by the British in 1897. A favourite art form was the cast head made from brass (an alloy of copper and zinc). Some of these were heads of ancestors which were placed on the altars of dead rulers known as Obas. Bronze, (using tin rather than zinc in the metal alloy) was sometimes used but other objects were made of wood, ivory and terracotta. Benin art is very rich in quality and it also provides us with many insights into everyday life. Another favourite product was the pictorial plaques cast in brass which showed many aspects of Benin life including events in their history. The lost wax process (*cire perdue*) was used in making sculptures (a method of bronze casting by filling space between the core and the mould after the wax coating the core has melted).

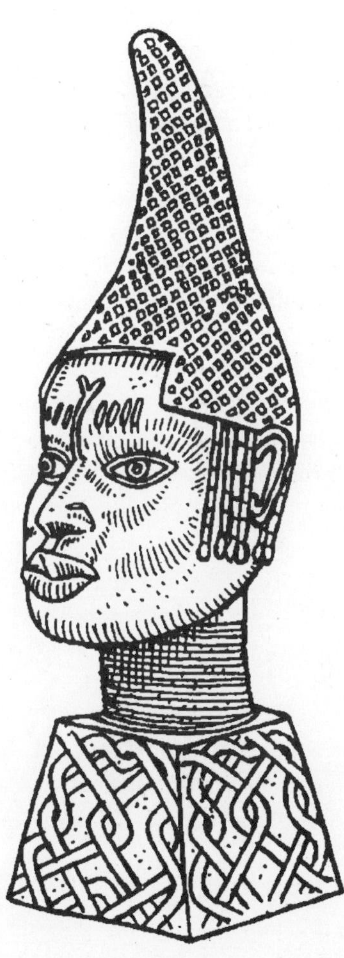

Preparation

Assemble some visual resources relating to Benin art including information about Benin plaques from the British Museum. Copy photocopiable page 157.

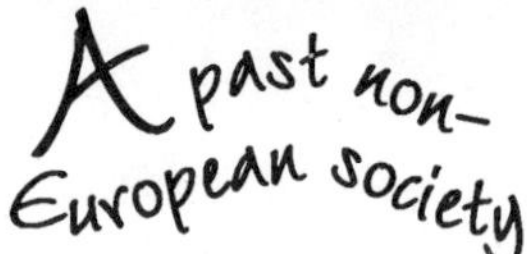

Resources needed

Picture books, postcards and posters depicting Benin brass sculptures and other artefacts such as those made from carved wood and ivory and those using coral beads. Drawing paper and pencils, gold wax crayons, sugar paper (black), tracing paper (as appropriate), photocopiable page 157.

What to do

Invite the children to observe closely one of the brass sculptures produced in Benin and to make a careful pencil drawing. Underneath the children could write some information which they have found out about the technique of lost wax sculpture (see page 115).

Suggestion(s) for extension

Children could repeat their drawings on black sugar paper using gold wax crayons.

Suggestion(s) for support

Some children may need to trace the outline of the sculpture as a starting point.

Assessment opportunities

As a form of summative assessment, give children a number of pictures of Benin artefacts and ask them to comment on them in terms of what they might be made of, how they were made and what they depict.

Display ideas

Children's art work separately displayed or alongside the results of the investigations on Benin Society (page 112).

Reference to photocopiable sheet

The photocopiable page 157 shows a variety of artefacts made in the kingdom of Benin. It could be useful with this activity and also Benin Society on page 112.

Some Benin artefacts

▲ Can you suggest what these objects are made of? Colour in the pictures with the colour you think should be used:
Brass = green
Ivory = yellow
Terracotta = brown
Wood = black
Coral = orange

▲ Choose one of these objects. Write two sentences to say who you think might have used it.
▲ Try making your own plaque using kitchen foil.

Photocopiables

The pages in this section can be photocopied for use in the classroom or school which has purchased this book, and do not need to be declared in any return in respect of any photocopying licence.

They comprise pupil worksheets and resource material for use by the children. Most of the photocopiable pages are related to individual activities in the book; the name of the activity is indicated at the top of the sheet, together with a page reference indicating where the lesson plan for that activity can be found.

Individual pages are discussed in detail within each lesson plan, accompanied by ideas for adaptation where appropriate – of course, each sheet can be adapted to suit your own needs, and those of your class. Sheets can also be coloured, laminated, mounted on to card, enlarged and so on where appropriate.

Change over time: Invaders and settlers, see page 32

Changes in Britain

▲ Cut out the pictures and arrange them in order. Start with the oldest.

Roman legionary

Viking ship

Norman castle-keep

Iron-age shield

Roman mosaic

Viking saga

Anglo-Saxon ruler

Iron-age hillfort

Anglo-Saxon helmet

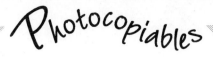

Roman roads, see page 35

What do you think about the new road?

- The road will bring noise and dust. ____________
- The transport system by the river is sufficient.
- The new road will bring goods from Rome including wine, food and fine glass and pottery.
- It will bring more soldiers into the area which will make life safer.
- You will be able to meet up with other tribes more quickly.
- The Romans will want to transport bigger loads of crops for their own use.
- More Roman soldiers will come into the area and interfere with the British way of life.
- The road will be a more direct route to other towns.
- The Britons will have to pay for the road through higher taxes.
- The forest will be disturbed and this will spoil the chance to hunt wild boar.
- Road building will provide lots of jobs.
- Life is alright as it is and there is no need for change.
- A new road will help trade between the towns and the country people.

▲ Read these arguments.
If you agree with them place a tick on the line beneath/next to them. If you disagree mark a cross.
How can the problem be solved?
▲ Write your solution on the back of this sheet.

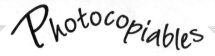

The revolt of Boudicca, see page 37

Supporting Boudicca

▲ Dio wrote a history of the Romans. This is what he said about Boudicca:

"Boudicca was a Briton of royal descent. The rebels thought her their best leader. She was much more intelligent than women usually are. She was tall, and she was terrifying to look at. She had a fierce look in her eyes and a raucous voice. A huge mass of yellow hair hung down to her hips. Around her neck she had a huge torque of gold and she wore a dress of many colours, pinned together with a brooch. This was how she normally dressed."

My name is Britorix. I am a soldier in Boudicca's army. We are fighting the Romans because.....

▲ Draw your own picture of Boudicca. How far will it be different from what Dio tells us?

A Roman town plan

aqueduct
cemetery
north gate
amphitheatre
ditch
baths
shops
forum
temple
west gate
east gate
temple
houses
baths
south gate
town wall

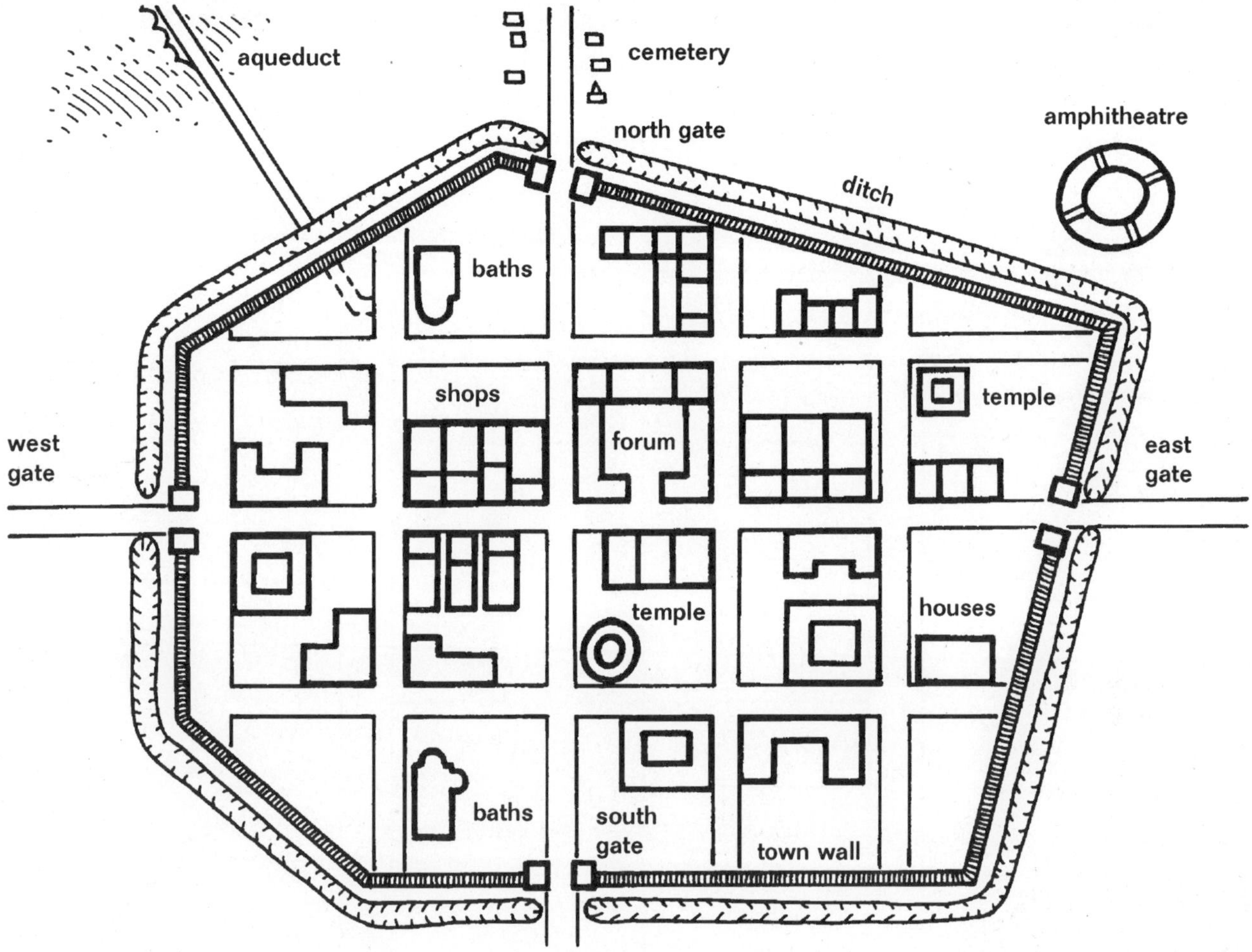

▲ The picture above shows a plan of a Roman town, try drawing a plan of your own town.

Make sure that you include the following:

Roads leading to and from the town	Boundary walls and ditches
Gates	Roads inside the town in a net pattern
Houses	Shops and workshops
A forum	Temples
A theatre or amphitheatre	Baths
Aqueduct	And finally, the Cemetery.

▲ Use this information to help you to decide where to put the Cemetery. It was always outside the town. Evidence of burials is usually found along the sides of roads which lead into Roman towns. Here is a town law which refers to this practice:

"It is against the law to bring a dead body into the city. Anyone who disobeys this law will be punished as soon as possible. A dead body may not be buried or burned within the town walls."

The Latin language, see page 42

Latin language

▲ Here are some Latin words. Draw arrows between the words to match the correct English word to the original Latin word.

VILLA	Slave
MAGISTER	Grass
SERVUS	Farmer
MILITES	Ship
FLORES	Soldiers
HERBA	House
AGRICOLA	Teacher
NAVIS	Flowers
LIBRI	Woman
MUS	Books
FEMINA	Mouse

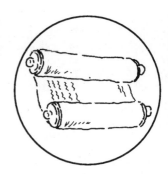

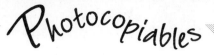

The end of Roman Britain, see page 44

An unexpected attack

▲ Read the descriptions below and use them to help you in writing about the invasion of your villa:

Source 1. (A contemporary Roman historian, Ammianus Marcellinus writing about the state of the Roman empire in between 367 and 368.)

"The Emperor Valentinian was very worried. He heard bad news about Britain. There was serious trouble. The Picts .... and Scots were everywhere and they were destroying everything they came across.

At the same time, along the coast of the Gaul*, the Franks and their neighbours, the Saxons, wherever they landed, were attacking people and cruelly robbing them. They set things on fire and murdered all those that they took prisoner."

* Now France

N.B. The Picts came from Scotland and the Scots from Ireland!

Source 2. Many Roman villas show signs of having been attacked about this time. Invaders would have rowed or sailed their ships up the river estuaries (such as the Severn) and along wide navigable rivers looking for places to land. Near to the River Avon near Bristol, there are a number of Roman villas which seem to have been attacked and destroyed. Archaeological excavation has shown that villas were set light to and violently destroyed. Human skeletons have been found in some cases and in two of the villas, bodies had been thrown down wells.

Early Angle and Saxon settlers, see page 46

Evidence for early Anglo-Saxon settlers

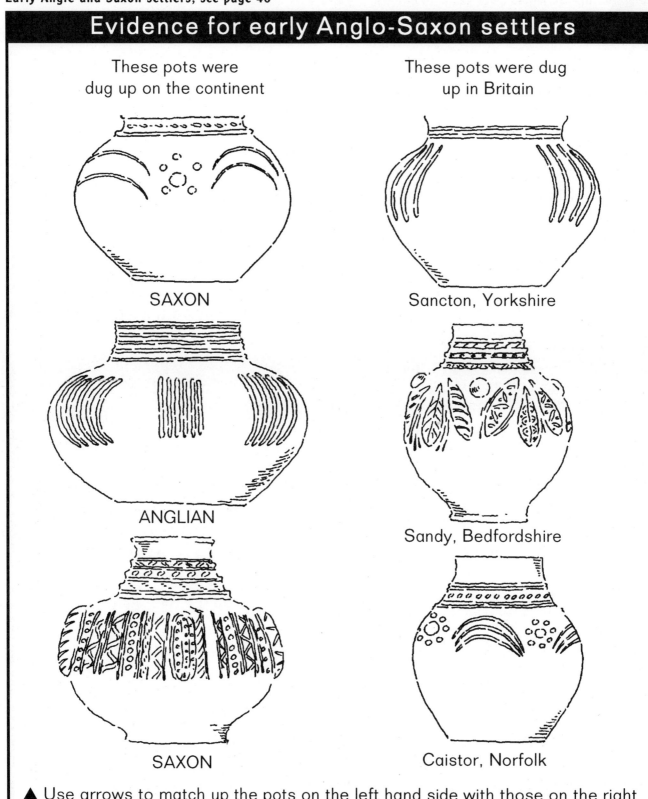

These pots were dug up on the continent

These pots were dug up in Britain

SAXON

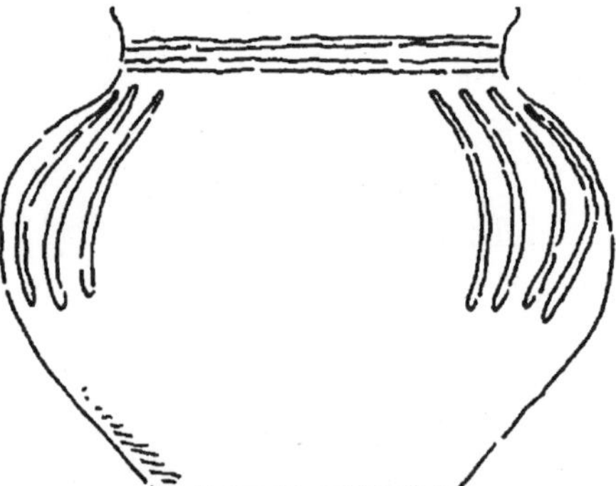

Sancton, Yorkshire

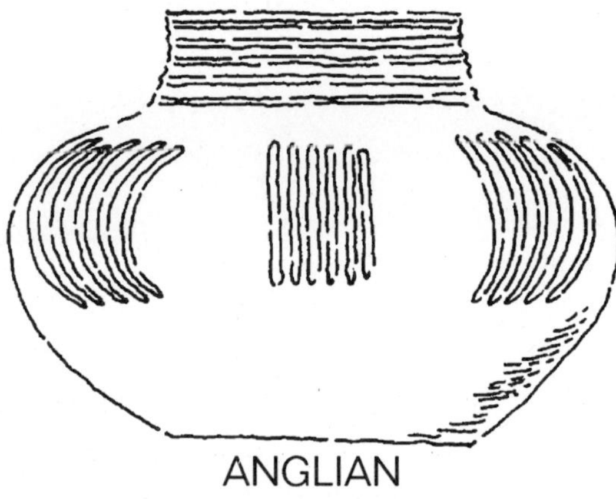

ANGLIAN

Sandy, Bedfordshire

SAXON

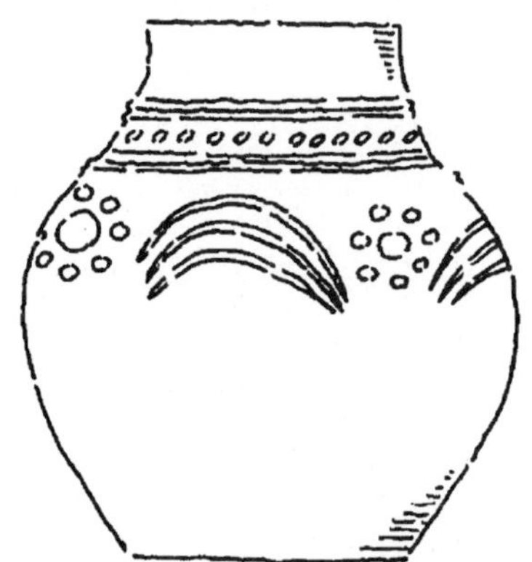

Caistor, Norfolk

▲ Use arrows to match up the pots on the left hand side with those on the right hand side. What does this tell you about the early Angles and Saxons?

▲ Now use a map of England to find all the place names you can which end in or include -ing, -ington and -ingham.

I have found ______ places where the Angles and Saxons settled.

King Ethelbert becomes a Christian

Here is the story of the conversion of King Ethelbert based closely on the account given by Bede:

"Pope Gregory sent the servant of God, Augustine and several other God-fearing monks into Britain to preach the word of God to the English. At first, they were afraid, and they even thought about turning back, rather than going to visit a barbaric, fierce and unbelieving nation, whose language they did not even know. Augustine and his friends some 40 of them, landed on the island of Thanet in the East of Kent. Augustine sent word to Ethelbert, the ruler of Kent, promising that those who obeyed the word of God would have eternal joy in heaven and a kingdom that would last for ever with the living and true God. The King, whose wife Bertha was a Christian from the Frankish royal family, and who had been allowed to marry Ethelbert on conditions that she should be allowed to worship the Christian God, gave permission to Augustine and his friends to stay on the isle of Thanet and sent supplies to them.

A few days afterwards, Ethelbert ordered Augustine and his friends to meet him in an open air place. They brought with them a silver cross and a picture of Christ painted on a panel. They chanted litanies and preached to the king. The king gave them permission to preach and gave them a place to stay in Canterbury, the capital of his Kingdom. Some people were converted to Christianity being impressed by the simple way of life which Augustine and his friends displayed. There was in Canterbury, a church dedicated to St Martin which had been founded in Roman times and in which Bertha used to pray. This became the church of the Christians, who began to meet there and where they chanted psalms, prayed, celebrated Mass, preached and baptised. Soon the king himself was persuaded to become a Christian. He was baptised and from then on, the Christians were allowed to preach wherever they wished and to build and restore churches."

▲ Choose any one part of the story and draw your own picture. Use bubbles to show what people are saying to one another.

Anglo-Saxon writing, see page 50

Using Anglo-Saxon writing

i j h p x s t b

n h w g k r o th u f

e ng m l d oe a ae y ea

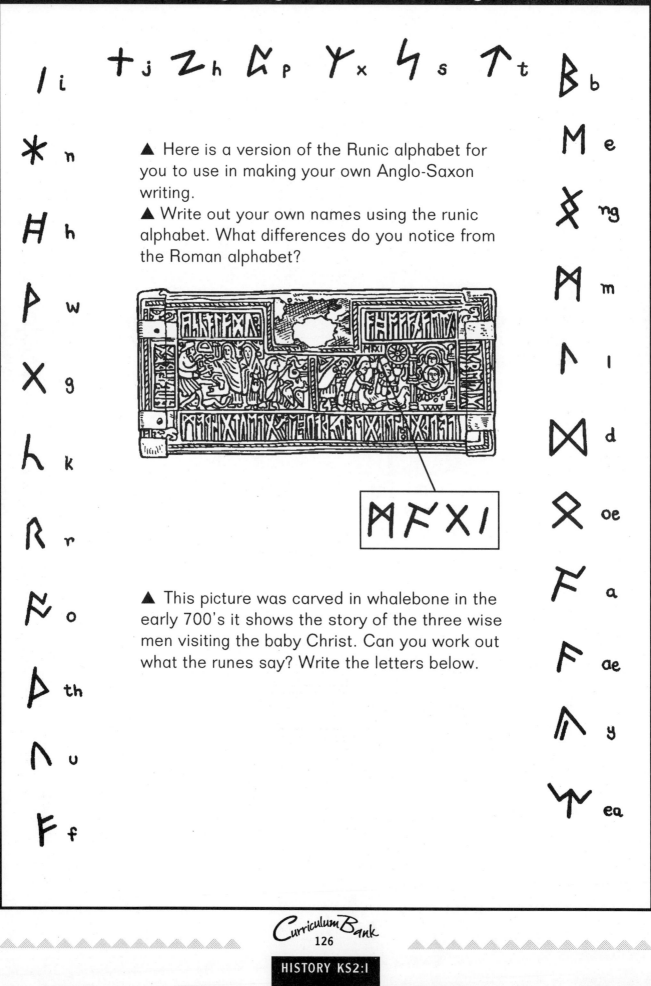

▲ Here is a version of the Runic alphabet for you to use in making your own Anglo-Saxon writing.

▲ Write out your own names using the runic alphabet. What differences do you notice from the Roman alphabet?

▲ This picture was carved in whalebone in the early 700's it shows the story of the three wise men visiting the baby Christ. Can you work out what the runes say? Write the letters below.

The Sutton Hoo burial ship, see page 51

A ship burial

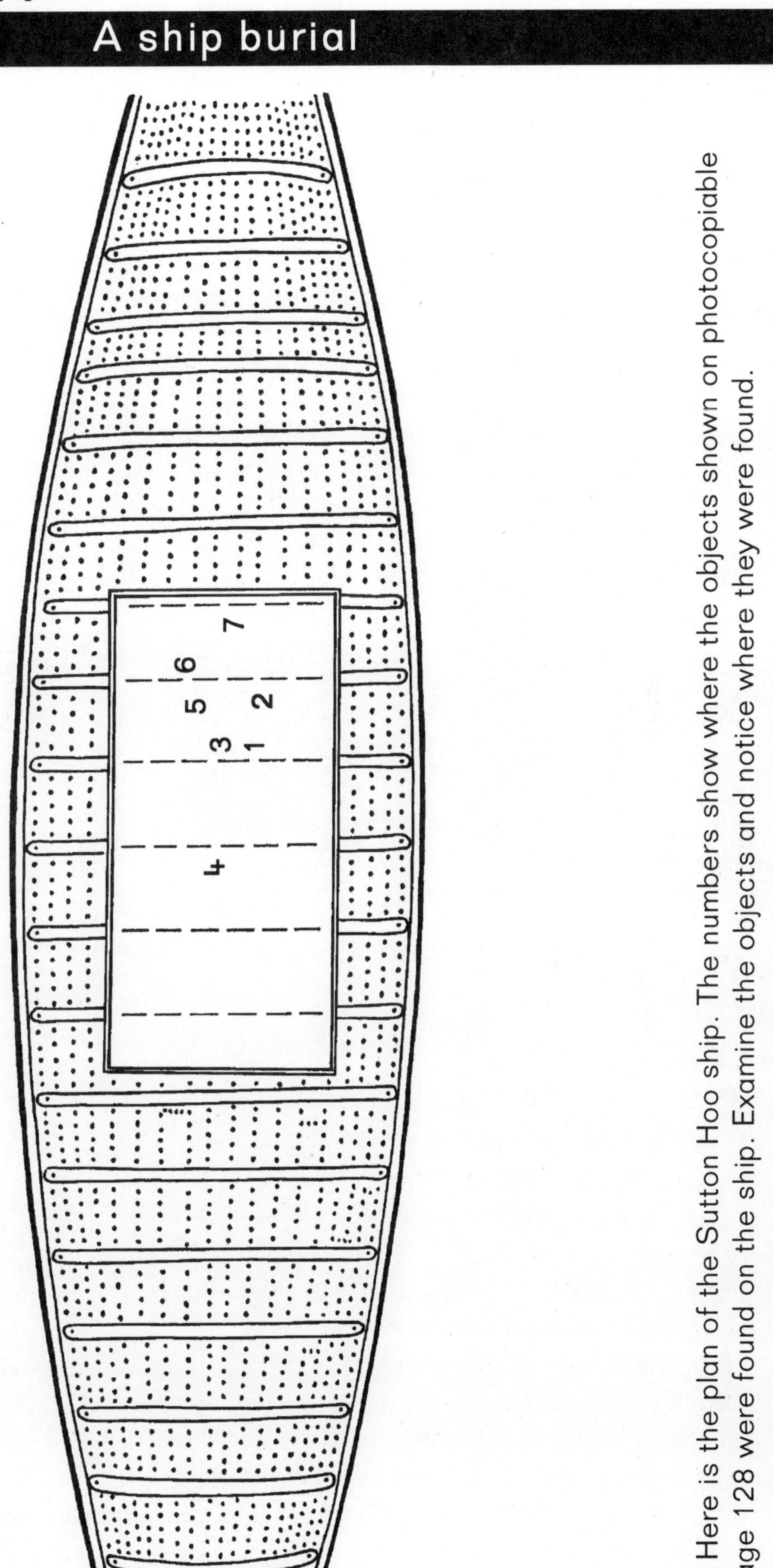

▲ Here is the plan of the Sutton Hoo ship. The numbers show where the objects shown on photocopiable page 128 were found on the ship. Examine the objects and notice where they were found.

The Sutton Hoo burial ship, see page 51

Items found on the Sutton Hoo ship

▲ Colour in the items. Think carefully about the colours you will use for each picture.

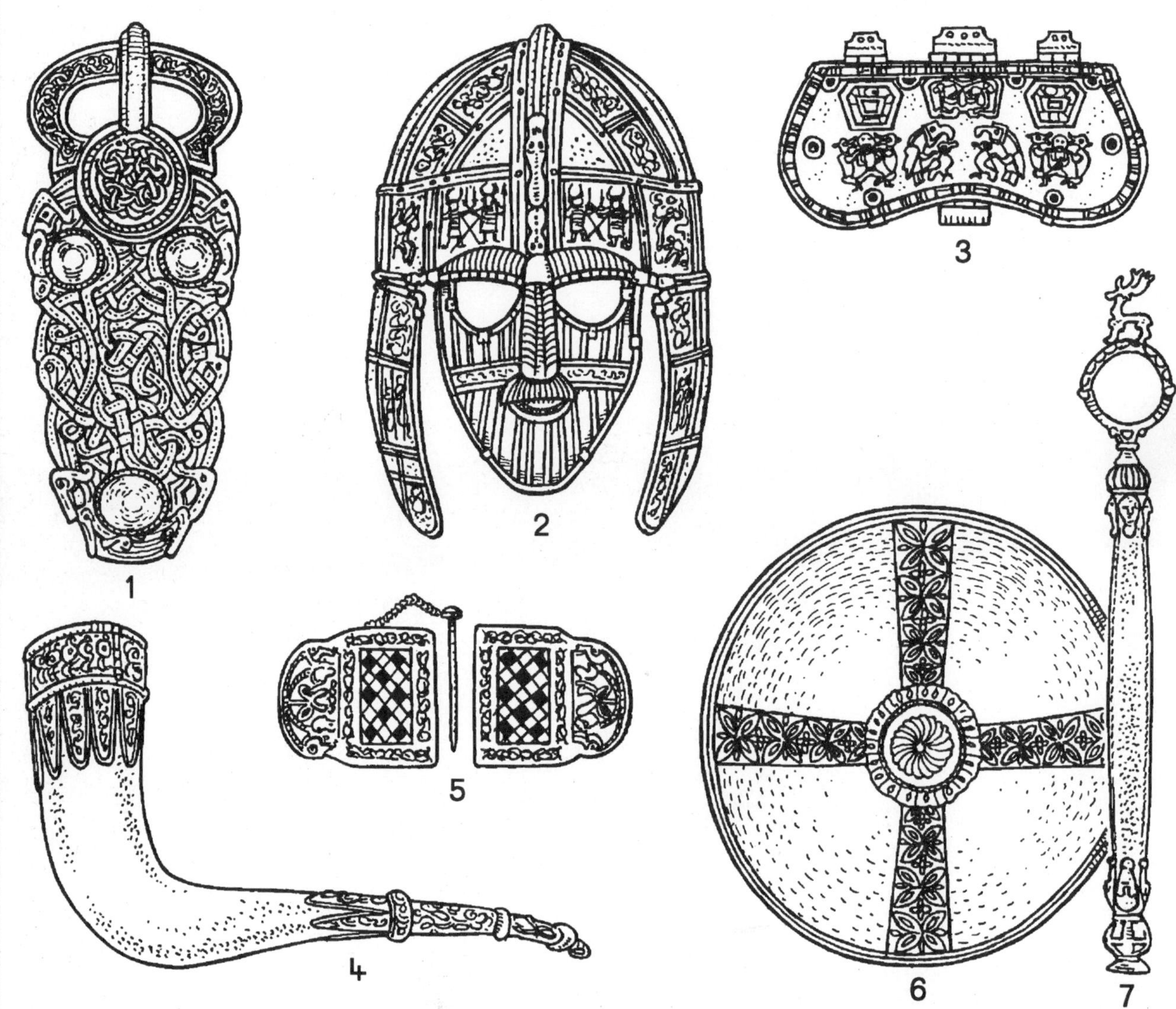

▲ When you have located the finds on your plan of the ship, (photocopiable page 127), read this account of the Danish King Scyld in the Anglo-Saxon poem called *Beowulf*. What things are the same? What things are different?

"Then Scyld's close friends carried him down to the sea, as he the Lord of the Danes has asked while he could still speak. That well loved man had ruled over his land for many years. There in the harbour stood the ship with its ringed prow, the ship of a prince covered in ice and keen to set sail. And then they laid their dear master the giver of rings, deep inside the ship next to the mast [in majesty]. There were many treasures and ornaments from places far and wide collected there. I never heard of a ship more finely equipped with weapons, with things for war and with swords and breast plates. On his chest lay so many fine things that one could not count them that were to go with him to the waves."

En ed the Great, see page 54

The deeds of Alfred the Great

These documents tell us about Alfred and about some of the things that he did during his reign.

Extracts from:
(a) **the Anglo-Saxon Chronicle** (which was written in Anglo-Saxon about the same time that Alfred was ruling Wessex).

878 In this year in the middle of winter after twelfth night, the enemy army came sneakily to Chippenham and they occupied the land of the West Saxons and settled there. Then they drove a large number of the people out into the sea and conquered most of the others. People gave in to them except for Alfred. He made a difficult journey through woods and fenland with a small army.

896 King Alfred had long ships built to oppose the Danish warships. They were almost twice as long as the others. Some had 60 oars and some had more. They were faster and steadier and higher than the other side's. Alfred fought against the enemy and drove them away. The enemy gave him hostages and swore that they would leave his kingdom and promised that their king would become Christian and they kept their promise.

(b) A much later account of Alfred in hiding in the fens of Somerset where he was sheltered by a pig farmer.
(This was written in Latin and is about a hundred years later than Alfred.)

"One day when the farmer was leading his animals to their usual pasture, the King stayed at home with the man's wife. She was worried about her husband's return and had left some kneaded bread in the oven. She then got on with her other housework. When she came to see how the bread was getting on in the oven, she saw it burning from the other side of the room. She became angry and said to the King (she didn't realise who he was): "Look here man, you don't bother to turn over the loaves which you can see are burning, yet you are more than happy to eat them hot from the oven."

▲ Read (a). What reasons are there for thinking that Alfred was a great ruler?
▲ Read the story told in (b). How likely is it that this really happened? What are the arguments for and against? Finish off the story and make a picture of it.

Viking raids, see page 56

The Vikings attack

▲ You are a monk who has escaped being killed during the attack on Lindisfarne. Write a letter to Bishop Alcuin telling him what happened. Make your own picture.

This account was written four hundred years later by Simeon of Durham. Do you think it is exaggerated? After all the monks managed to keep going and did not leave until 875 when they were worried about further attacks.

"793 terrible and amazing things happened which terrified the English nation. Horrible lightning storms and dragons were seen in the air. Fiery flashes darted this way and that. These signs meant that there was to be a great famine and horrendous and indescribable murder of many people took place after this...

In the same year the pagans from the north came with their ships to Britain like stinging hornets and spread out on all sides like frightening wolves. They robbed, tore and killed not only the beasts of burden, sheep and oxen, but even priests and deacons and groups of monks and nuns. And they came to the church of Lindisfarne, laid everything waste with their dreadful plundering, trampled all over the holy places, bringing pollution to the place. They dug up altars and seized all the treasures of the holy church. They killed some of the brothers and took away some in chains, many they drove out naked and bombarded with insults and some they drowned in the sea."

▲ This carved stone was found at Lindisfarne. What do you think it shows?

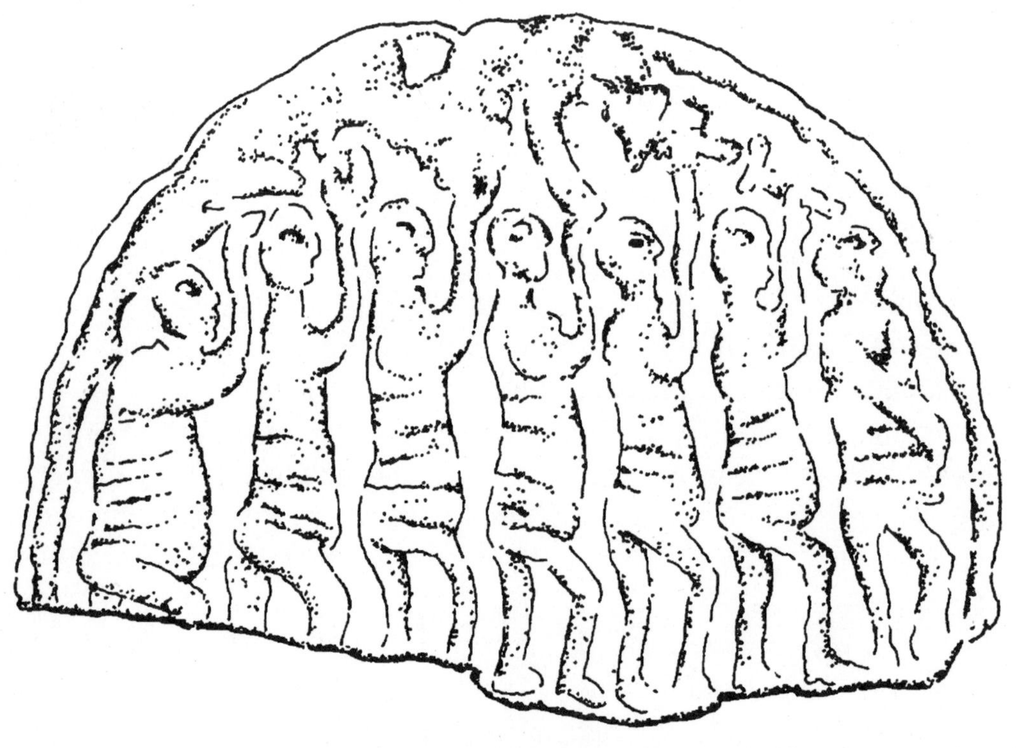

The Viking way of life, see page 58

The Viking way of life

▲ How many of these things have you found out about? Match the object with the trader by drawing an arrow between them.

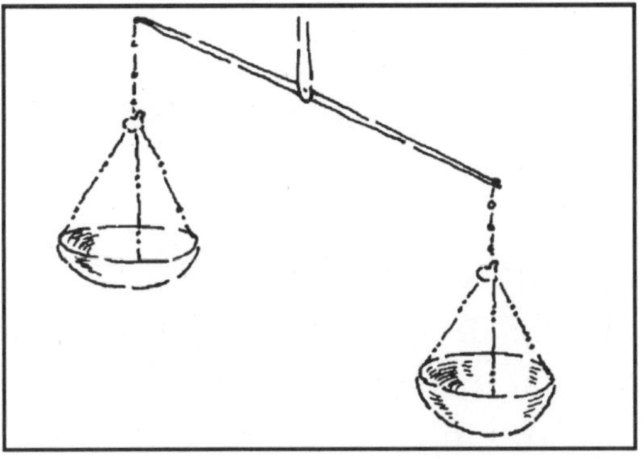

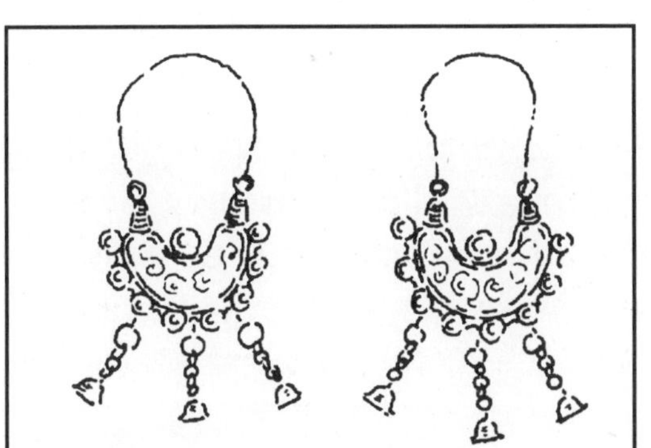

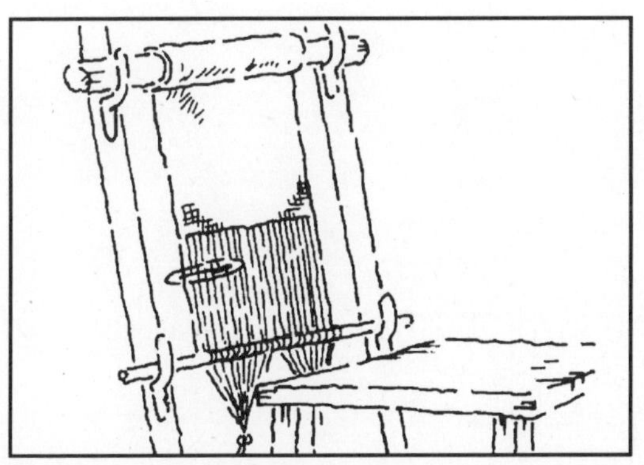

Alfred, the Danes and Danelaw, see page 59

Map of Danelaw

Boundary of Danelaw

York

Lincoln

Oxford

London

Here are some words which go back to the time when the Viking people invaded and settled in Britain.

Thorpe	a farm
Toft	site of a house, homestead
Hulme	an island
By	a farmstead or village
Booth	a shelter

▲ Look at a map of England and see how many place names you can find which include these words. Mark on your map with an X the position of each place that you can find.

▲ Are most of these names inside the area of Danelaw? What does this tell us?

Ancient Greek timeline, see page 65

Things that happened in ancient Greece

All dates are BC.

▲ Cut carefully along the dotted lines and arrange the pictures in the order that they happened.

First recorded Olympic Games 776

Greek alphabet invented about 750

Cleopatra dies: the Romans conquer Egypt 30

Greek settlements in the Mediterranean 750 to 550

Pericles makes Athens more democratic 462

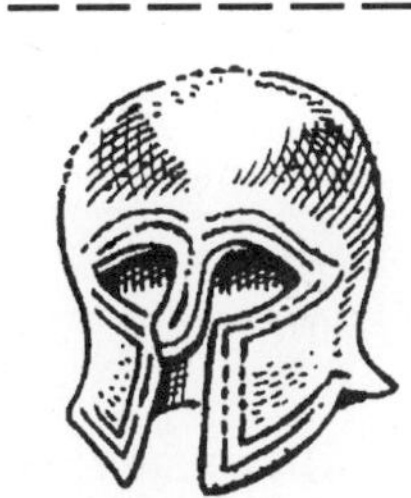

Peloponnesian War 431 to 404

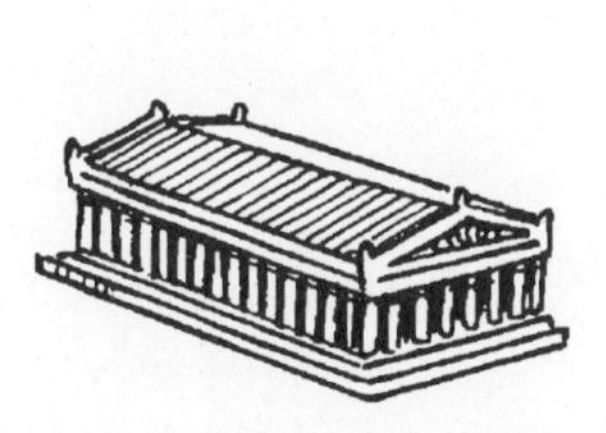

The Parthenon is being built about 440

The Ionian Greeks rebel against the Persians 499

The Battle of Salamis (second Persian War) 480

The Battle of Marathon (first Persian War) 490

Alexander the Great's conquests and settlements 336 to 323

Pericles makes Athens more democratic 462

Heroes and heroines, see page 69

Daedalus and Icarus

Daedalus and his son Icarus had long been held prisoners on the island of Crete by King Minos.

Daedalus loathed Crete and his long exile. He longed to see his homeland again, but was cut off from Greece by the sea.

'Minos may stop us escaping by land or water, but not by sky. I shall go that way,' he said to himself. 'Minos may rule everything, but he does not rule the sky.'

So saying, Daedalus started to work on something that no one else had tried. He began by laying feathers in rows, starting with the smallest ones. Then he fastened the feathers together with string and wax. He then bent them in a gentle curve so that they looked like the wings of real birds. As he worked, his son, Icarus watched him. He found it hard not to play about. He caught the feathers as they were blown about in the air; he pushed his thumb into the wax, while his father patiently continued his amazing work.

At last Daedalus put the finishing touches to his work. He had made two pairs of wings. Daedalus tried his on and, balancing his body on the two wings, he flapped them and hovered in mid-air. Icarus cried out in astonishment. He could not wait to have a go. As Daedalus fitted the wings to Icarus he spoke to him. 'Listen to me, Icarus, fly on a middle course. If you fly too low, the spray of the sea will make your wings too heavy; if you fly too high, the sun may burn them. Fly between the two. Do not steer your course by Bootes or Helice or by the drawn sword of Orion, but follow closely behind me.'

As he worked and talked, he began to cry and his hands trembled. Then he kissed his son, and rose up on his wings. He told his son to follow him. He flew on ahead, as anxious as a mother bird over a baby fledgling. A fisherman saw them as he angled for fish. Then a shepherd saw them as he stood leaning on his crook, as did a ploughman holding the handles of his plough. They stood there in amazement thinking, anyone who flies through the air must be a god.

As they flew Icarus grew more confident; he made for the open sky and began to fly higher and higher leaving his father far behind. Foolish Icarus had forgotten his father's wise words.He did not notice the scorching rays of the sun beginning to melt the wax with which his wings were held together. Icarus beat his bare arms up and down, but without wings they could not catch the air and he fell from the sky into the sea below. His poor father called out 'Icarus, where are you? Where shall I look for you, Icarus?'. Then he saw feathers floating on the waves and cursed his invention.

From this time on the sea took its name from Icarus and the land where his body was buried was called after the boy who was buried there.

Heroes and heroines, see page 69

The twelve labours of Heracles

Heracles performed twelve heroic labours for the king of Mycenae, Eurystheus. He was advised by the Delphic Oracle that if he were to spend twelve years serving Eurystheus in this way, he would be rewarded by being made immortal.

First Labour: To kill and skin the Nemean lion, a giant animal with a hide that no iron, bronze or stone point would go through.
Solution: His sword bent like a piece of lead against the lion and his club shattered, but Heracles trapped the animal in its own cave with a net before strangling it with his bare arms.

Second Labour: To destroy the Lernaean Hydra, a monster with the body of a dog and nine snake-like heads one of which was immortal. It was so venomous that even one whiff of its breath or the smell of its footprints could be lethal.
Solution: Every time he cut off one head, three more grew in its place. But Heracles was able to cut off the head that was immortal, burying it in the ground while it still hissed. Then he cut the animal to pieces with his sword, dipping his arrows in the animal's gall to make them deadly.

Fifth Labour: To clean out the filthy Stables of Augeias in one day. The dung in Augeias' cattle yard had not been cleared away for many years and the stench from them spread all over southern Greece.
Solution: Heracles first cut a hole in the wall of the yard in two places. Then he diverted the two nearby rivers so that they rushed through the yard, sweeping it clean. He then went on to clean the surrounding areas too.

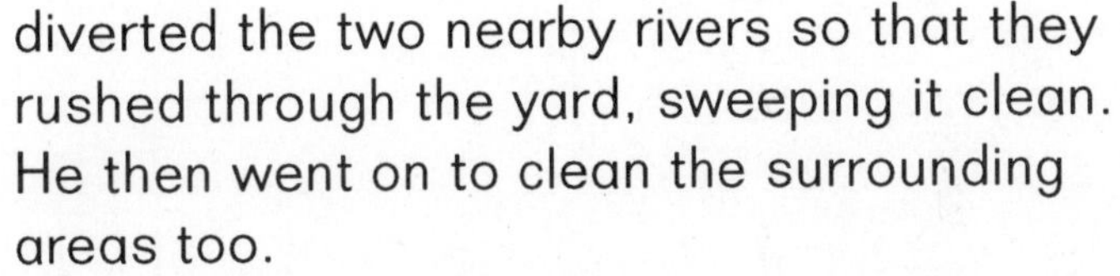

Twelfth Labour: The last and most difficult task was to bring back the three-headed dog, Cerberus from the underworld.
Solution: Heracles descended to the underworld near to Sparta. Charon ferried him across the River Styx. He found the dog chained to the gates. He gripped the dog by its throat. Although its three heads had snakes for hair, Heracles choked the creature until it gave in. Heracles was protected by his thick lion's skin. He dragged the dog bound with chains of adamant up into the upper air. As it reached the light, the dog barked wildly slavering from its three mouths.

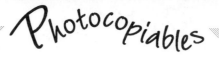

Heroes and heroines, see page 69

Which stories do these come from?

▲ All these pictures were made by ancient Greek artists. Find pictures of some of these stories made by modern artists. In what ways are they different? Why do you think this is so?

Jason and the dragon

Odysseus blinds the cyclops

Theseus kills the minotaur

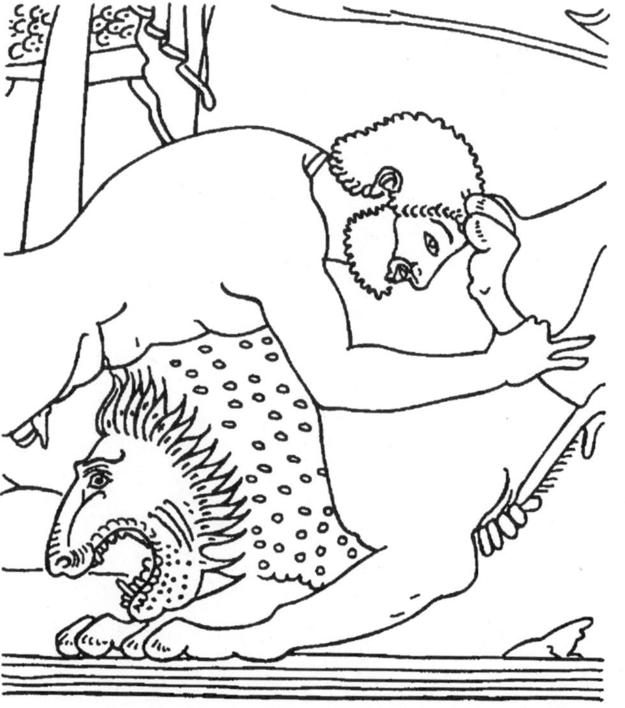

Heracles and the Nemean lion

Everyday life, see page 71

Map of Attica

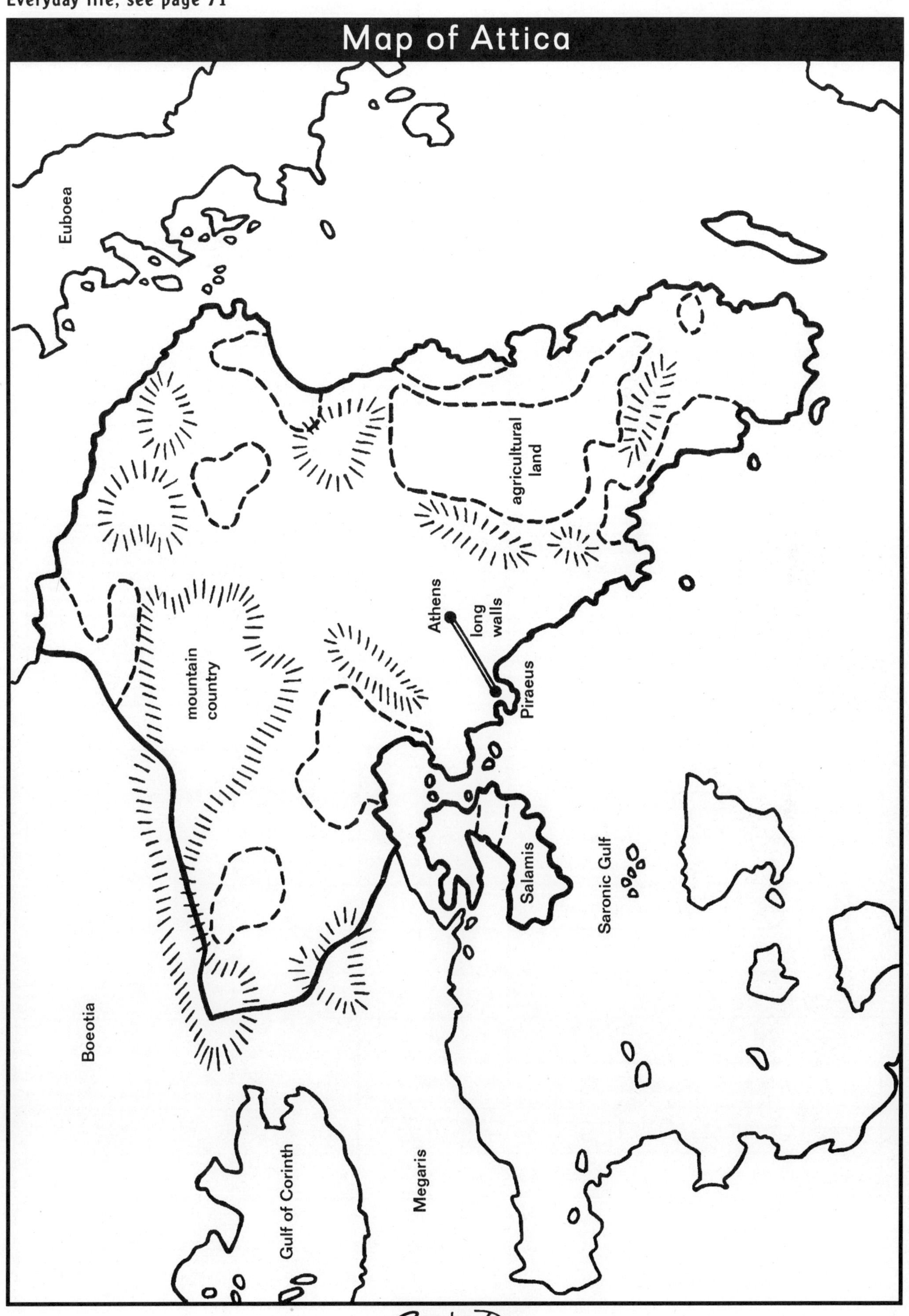

Everyday life, see page 71

Occupations

Occupation	Locality				
	town	port	mountain	coast	flat lands
Greengrocer (G)					
Beekeepers (B)					
Charcoal burners (CB)					
Farmers (F)					
Fishermen (Fi)					
Armourers (A)					
Dock and shipyard workers (D)					
Sculptors (S)					
Hill farmers (HF)					
Leather tanners (LT)					
Potters and pottery painters (P)					
Ship builders (SB)					
Sailors/oarsmen (SO)					
Lawyers (L)					
Seafaring merchants (SM)					
Market traders (MT)					
Actor (Ac)					

▲ Tick on the table where you would have seen these occupations. Transfer your findings onto the map of Attica on page 137 using the abbreviations listed.

Sparta, see page 75

Spartan soldiers

The Spartans were prevented from bringing up their sons in their own way. Lycurgus ordered all boys aged seven to be taken away from their families and to be put into 'military units' where they would be brought up and looked after together. They had a very basic training in reading and writing. The rest of their education was concerned with making them obey orders, putting up with hardship and winning battles.

'A young man aged 20 is in charge of each unit of boys. It is his job to supervise mock battles and the boys have to serve him his meals indoors. He makes the bigger boys fetch firewood while the smaller ones have to gather herbs. The boys steal from what they fetch and anyone who is caught stealing is given several lashes with a whip, either because he has been careless or because he is not a clever enough thief. They also steal what food they can and learn how to be good at attacking people who are asleep or not paying attention.

There is a story that once upon a time a boy who had stolen a fox was carrying the animal under his cloak. Rather than let himself be found out he let the animal tear out his insides with its teeth and claws.'

Ships and Seafarers, see page 76

Map

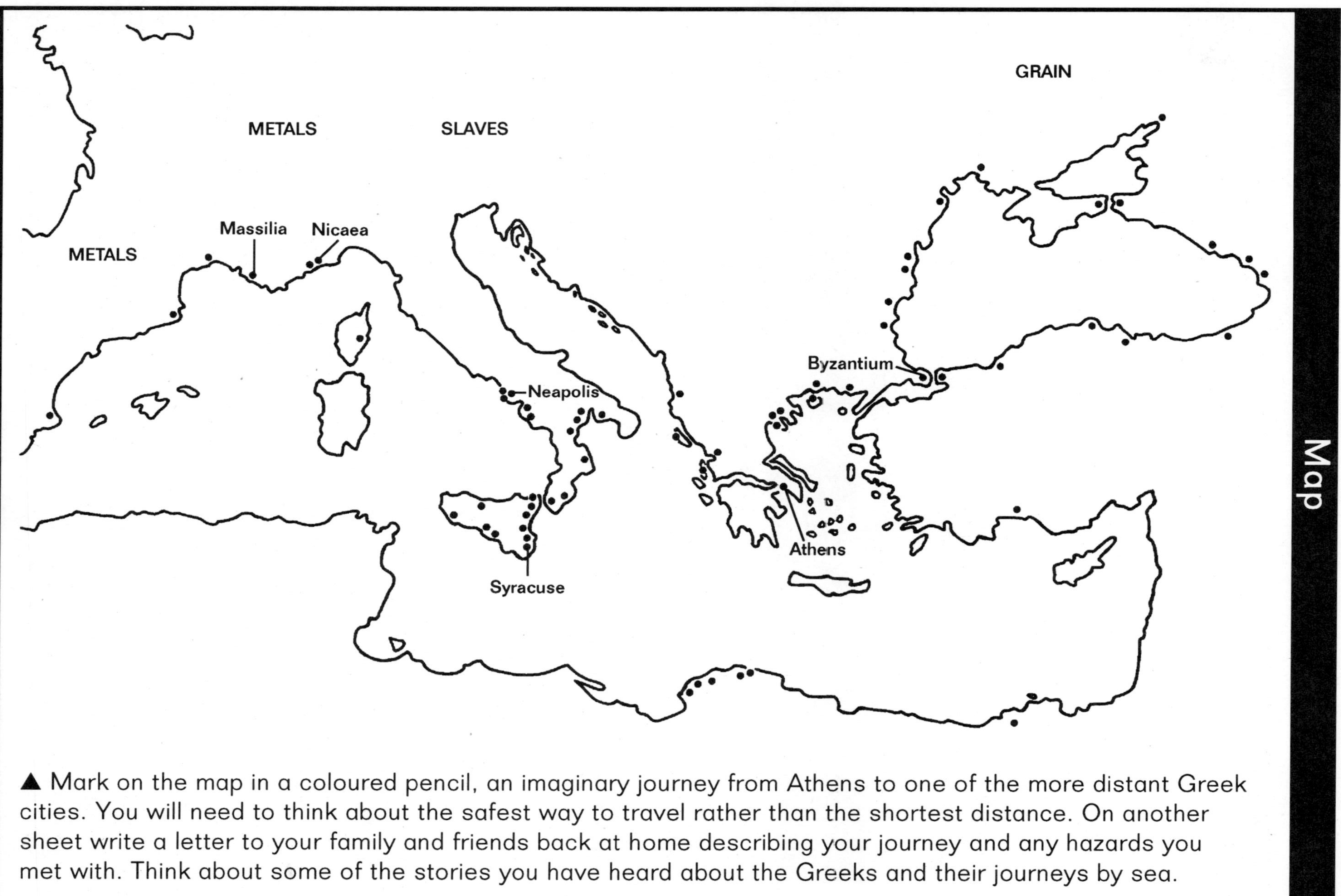

▲ Mark on the map in a coloured pencil, an imaginary journey from Athens to one of the more distant Greek cities. You will need to think about the safest way to travel rather than the shortest distance. On another sheet write a letter to your family and friends back at home describing your journey and any hazards you met with. Think about some of the stories you have heard about the Greeks and their journeys by sea.

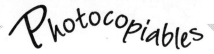

The Greeks and Persians, see page 78

Maps of the Persian Empire

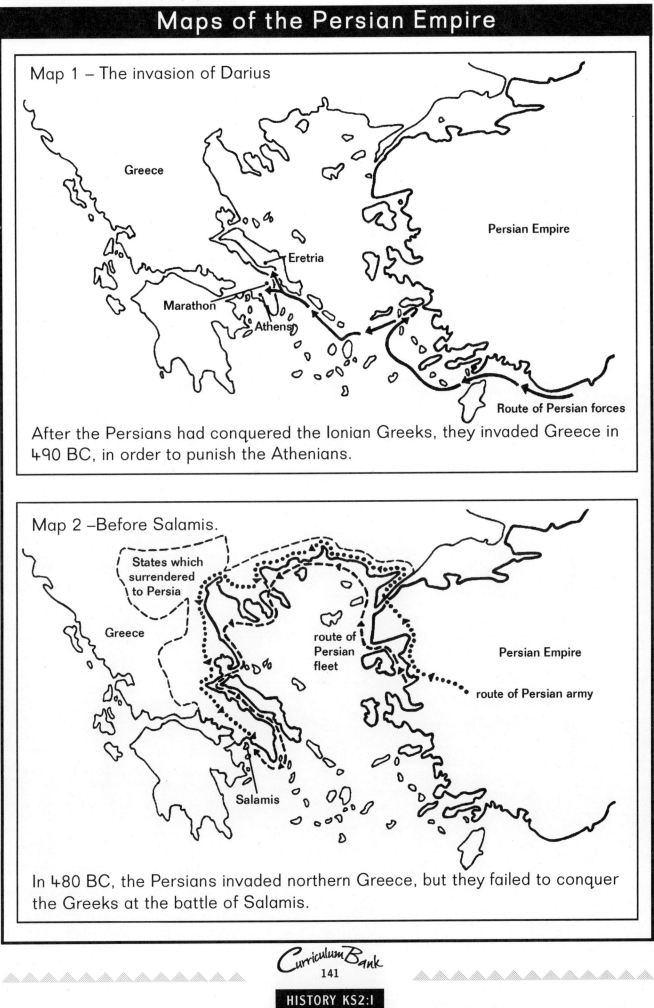

Map 1 – The invasion of Darius

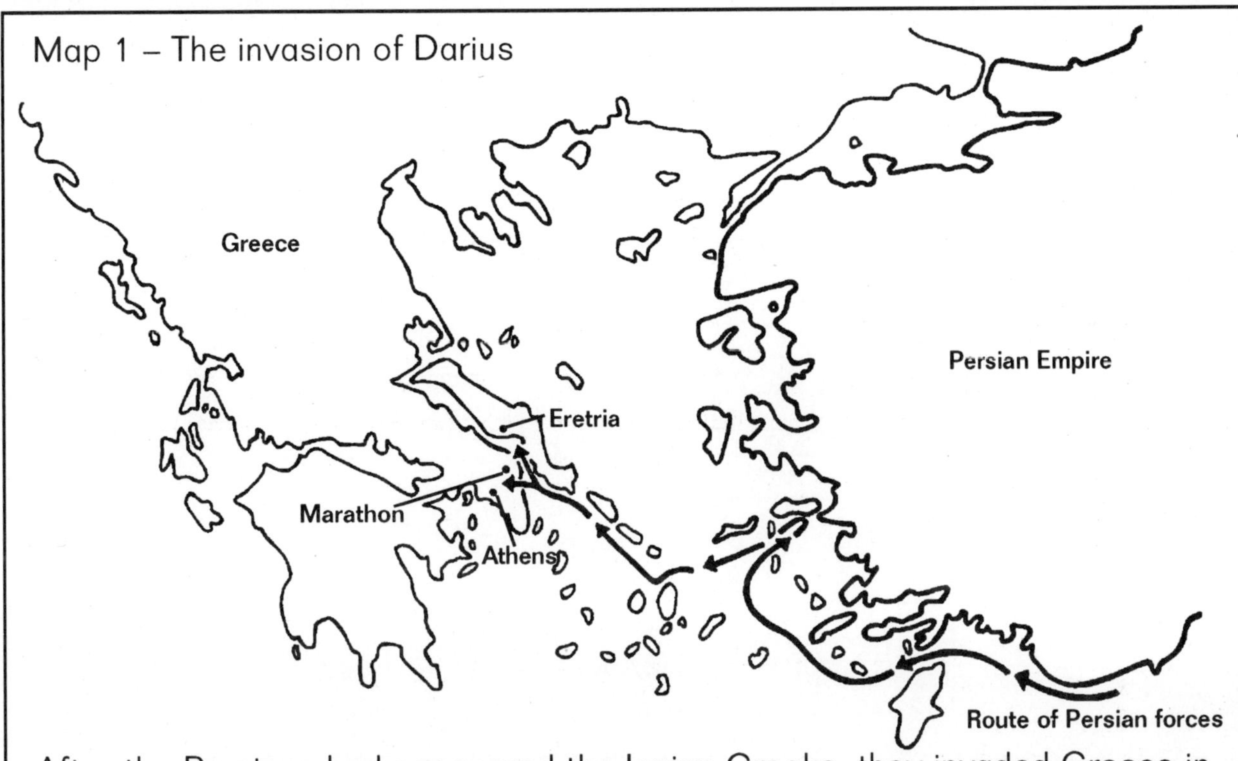

After the Persians had conquered the Ionian Greeks, they invaded Greece in 490 BC, in order to punish the Athenians.

Map 2 –Before Salamis.

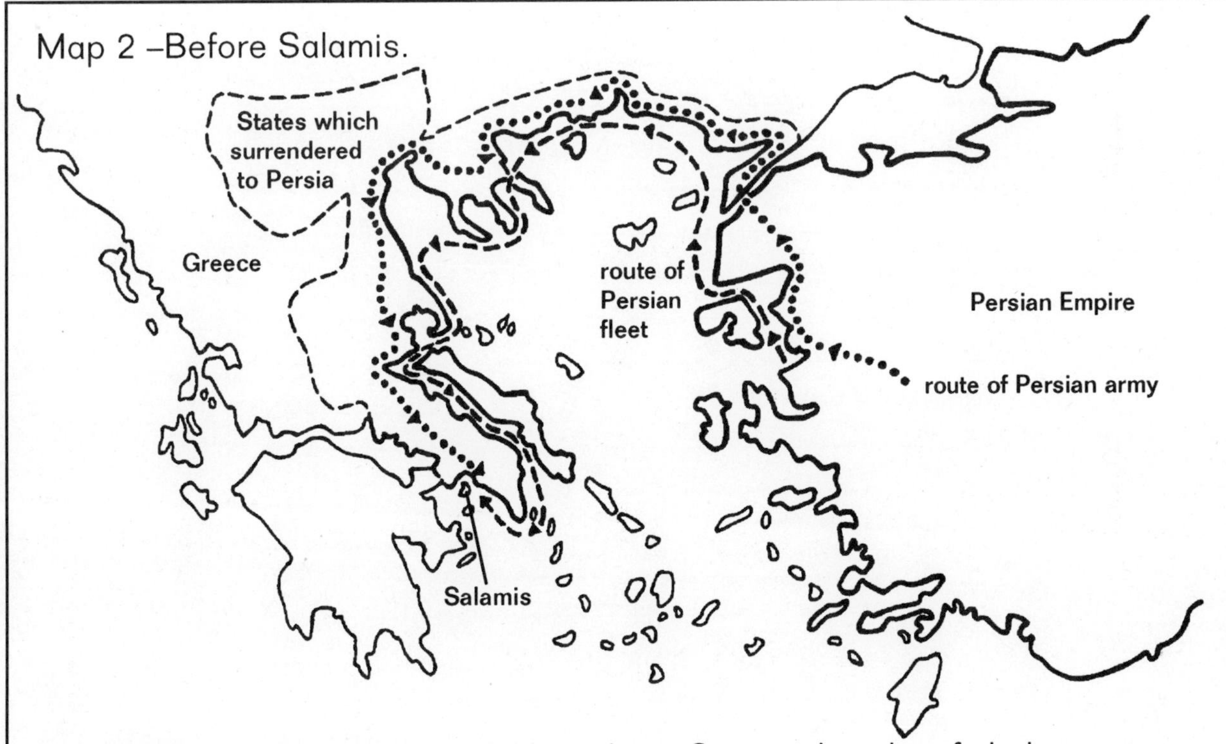

In 480 BC, the Persians invaded northern Greece, but they failed to conquer the Greeks at the battle of Salamis.

The Greek and Persians, see page 78

Linking events (cause and effect)

▲ Cut out these sentences and place them in the order that they happened.

✳ Xerxes' army marches into Greece demanding earth and water

Pheidippides runs to Sparta for help

Darius shoots an arrow into the air

The Athenians beat the Persians at Marathon

✳ The pass of Thermopylae is betrayed

✳ Xerxes cuts a canal through Mount Athos

Darius and his army camp at Marathon

The Ionian Greeks revolt against the Persians

✳ The Greeks defeat the Persians at Salamis

Athens sends twenty ships to help Ionian Greeks

✳ The Persians invade Attica

✳ Xerxes flogs the Hellespont

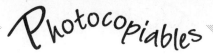

Painted pottery, see page 82

Finding out about the Greeks from pottery

Circe gave this warning to Odysseus:

'The Sirens cast their spell over everyone who comes near to them. If any man is so unlucky as to sail close enough to their island to hear their voices, he will never see his home land again. This is what the Sirens used to bewitch sailors. They sit together, surrounded by large piles of rotting human skeletons and when a ship goes by, they sing their songs which are so beautiful that the men cannot resist them.'

Then Circe advised as follows: 'Sail your ship past the Sirens but you must make sure that none of your crew hears them. In order to do this, you must soften some wax and plug everyone's ears with it. If you yourself wish to listen to song, make your crew tie you very firmly to the mast using strong ropes. You can then listen to the Sirens but you won't be able to reach them, however hard you try to struggle free. Tell your men to tie you up even more strongly when you start begging them to let you go.'

Odysseus did as Circe had instructed him and both he and his crew sailed past in safety.

This pot was made in ancient Athens:

- it tells us about Greek ships;
- it shows us how pots were painted using red figure style;
- it shows us the patterns that were used for borders;
- it tells us the story of Odysseus and the Sirens.

▲ Here are some things you can do:

- colour in the white areas of the picture with orange coloured crayon;
- make your own picture of a Greek pot using black and orange colours;
- find out more about the story of Odysseus and the Sirens.

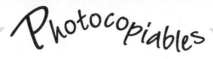

Greek temples and the Athenian Acropolis, see page 84

Temples – a history

Early temple made of mud/brick or stone

Next a porch was added with two columns to support the roof

More columns and decoration were added

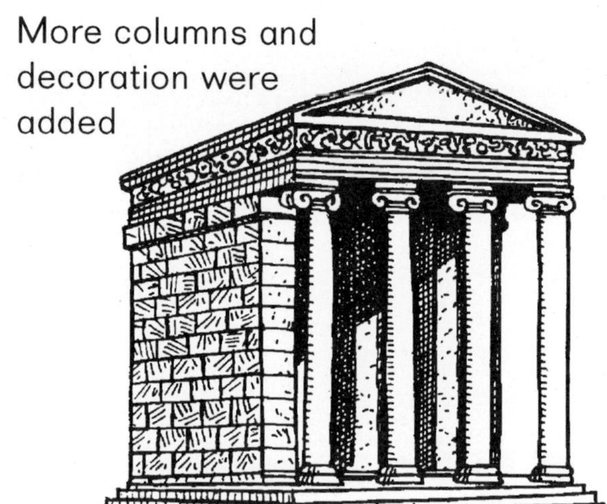

Athenian Acropolis

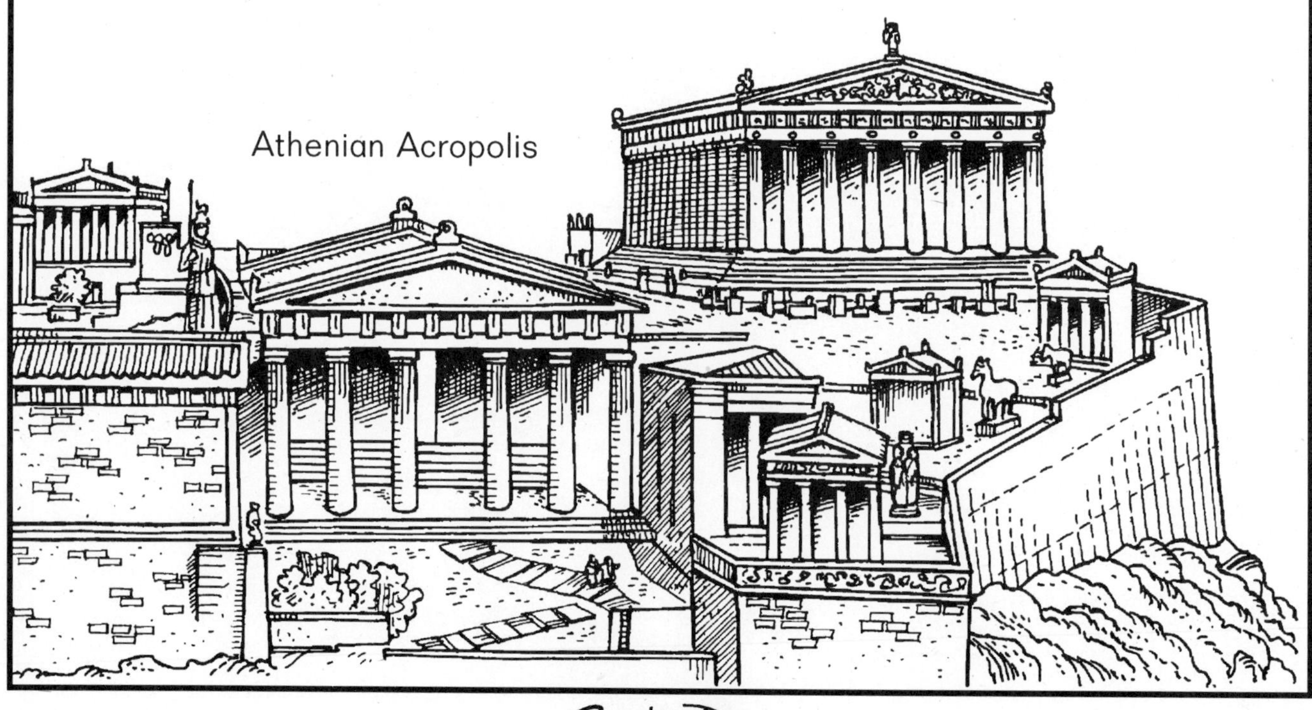

The Greek alphabet, see page 85

The ancient Greek alphabet

	GREEK	ROMAN
Alpha	Α	A
Beta	Β	B
Gamma	Γ	G
Delta	Δ	D
Epsilon	Ε	E
Zeta	Ζ	Z
Eta	Η	E
Theta	Θ	TH
Iota	Ι	I or J
Kappa	Κ	K or C
Lambda	Λ	L
Mu	Μ	M
Nu	Ν	N
Xi	Ξ	X
Omicron	Ο	O
Pi	Π	P
Rho	Ρ	R
Sigma	Σ	S
Tau	Τ	T
Upsilon	Υ	Y, U or V
Phi	Φ	PH
Chi	Χ	CH
Psi	Ψ	PS
Omega	Ω	O

▲ Now try deciphering these pieces of Greek writing.

Here are some Greek names you may have met:

ΘΕΜΙΣΤΟΚΛΗΣ

ΠΕΡΙΚΛΗΣ

ΔΙΟΔΟΤΟΣ

ΚΛΕΩΝ

Here are some Greek names used in inscriptions carved in stone:

ΑΛΕΧΑΝΔΡΟΣ

ΚΛΕΟΠΑΤΡΑ

ΤΙΜΟΘΕΟΣ

ΦΙΛΙΠΠΟΣ

ΠΗΝΕΛΟΠΗ

Here are some Greek names scratched on pieces of pottery and used by the Athenians for voting:

The Olympic games, see page 87

The Olympics

▲ Compare the ancient Olympics with today's games. Write/draw in the boxes.

Here are some events that are the same.

Here are some events that are different.

Here are some other things that are the same (for example,prizes).

Here are some other things that are different.

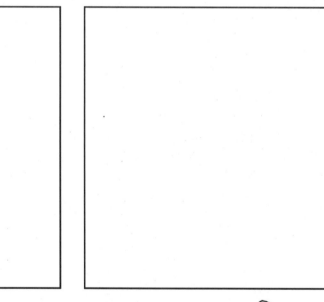

▲ Consider these questions:

- Where did the athletes come from?
- What prizes were there for the winners?
- How often were the games held?
- Did women and men take part?

What did they look like?, see page 92

Reconstructing pottery

▲ These pieces all belong to one pot. Cut the pieces out and make it up again. There is a piece missing, see if you can draw it in to complete the pot.

Making sense of the evidence, see page 96

What I have found out

▲ Consider these topics and write on a separate sheet of paper what you have found out about the civilisation which you have been studying.

Government (How were they ruled?).

Transport (How did they get about/carry goods?).

Trade (What did they buy and sell?).

Religion (Who did they worship?).

Buildings (What were these like?).

Metal working (What did they make?).

Jewellery (What kind did they make and wear?).

Arms and armour (What were these like?).

Graves (What kind did they use?).

Paintings (What forms of art did they produce?).

▲ How do we know about these people who lived so long ago?

▲ What is the evidence (How do we know?).

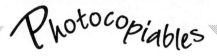

Ancient Egypt, see page 97

Tutankhamun's tomb

The ancient Egyptians buried their rulers with all their belongings. These tombs had once been full of gold and many other riches. Most of the Egyptian tombs had either been robbed a long time ago or had been found by archaeologists. Howard Carter was an English Egyptologist who explored the area called the Valley of the Kings. In 1922 Carter was about to give up looking, but he decided to look in just one more place.

▲ Here are some of the things which were found in Tutankhamun's tomb. Can you name them?

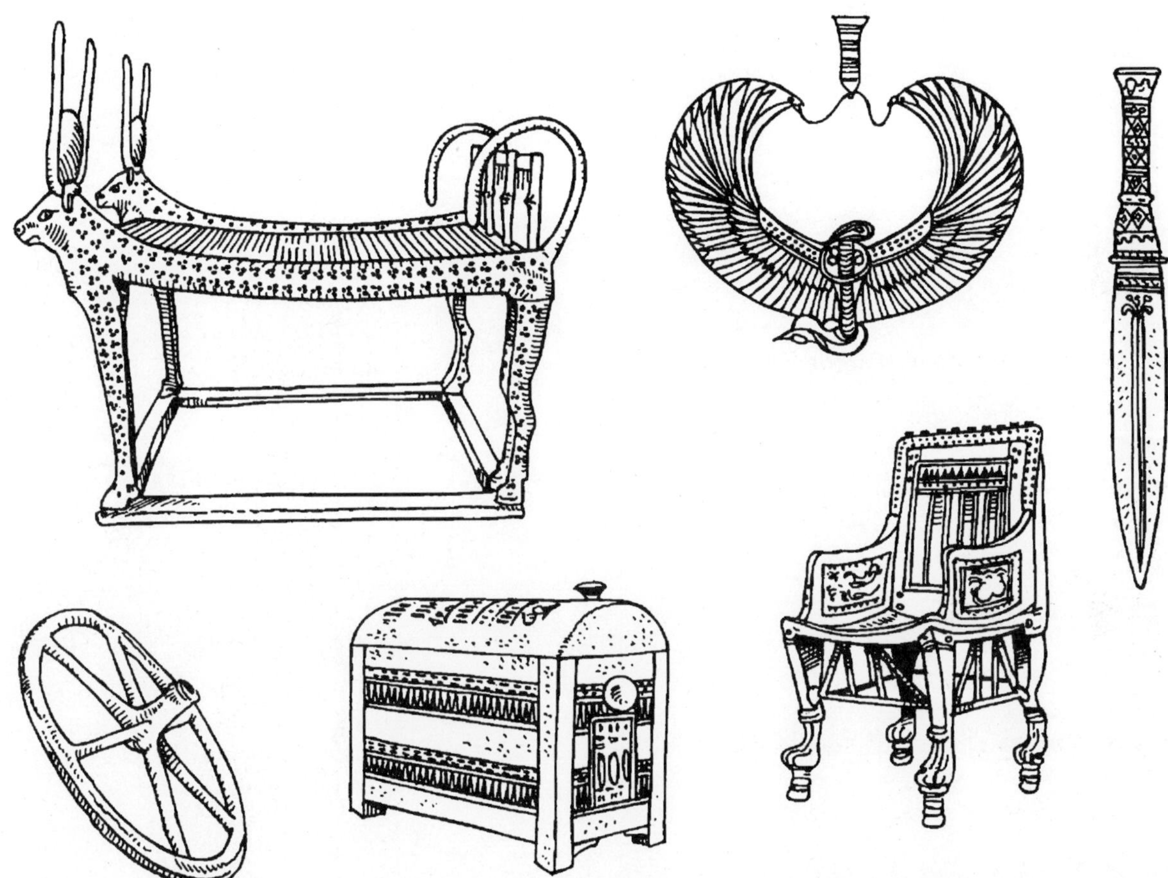

Beneath some ancient huts, Carter's workmen found first one step cut in the rock, then more steps. Finally, he uncovered 15 steps which led down to a door covered with plaster. They found that someone else had already got there, but they found another room behind, which was still untouched. Inside they saw gold and silver objects, brilliant jewellery, a throne, and other furniture. It took them a very long time to clear out the room, but they found yet another room beyond. In this room they found the buried king who was only 19 when he died. His body was in a stone coffin, but it was covered in no less than four gilded shrines made of wood.

Investigating a dead Egyptian, see page 99

Hieroglyphics

▲ Use the Egyptian alphabet to write out your own name and to make messages.

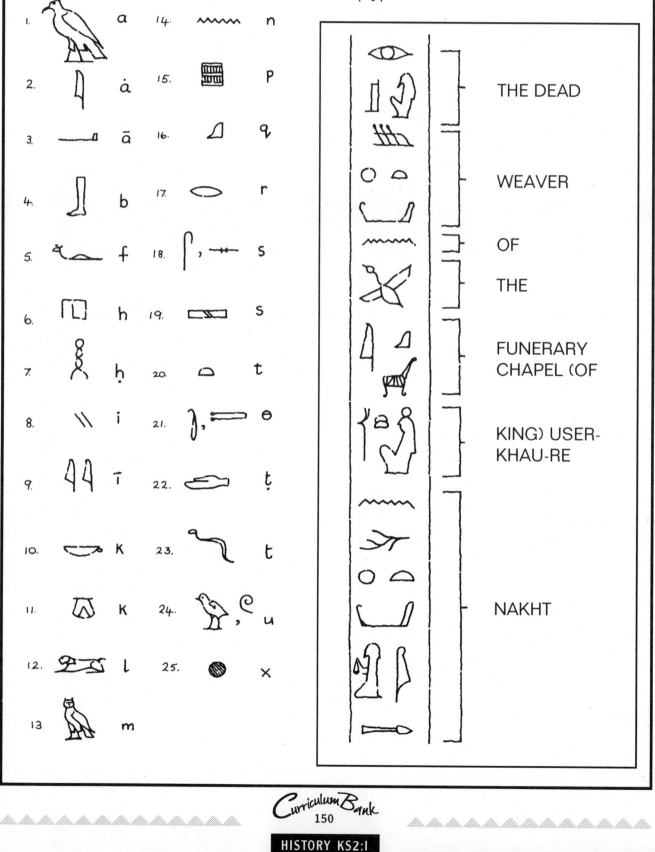

1.	a	14.	n
2.	ȧ	15.	p
3.	ā	16.	q
4.	b	17.	r
5.	f	18.	s
6.	h	19.	s
7.	ḥ	20.	t
8.	i	21.	θ
9.	ī	22.	ṭ
10.	k	23.	t
11.	k	24.	u
12.	l	25.	x
13	m		

▲ Here is a piece of Egyptian writing. It is a copy of the inscription on Nakht's tomb.

▲ Can you recognise any of the hieroplyphics?

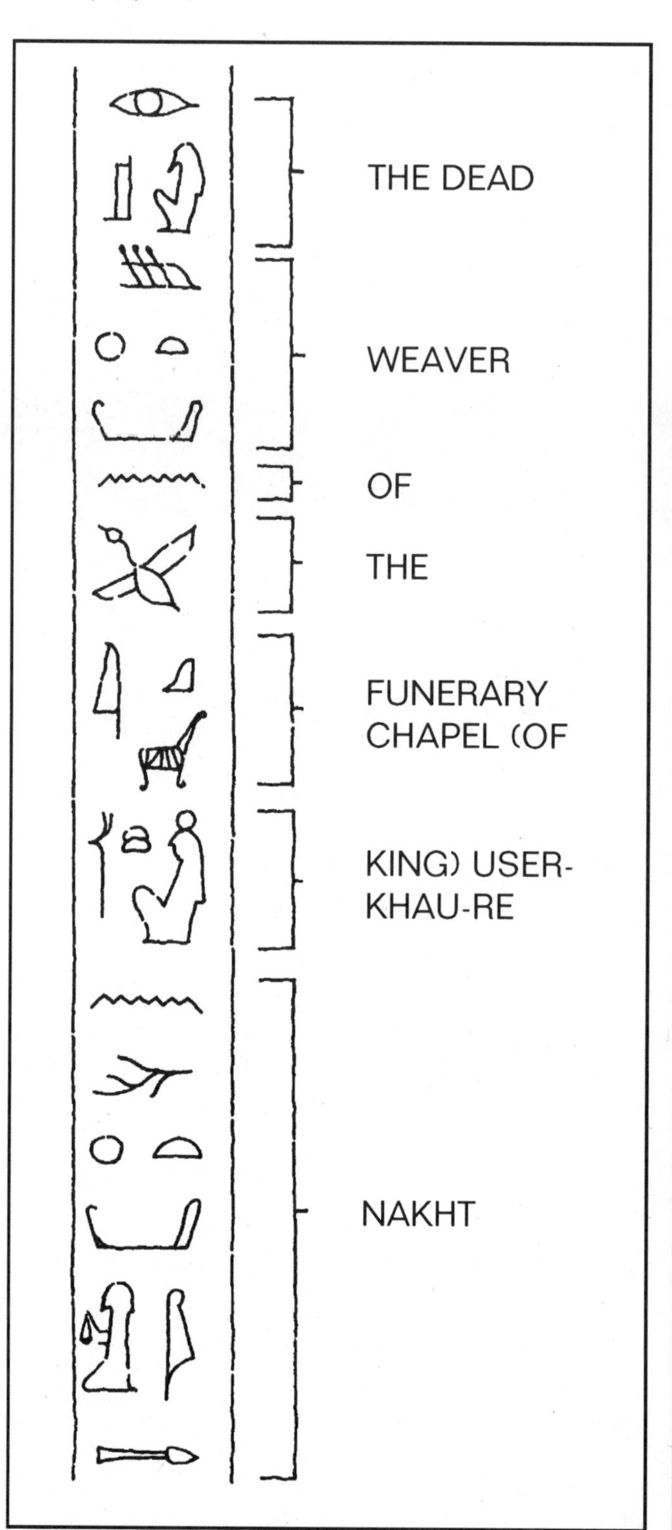

Ancient Sumer – the people of Sumer, **see page 102**

Royal Standard of Ur

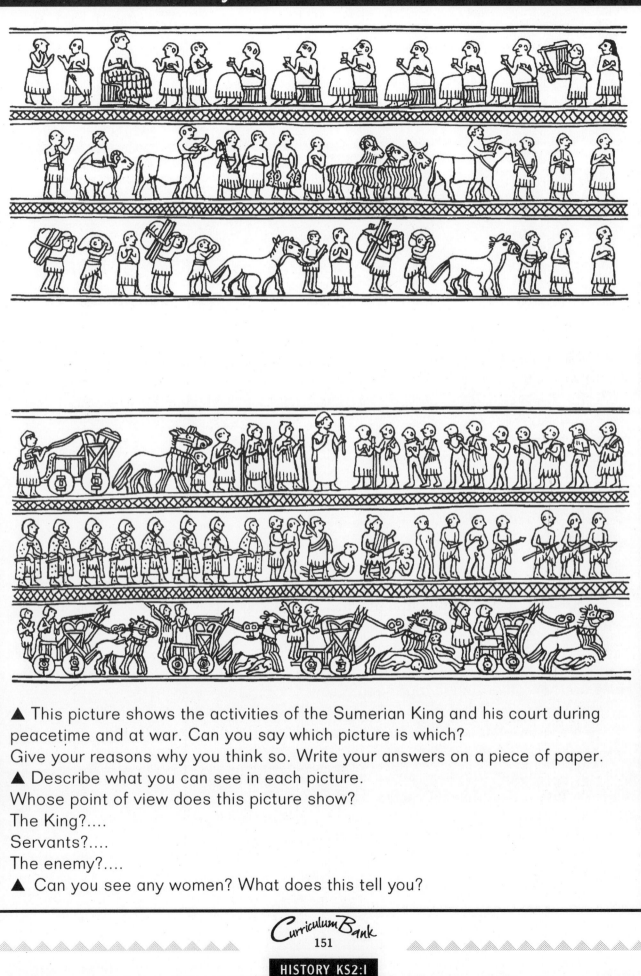

▲ This picture shows the activities of the Sumerian King and his court during peacetime and at war. Can you say which picture is which?
Give your reasons why you think so. Write your answers on a piece of paper.
▲ Describe what you can see in each picture.
Whose point of view does this picture show?
The King?....
Servants?....
The enemy?....
▲ Can you see any women? What does this tell you?

The Assyrian Empire, see page 104

King Ashurbanipal

"I killed 450 big lions, 390 wild bulls and 200 ostriches. I caught alive also 30 elephants, 50 wild bulls, 140 ostriches and 20 big lions."

Esarhaddon, king of Assyria boasts of his conquest of Sidon in Palestine
"I tore down its walls and threw them into the sea and I destroyed the king's palace. The king had run away. I caught him out at sea just like a fish and cut off his head. I captured his belongings, his gold, his silver, his jewels, his elephant hides, ivory and cloth of every kind which was stored in his palace."

Here are two other things that people said about the Assyrians.

1) Isaiah, a prophet in the Old Testament warns the Jews who were near neighbours:
"Do not be afraid of the Assyrians. They will beat you with rods and will raise their staffs against you just like they did against Egypt."

2) The English poet Lord Byron wrote in the last century:
"The Assyrian came down like a wolf on the fold,
And his cohorts were gleaming in purple and gold."

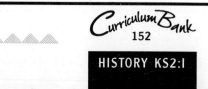

The Indus Valley – life in towns, see page 105

Buildings in the Indus

Great bath at Mahenjo-Daro

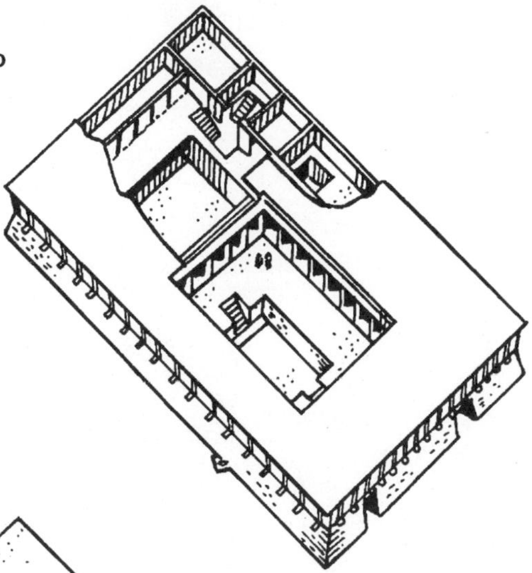

house

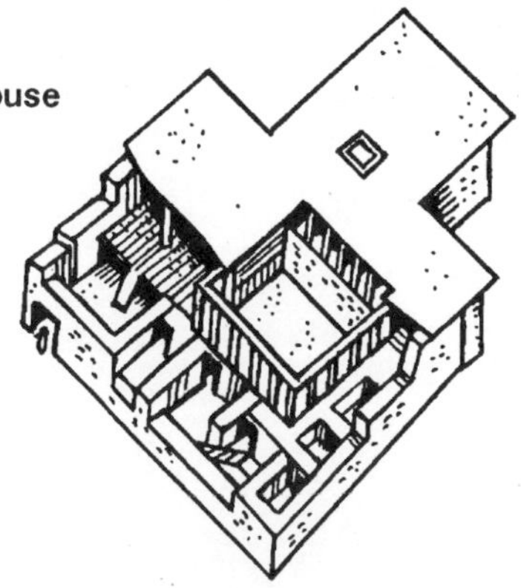

a toilet

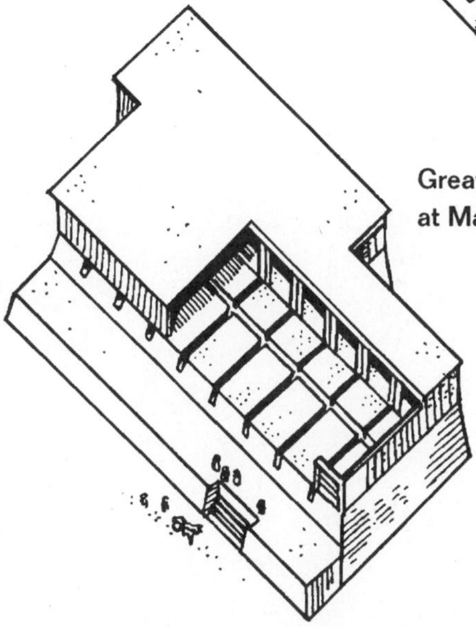

Great grain store at Mahenjo-Daro

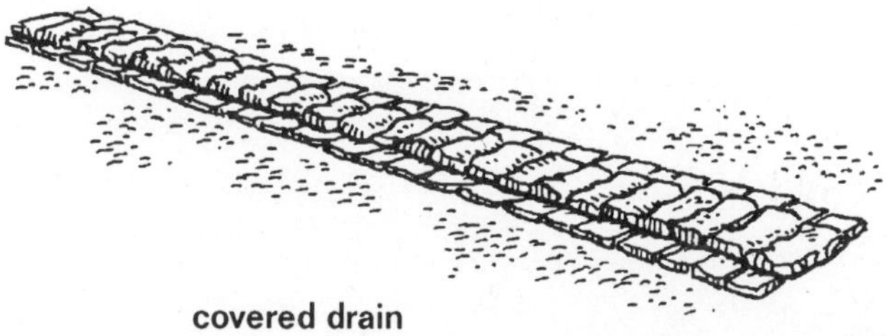

covered drain

Here are some of the things that archaeologists have found:

- The cities were carefully planned.
- Fortified walls of baked mud brick and towers protected the cities.
- The great bath at Mohenjo–Daro was probably used for religious purposes. There were rooms for priests nearby. There were brick steps down to the water and the bath was made waterproof with asphalt. A large well supplied water for the bath.
- Drains were built of bricks and had holes for inspection.
- Some houses were very large. They were arranged around a courtyard and had an upstairs. Other houses only had one room.
- Many houses had their own bathrooms and some had toilets connected to sewers.

▲ Use the information on this sheet to write about the people of the Indus Valley. Why was the Indus Valley civilisation important?

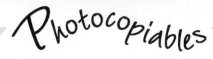

Making Indus Valley amulets, see page 107

Amulets from the Indus Valley

▲ How to make one of the amulets: 1) Paste the sheet onto card. 2) Draw an animal like one of these onto the amulet, colour it in and then cut out the whole circle. 3) Pierce a hole in the amulet and attach a piece of string. 4) You can now wear this round your neck to keep away evil spirits.

Archaeologists have found many of these objects. They were made from stone and probably belonged to individuals and were used as seals to mark personal belongings. It was not possible to decipher the writing found on them but it is thought that it gives the owner's name.

▲ Try designing your own seal or amulet using clay or Plasticine. Make a rough drawing on paper, then make the shape of your seal in clay. Press the letters and picture that you make into the clay. Find a way of attaching the string.

The Maya and everyday life, see page 108

The Mayan ball game

This account is based on archaeological evidence and on what people wrote after the conquest of Mexico by the Spaniards.

"It is baking hot. The ball player straps on his chunky belt, his hip pads and knee pads made of cotton and leather. This will help to protect the players from the hard rubber ball. The players are from important families.

There is a perfumed smell of resin coming from incense burners. Priests meet the players as they reach the main door of the temple. Prayers are offered up to Tlaloc, the rain god. They pray for lots of rain and a good harvest of maize during the summer ahead. Priests and players together process to the hill where the great palace of the ruler stands. The ruler cuts himself in honour of the gods and then joins the procession. They all go towards the ball court. They cross an area which is covered in white plaster. As they do so they pass buildings that are plastered and painted bright colours. They reach the ball court. The priests and all the important people climb the stairways at the back of the ball court and sit down in a place from which they can watch the game.

Then the players take up their places at opposite ends of the court. The two chief players stand in the alley and the rest of their team stand behind them at the far ends of the court. Then the large hard ball made from the sap of a rubber tree is brought out. The players have to hit the ball through rings which have been arranged high on each side of the court. Each team aims for one of the rings. They can only play in the narrow alley down the middle of the court. The players must use their bodies to hit the ball but they must not use either their hands or their feet. After many tries, one player gets his chance. He makes a beautifully placed shot from his hip. The ball bounces off the wall, goes through one of the rings and the game is over."

This was no ordinary sport. There is evidence that the leader of the winning team was rewarded with a jade necklace, but the leader of the losers was tied up with ropes and dragged to the temple. Here his head was cut off by one of the priests and his body was rolled down the temple steps.

An Aztec market

This is how the Spaniard Diaz described the market in the Aztec capital. He wanted to let people in Spain know what life was like in Mexico:

'I will start by telling you about the traders in gold, silver and jewels, feathers, cloaks, embroidered goods and the male and female slaves who are sold there. They bring to sell in the marketplace all black slaves that the Portuguese have brought from Guinea. Some of them are brought along tied with collars fixed to long poles to stop them escaping, but others are loose. Then there were those who sold coarser cloth, things made of cotton and cloth made from twisted threads. There were also chocolate sellers with their chocolate.

Some people were selling sisal ropes and sandals to wear on the feet, both made from the same plant. All these were in one part of the market. In another place there were the skins of tigers, lions, otters, jackals, deer, badgers, wild cats and other wild animals. Some of them were tanned.'

These drawings were made by Aztec artists after the conquest. They were used to illustrate a form of book which we call a 'codex'.

▲ Write out a list of all the items shown in the pictures that you can also find in the written account of Diaz.

Benin – art and technology, see page 115

Some Benin artefacts

▲ Can you suggest what these objects are made of? Colour in the pictures with the colour you think should be used:

Brass = green
Ivory = yellow
Terracotta = brown
Wood = black
Coral = orange

▲ Choose one of these objects. Write two sentences to say who you think might have used it.

▲ Try making your own plaque using kitchen foil.

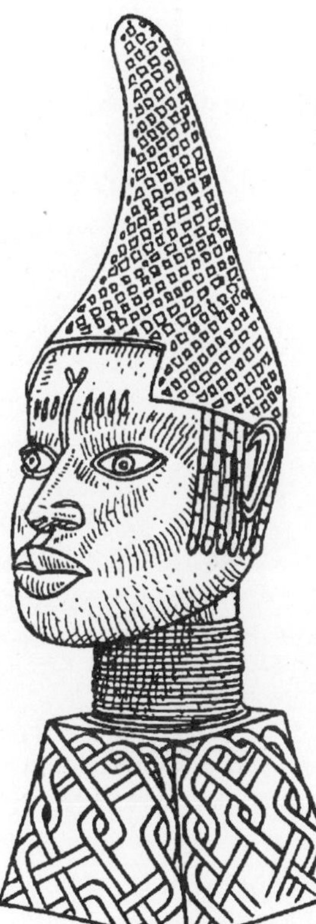

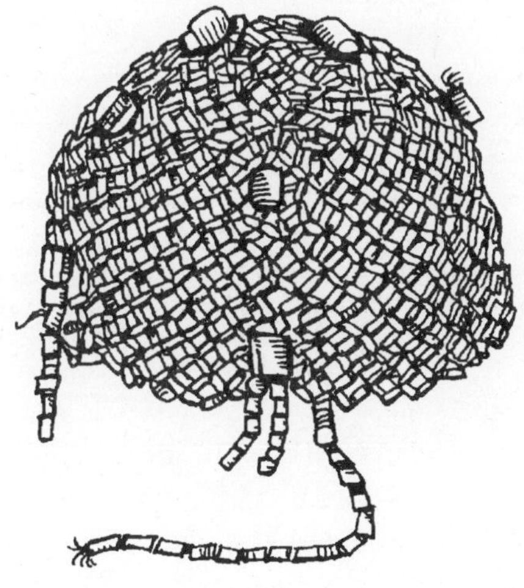

INFORMATION TECHNOLOGY WITHIN HISTORY AT KEY STAGE 2

History provides teachers with many opportunities to use IT both to develop children's IT capability through communicating information, modelling and simulations but also to enrich children's historical knowledge and understanding. New software related to the National Curriculum History Study Units appears regularly, particularly in the area of CD-ROMs and it has been possible to mention only a few of the more relevant and useful titles within the activities. Teachers may want to supplement the activities with other software or CD-ROMs as they become available.

Main IT focus

The main emphasis for the development of IT capability within these activities is on communicating information and modelling through the use of simulations and adventure games.

CD-ROMs

There are now an ever-growing number of CD-ROMs available for schools designed to complement the History Study Units at Key Stage 2. They vary in quality and suitability for children at Key Stage 2 and it is worth trying to look at specific CD-ROMs before purchasing them. CD-ROMs fall into three broad categories.

The first are those which provide an encyclopaedia type of environment. The CD-ROM will contain text and pictures and some of the more up-to-date CD-ROMs also include moving pictures and sounds such as music, sound effects and speech. Children can access the information in a number of ways. They may be able to make a simple search for the topic they are interested in, by typing the word *Tutankhamun*, for example. This will then take them to the relevant part of the CD-ROM. When they read the page they may also find some of the words highlighted in a different colour. By clicking on these words they will be taken to another section of the encyclopaedia which has more, or linked, information. Moving from one part to another via these 'hot links' is called browsing. There are a wide range of such CD-ROM encyclopaedias which provide varying levels of information.

It is often possible to save the text from searches or pictures from the CD-ROM which can be used in later work. However, when children save large quantities of text from the CD-ROM it is important that they read and sort through it to find the key points relevant to the topic being studied. Make a printed copy which children can use away from the computer, marking the key points with a highlighter pen. They can then load the text into a word processor and reorganise and edit it to present just the useful information.

CD-ROMs usually contain such a vast quantity of information that it is important to try any new CD-ROM in advance of its use with children. Check the quality and relevance of the information, the readability of text, where and how the information can be found and whether it is possible to extract pictures or text for use in other work. It is often useful to set up some simple questions to direct the children's use, ensuring it is relevant and not just unproductive time spent browsing.

A second form of CD-ROM is an interactive one, where children make a decision that then takes them to another part of the CD-ROM. These types may be in the form of adventure games or interactive stories. *Frontier 2000* which looks at the area around Hadrian's Wall is probably one of the most well known in this category. There are also many 'living book' type CD-ROMs which are story books which the children can either read for themselves or hear the words read to them. They can re-listen to a section by clicking on the sentence or even individual words, and there are usually animated pictures and sound effects.

The third type of CD-ROM is usually a large collection of pictures or other resources which can be used within the children's own work. There may, for example, be collections of 'clip art' or photographs of artefacts and other documentary evidence which are linked to a particular topic such as the Vikings.

Simulations and adventure games

History is one area of the curriculum which has generated a number of interesting and useful simulations which can give children an interactive feel for the period of history they are studying. It is, however, important that the use of such software is integrated fully into the work of the classroom. There is limited value by simply sitting children with the software and letting them 'play' without a proper introduction and follow-up.

If you decide to use simulation software make sure that you try it out in advance to give you a clear understanding of the aims and the structure of the simulation and how children will be able to interact with the text and pictures. Look at ways to extend the work started at the computer. Children could keep diaries/record their turns at the computer.

Try to avoid siting the computer in a corridor or situation away from the classroom where you cannot see what is happening, intervene or interact with the children as they are using the software. Take some time at the start of the project to talk to the whole class about the simulation, what it is about and what they are going to do. Show them how to load the software, perhaps working through the first few screens together to give them a feel for the routines and conventions and avoid time-consuming mistakes later on. Show the children how to save their position in the simulation so that they can return to the same point later on.

Apart from supporting the work in history you can help children to develop an understanding of the simulation itself, how the model works, how to make decisions and what is likely to happen as a result of a particular choice. Discuss the limitations of the simulation or adventure, how choices are limited by the information held in the computer or the ways that questions are asked by the children. These are important issues in developing children's IT capability in the area of modelling. It will also be useful to discuss other models the children may have used, in school or in the wider world.

GRID 1

AREA OF IT	SOFTWARE	ACTIVITIES (PAGE NOS.)		
		CHAPTER 3	CHAPTER 4	CHAPTER 5
Communicating information	Word processor	32, 35, 37, 42, 44, 48, 58	65, 69, 75, 85	**90**, **96**, 100, 105, 108
Communicating information	DTP	32, 54	75, **87**	90, 96, 100, 105, 112
Communicating information	Art/graphics	35, 39, 41, **50**	82	
Communicating information	Framework software	32	82	90
Communicating information	Authoring software	48, 54, **56**	**66**	100
Information handling	Database	32	66	
Information handling	Branching database		**66**	
Information handling	CD-ROM	35, **48**, 54	65, 66, 75	92, 94, 96, 100,112
Modelling	Simulations	**44**, 46, 61		92, 94, 97, 109
Control	ROAMER/PIPP	39		

GRID 2

SOFTWARE TYPE	BBC/MASTER	RISCOS	NIMBUS/186	WINDOWS	MACINTOSH
Word Processor	*Pendown* *Folio*	*Pendown* *Desk Top Folio*	*All Write* *Write On*	*Word for Windows* *Kid Works 2* *Creative Writer*	*Kid Works 2* *EasyWorks* *Creative Writer*
DTP	*Front Page Extra*	*Desk Top Folio* *Pendown DTP* *Bearword*	*Front Page Extra* *NewSPAper*	*Creative Writer* *NewSPAper*	*Creative Writer*
Framework		*My World*		*My World*	
Art Package	*Image*	*1st Paint* *Kid Pix* *Splash*	*NewSPAint*	*Colour Magic* *Kid Pix 2* *Fine Artist*	*Kid Pix 2* *Flying Colours* *Fine Artist*
Multi-media Authoring		*Magpie* *Hyperstudio* *Genesis*		*Genesis* *Hyperstudio* *Illuminus*	*Hyperstudio*
Database	*Grass*	*Junior Pinpoint* *Find IT* *KeyNote*	*Grass*	*Sparks* *Claris Works* *Information Workshop*	*Claris Works* *EasyWorks*
CD-ROM		*Children's Micropedia* *Hutchinsons*		*Encarta 96* *Children's Micropedia* *Grolier*	*Encarta 96* *Grolier*
Timeline	*Timelines*	*Timelines* *Time Traveller*	*Timelines*	*Timelines*	
Simulations		*Arcventure* *Time Detectives* *Landmarks*		*Arcventure* *Landmarks*	

Cross-curricular links

	ENGLISH	MATHS	SCIENCE	GEOGRAPHY	D & T	IT	ART	MUSIC/PE	RE
ROMANS, ANGLO-SAXONS AND VIKINGS IN BRITAIN	Discussion and debate. Role-play, drama. Speaking and listening, story, saga. Writing. Language awareness; derivations, transliteration (Runes). Extracting information. Using an index. Using reference books.	Dating BC/AD. Lines on maps. Tesserae/ tessellation. Roman numerals. Sizes/weights of finds.	Hydraulics. Survival of archaeological evidence. Writing materials.	Distribution of settlements. Pre-Roman perceptions of Britain; Roman roads. Army movements. Town layout. Villa sites; rivers. Distribution of finds. Campaigns map. Spread of Vikings. Danelaw and place names. Sea routes.	Surveying and construction of roads. Making a torque. Water supply. Designing and making mosaics. Designing and making ship's prow. Ship's construction. Sculptures. Artefacts.	Newsroom simulation. Data base.	Timeline. Frieze and collage. Activities in town trades etc. Drawing mosaic. Wall painting: marbling/sponge. Making pots. Crosses. Rubbings. Jewellery; arms/ armour. Pictures of Alfred story. Viking pictures. Textiles.	Roman music (Archaeo–logica Musica), tapes. Funeral music. Viking Music.	Morality of conquest. Religious themes. Pre-Christian burials. Spread of Christianity. Magi in Christian art. Pre-Christian burials. Conversion. Christianity and Vikings.
ANCIENT GREECE	Biographies; retellings; derivations. Story boards. Recording information. Debate and discussion. Writing and recording. Writing reports/ commentaries. Language awareness. Speaking and listening.	Dating BC. Symmetry and design. Comparison of distances etc.	Forces. Evidence of survival. Writing materials.	Pâpier maché map. Map of occupations. Settlements and sea battle sites. Sites of temples.	Mobile. Work done by slaves. Hoplite's equipment. Design and construction.	Timeline. Data base.	Timeline. Display/big book. Visual interpretations. Hoplite's equipment. Artefacts in graves. Illustrating battles. Designs; paintings. Collage. Making Greek signs.	Training; marching; music to beat time. Rowing in time. Running and field events.	Belief in many gods. Purpose of temples. Celtic burials. Nature of temples. Religious origins.
A PAST NON-EUROPEAN SOCIETY	Recording; discussion; questioning; investigation. Planning; creating narratives; listening. Investigating early writing (cuneiform). Writing, comparing.	Dating BC/AD. Pyramids. Number base 60. Bricks measurement.	Evidence. Writing as evidence. Human remains. Impact of flooding.	Locating societies. Aerial photographs. Desert; Nile. Mesopotamia. River Indus. Central America. Plants native to America. Rain forests.	Removal of monuments. Pyramids. Bricks construction. Lost wax casting.	Data base. 'ROAMER'	Timeline. Reconstructing pottery. Jewellery; death masks. Interpreting visual evidence. Model making. Market picture. Close observation drawing.	Funeral procession and music.	Religious artefacts. Belief in afterlife. Funeral gods and beliefs. Burials. Flood/Noah. Benin gods: creation story.